Cooperatives and Mutuals in the Market System

Cooperatives and Mutuals in the Market System

Richard B. Heflebower

THE UNIVERSITY OF WISCONSIN PRESS

Published 1980

The University of Wisconsin Press
114 North Murray Street
Madison, Wisconsin 53715

The University of Wisconsin Press, Ltd.
1 Gower Street
London WC1E 6HA, England

First printing

Printed in the United States of America

For LC CIP information see the colophon

ISBN 0-299-07850-7

Contents

Contents

List of Tables and Figures

Figures

Preface

In this volume cooperatives are studied as enterprises whereby groups of consumers, farmers, or relatively small nonfarm businesses integrate as groups into the activity of which they would otherwise be customers or suppliers. Consequently, the cooperative is usually an entrant into a vertically adjacent activity in which existing enterprises are investor-owned firms.

Vertical integration is widespread in modern economies, much of it carried out by substantial-to-large corporations. The unique feature of this study is the analysis of vertical integration by groups of relatively, and usually absolutely, small customers or suppliers organized as cooperatives.

Viewed as just described, financial mutuals also fit into the study. Typically they enter an established activity of which members have been patrons of investor-owned firms. As the mutuals become older and larger the members' influence fades except as they do or do not continue patronage.

The first three chapters are introductory. After presenting the quantitative importance of patron-owned enterprises in various sectors of the economy, chapter 1 compares the patron-owned cooperative with the usual investor-owned firm. From this emerges the concept of the cooperative stated above. Given the economic characteristics of cooperatives as developed in chapters 1 and 2, chapter 3 adapts the theory of entry to entry by cooperative vertical integration, which is the role of the cooperative.

Building on the introductory chapters, the development and performance of cooperative and mutual enterprises in various economic activities is examined in chapters 4-13. Two chapters are devoted to farmer-owned marketing cooperatives and a similar number to farm supply cooperatives. New to many readers will be the substantial development of cooperatives owned by groups of nonfarm business enterprises, described in chapter 8. Readers may be surprised at the nominal role of consumer retail cooperatives, reported in chapter 9, and the reason therefor. An exception is the very successful rural electric and telephone cooperatives, which are classified here as consumer cooperatives.

Chapters 10-12 consider the origin and performance of cooperative and mutual financial enterprises in the variety of economic activities, while chapters 11 and 15 summarize two aspects of patron-owned enterprises. One is the limited equity capital subscribed by members, which restricts the type of activity which cooperatives and to some degree mutuals can enter. But once well started, these enterprises add to capital by reinvesting all or much of their net income. Second, and parallel, is the question of entrepreneurship in starting and later directing the cooperative or mutual, the subject considered in chapter 14.

The last three chapters serve as summaries. Chapter 13 appraises the effects of cooperatives and mutuals on the markets entered, chapter 14 reports some of the handicaps and accomplishments of patron-owned enterprises, and the final short chapter appraises the entry by cooperatives and mutuals as reported in preceding chapters that augments the performance of the markets entered.

In the years during which work on this volume has proceeded, much help has been provided by government agencies, particularly the federal Farmer Cooperative Service, by academic economists, and by individuals and trade associations in the industries studied. Much empirical information was obtained by interviews with officials of cooperatives and of trade associations of cooperatives and mutuals as reported in the chapters. Several field studies were made of cooperatives owned by nonfarm businesses. The assistance of the respondents is appreciated. Early work on the project was financed by the Merrill Foundation for the Advancement of Financial Knowledge, assistance that was useful in financing surveys and in relieving me for a time of part of my academic duties.

R.B.H.

June 1979
Evanston, Illinois

Cooperatives and Mutuals in the Market System

1

The Cooperative Form of Enterprise

Cooperatives and mutuals owned by groups of customers or suppliers strongly influence major sectors of the American economy.[1] Their influence is not as a means of social change but stems from their unique form of enterprise organization. In contrast to the usual corporation or partnership in which persons invest to gain in proportion to ownership, groups of patrons as suppliers or as customers own the cooperative or the mutual[2] and share net gains of the enterprise in proportion to patronage. Patronage may be the act of selling commodities through the cooperative for processing or marketing or through the mutual of savings for investment. Alternatively, the members may be buyers of commodities, services, insurance, or loanable funds through an enterprise they own as a group.

Monetary gain from being a patron-member is obtained to the extent that the cooperative's or mutual's net price after patronage dividends[3] is preferred to the offer of investor-owned concerns. Where enterprises owned by groups of patrons have succeeded in this fashion, rivals are pressed to improve their terms of sale or of purchase to avoid loss of volume. In this process is found the economic significance of patron-owned enterprises as their role is developed in this study. These conclusions will be buttressed by consideration of the conditions under which the cooperative or mutual form of enterprise has not succeeded.

Economic analysis of patron-owned enterprises involves three steps.

3

The full import of the distinction between patron-owned and investor-owned is spelled out in this and the next chapters, where the cooperative or mutual is portrayed as an enterprise entering a market composed of

Table 1.1. Cooperatives' and Mutuals' Share of Volume by Areas of Economic Activity, Circa 1970–1975[a]

Area of economic activity	Cooperatives' or mutuals' percentages of respective markets
Marketing farm products[b]	29%
Farm purchasing of[c]	
Farm supplies	18
Farm equipment	Nominal
Consumer cooperatives	
All retail[d]	0.25
Food retailing only[d]	0.36
Rural electric (of which a significant percentage is generated)[e]	50
Retailer-owned wholesale enterprises[f]	
All wholesaling	4
General line groceries	25
Building supplies (except lumber, brick, cement)	5
Drugs	10
Hardware	10
Department stores	Significant
Manufacturer purchasing	
Nonlocal news gathering	Majority
Small bakery company purchasing[g]	Substantial
Other	Nominal
Nonagricultural service industries	
Railroad express service[h]	(96)[h]
Long-distance moving of household goods[i]	4
Freight forwarding	Significant
Mutual investing or borrowing	
Mutual investing of saving deposits[j]	51
Mutual investing of variable dollar value type	100
Collective borrowing	
By farmers, varying by type of loans[k] from	21–33
By consumers[l]	12
Mutual nonlife insurance[m]	
Mutual insurance: fire	20
Automobile casualty insurance	33
Workmen's compensation	33

[a]Except where indicated otherwise in the following footnotes, the percentage of non-quantitative estimates were made by me on the basis of my study of the particular areas of economic activity.

[b]Estimates of the Farmer Cooperative Service of the Department of Agriculture for 1974–75. Percentage ranges by commodities from 10 to 76 percent of total.

^cSame reference as for products marketed. Supply cooperatives also manufacture varying percentages of some types of supplies.

^dSee table 9.1.

^eSee pages 122–25.

^fSee table 8.1. Wholesaling by farmer cooperatives is omitted.

^gExclusive of flour and sugar.

^hRailway Express operated for decades as a cooperative owned by the railroads. In 1969 it became an investor-owned company and in 1974 went into receivership and suspended operations.

ⁱThe largest cooperative hauler of household goods announced in 1969 that it was converting into an investor-owned enterprise. The percentage in the table is an estimate for a small hauler which remains a cooperative.

^jComputed from data on page 15 of *Savings and Loan Fact Book* (Chicago: United States League of Savings and Loan Association, 1974).

^kSee chapter II.

^lSee pages 135–40.

^mFrom *Best's Aggregates and Averages: Property-Liability* (Oldwick, N.J.: A.M. Best Co., 1971).

established investor-owned firms. The conditions that make such entry possible are discussed in the third chapter. The following nine chapters report empirical studies of conditions existing in the sectors of the economy in which cooperatives or mutuals have entered and gained varying market shares. The concluding chapters appraise the entry role patron-owned enterprises have played in some sectors and the economic significance of this form of enterprise.

A Preview of the Record

The recent market shares of cooperatives and mutuals in various types of economic activity, portrayed in table 1.1, are the outcome of many years of trial and error. For decades failures far out-numbered successes, particularly of commodity-handling cooperatives. Their struggle for survival and growth was not always a peaceful market-testing process, in part because their sponsors often hailed cooperatives as a means of changing the economic system. This diverted attention from the economic basis for success, the obtaining of better prices for members, and also enabled established enterprises losing patrons to the cooperatives to appear before the public as knights defending the established order. Often cooperatives' rivals engaged in economic warfare by temporary price offers that cooperatives could not match. On occasion, established concerns developed schemes to bar cooperatives from access to markets from which they bought or in which they sold. Financial mutuals faced much less vigorous opposition.

From the historical process just sketched emerges a clearer view of the economic role of patron-owned enterprises. Instead of promoting them as a means of social reform, as was often claimed in the last century, those new organizing cooperatives emphasize the expected gain from entering by means of an enterprise the patrons own, the particular market in which the members would otherwise buy, sell, or borrow. Rather than appealing to nonpecuniary motives, patron-owned enterprises are usually portrayed as the means of augmenting the real incomes of members. To the extent this gain is realized, the investor-owned firms are pressed to make better offers, the familiar result of rivalry among enterprises. But it has become obvious to nonmembers that the private property, market-directed character of the economy has not been altered thereby. Not surprisingly, opposition to cooperatives has simmered down to a controversy as to whether they receive government favors, particularly under the federal income tax laws.

Table 1.1 shows the widely differing shares of total volume of various economic activities that cooperatives and mutuals have obtained. To Europeans, the insignificant role of consumer-owned retail stores will be a surprise, but perhaps the almost complete absence of worker (or production) cooperatives will not. Many farm marketing and supply cooperatives and rural electric cooperatives have obtained large market shares. What is less well known is the extent of development of cooperatives owned by nonfarm business enterprises to purchase supplies for their member-owners or to provide transport or other services. But cooperatives that market the output of nonfarm businesses appear not to exist. Few farm marketing cooperatives engage in manufacturing except to convert perishable products into storable or transportable forms. Some large buyer-owned cooperatives have integrated into manufacturing of the goods they handle. Financial mutuals and cooperatives enjoy very strong positions in insurance and in some investment and banking-like operations. More detailed information about cooperatives' and mutuals' volumes and shares of the activities in which they engage will be found in chapters 4–12 inclusive.

Patron-Owned Versus Investor-Owned Enterprises

Much of what follows turns on the characteristics of the cooperative and of the mutual that distinguish them from the more usual investor-owned enterprise. The critical similarities or differences are found in the purpose of ownership and the relation of the owners to the enterprise.

Consider first the features of the investor-owned corporation whose owners expect to gain in proportion to ownership. They are not necessarily nor often to a significant degree patrons as sellers to or buyers from the corporation. In one sense the owners are supplier-patrons, for they provide the equity capital of the enterprise and receive dividends and increase in value of their stock in proportion to their equity capital patronage. Each such corporation might be viewed as a production cooperative owned by suppliers of capital (but not of labor) were it not for another feature. The stockholder in the investor-owned corporation may not at will withdraw his "patronage," that is, the capital, he supplied. He does not expect to have that privilege. Ordinarily he may sell his ownership share at any time, but doing so does not alter the total equity capital of the corporation. That may be done only by the vote of the holders of the majority of the stock who approve the sale of additional stock or retirement of some previously authorized. In contrast, transfer of membership in a cooperative or mutual is rarely if ever permitted. A member may cease to be a patron unless bound by a term contract, but he may not be able to withdraw his share of the enterprise's equity capital.[4]

What is often termed a voluntary worker or production cooperative is similar in one basic regard to the investor-owned corporation, but not in other ways. In a sense the worker-owners are labor-investors, and they receive their labor-input shares of the excess of the cooperative's receipts above costs, with wages not included in costs. (By agreement some of the net savings may be withheld for investment in the enterprise.) Unlike the usual corporate stockholder the worker-member of such a cooperative participates directly in its activity and usually his entire income consists of his share of the enterprise's receipts above other costs. The member may withdraw his labor investment at will and need not find a replacement even though the producing capacity of the cooperative is thereby altered. The continuing members may admit or reject new members at will. All these features are corollaries of the fact that the members are the cooperative's owners as well as its work force and that each member relies on his patronage dividend, part of which may be paid in a periodic wage, for his income. Very few worker cooperatives exist in this country.

In sharp contrast to investor-owned corporations are the widespread cooperatives and mutuals whose market shares were shown in table 1.1. Their members do not ordinarily participate in the enterprise's operations though some may be employees for a contract wage. It is not inconsistent with sharing benefits on a patronage basis for the cooperative to pay part of its net savings to members as a return on their investment in it at a rate that approximates what the funds could earn in alternative uses. There is no net gain from patronage over a period of time unless the cooperative's net savings exceed such a return on the members' equity.

Financial mutuals are included in this study even though to varying degrees they are not controlled by their members or fully share net savings with them. Nevertheless they do affect the performance of the markets in which they operate.

A corollary of patron ownership as a form of enterprise organization is that it is usable regardless of the source of the economic interest of potential members. They frequently are households as purchasers of commodities, services, and insurance, or as borrowers or investors of savings. In other cases the owners are relatively small investor-owned enterprises such as farms or retail stores. But in some markets quite large corporations are members of enterprises that meet the test of the cooperative, that of sharing net gains on a patronage basis.

While members of a cooperative may join for reasons other than individual gain the assumption here is that their motive is an expected increase in real income. The primary test is whether more money is received for what is sold or less paid for what is bought by being a patron-member of a cooperative than a patron of an investor-owned firm.

Two qualifications are in order. As noted earlier better net price does not add to real income unless that gain exceeds what could have been earned in the best alternative use of the funds the member invests in the cooperative. In buying, the quality of goods and of retailing service, of health service, of insurance, or of terms of borrowing are considerations. Presumably each buyer weighs these considerations against price differences. In selling commodities, price is apt to dominate. In providing labor, working conditions and future opportunities on the job may offset quite marked differences in the wage income. Sellers of savings as direct investors or through financial intermediaries are interested in the safety and liquidity of principal as well as the rate of return. Hereafter gain in real income from cooperative membership will be referred to as obtaining a better net price.

Each type of purchase or sale is related to a primary interest of the patron-member. The primary interest of the household as a buyer has to do with its consumption of commodities and services with its protection (through insurance) against financial loss from calamitous events or with enlarging its funds temporarily by borrowing. As a seller the household's primary interest includes the income from and the conditions under which its members work, or the income from investment of savings. If the member is an investor-owned enterprise, whether a farm, a retail store, or a sizable corporation, its primary interest ordinarily covers a lesser range because its activities are more specialized than those of the household.

Interest in joining a cooperative can be expected to vary according to the percentage by which the potential member anticipates that his real income (as defined above) will be increased. This is a function of the percentage of the potential member's purchases or of his sales that are made through the cooperative. For example, this interest may be very small, as for the typical household purchase of gasoline, but petroleum products are a large item in a farmer's expense. Second, the potential gain is also a function of the percentage by which the cooperative's net price is better (as defined above) than the price of investor-owned firms. Variations in expected individual gain from patron-membership must influence the extent of the member's willingness to participate in forming a cooperative and in providing leadership after its establishment. These topics are considered in chapter 2 and more fully in chapter 13.

To recapitulate, when a buyer or seller becomes a patron-member of a cooperative that organization becomes his agent for purchases or sales which are made through the cooperative. Except for bargaining cooperatives to be considered below, the cooperative is the means whereby members by-pass the market adjacent, vertically, to them and in which they would otherwise make individual arms-length transactions with investor-owned enterprises. As such, a cooperative is a means of "vertical integration" to reach a better market.

The Cooperative As Vertical Integration

What the cooperative does for its members can be visualized by considering first the series of steps, vertically arrayed, that are involved in most economic activities. The earliest step for commodities that consumers purchase at retail is the production of raw materials. Subsequent processing and distributive steps land the goods on the retailers' shelves. A similar vertical chain exists in the opposite direction, as when farm products are prepared for shipment to consuming markets in fresh form or are processed and then sent through distributive channels. Savers need not invest their money directly in producing enterprises or home mortgages for they can place their funds in financial intermediaries which do the investing. Nor do borrowers necessarily obtain funds directly from savers, for a financial institution usually operates between them. Insurance is somewhat different, as will be seen later. One can look at these vertical steps as "downstream" from the user or "later," or from the user's point of view "upstream" toward "earlier" stage operations.

In contrast to market transactions between vertically placed and independent operations two or more of these operations are often combined in a single ownership, that is, they are vertically integrated. Often a large chain food store company integrates upstream to perform the wholesaling function and even to manufacture part of the goods it sells. A petroleum refiner often owns oil wells and pipe lines to transport the crude oil and downstream owns product pipe lines and wholesale and even retail outlets to distribute refined products. Examples can be multiplied.

Usually buying or selling in a more distant market vertically can be done efficiently only on a scale far larger than the size of any one patron's primary interest. In order to solve this problem, buying at an earlier transaction step or selling at a later one is undertaken by a group of patrons through a cooperative. Small savers rarely lend money directly to borrowers but do so through a mutual savings and loan association or a mutual savings bank.

Quite different in organization and method are the "bargaining cooperatives" or "bargaining associations" that have become widespread in American agriculture. If all that an association of this type does is to bargain with buyers, backed by the threat to withhold its members' output from the market in order to obtain a better price, its function is analogous to that performed by a labor union for its members. Instead of bypassing by vertical integration the adjacent market that performs unsatisfactorily for its members, the bargaining association seeks to force the buying (or selling) firms to agree to a better price. It is a collective endeavor on the part of the autonomous members. Because these associations may be an alternative to cooperative vertical integration, they will be considered at the appropriate points in later chapters.

Entry by the Cooperative

With rare exceptions cooperatives are established to carry on an activity in which investor-owned firms are already engaged. The cooperative enters a going market. To succeed the cooperative must add to its members' incomes when in competition with established investor-owned firms. Clear recognition of this character and role of cooperatives has not been evident in much of the literature on these enterprises, which portrays them as instruments of social reform. Those who take this view often stumble because they ignore the fact that cooperatives operate in a market system and that they, like any enterprise, may earn profits or incur losses.

The economic significance of the cooperative stems from its form of enterprise organization, which is designed to augment the economic welfare of its members by becoming itself a participant in the market in which members would otherwise buy or sell. The cooperative is an "entrant" in the economist's terminology and, particularly if it adds capacity, can be expected to disturb the previous situation in the market. It is also an "innovation," as J.A. Schumpeter used that term, for he included new forms of enterprise organization among innovations.[5] It disturbs the status quo to the degree that its net price after patronage dividends is better than that of its rivals and thereby attracts patronage. Its rivals are then under pressure to revise their prices to thwart added loss of volume. These adjustments are to the disadvantage of these firms' investor-owners but to the advantage of their patrons. Such is the process of competition and also the typical effect of the cooperative.

In the turmoil that follows it is by no means certain that the cooperative will survive and often it has not. Its survival and growth will depend on the validity of the founders' estimate of the extent to which rivals' prices are out of line with necessary costs, on the efficiency of the cooperative venture, and on the fighting capacity of the established enterprises.

So far the emphasis has been on entry by cooperative vertical integration made possible by failure of the market entered to have performed efficiently and competitively. This is the gist of the economic theory of entry to be presented in chapter 3. It is possible, however, that the purpose of cooperative entry may be to obtain such a large share of the vertically adjacent market as to make it less competitive, as has occurred in some markets for farm products. Even in such a case the cooperative is an entrant in order to obtain higher real income for its members.

An analysis with the focus just sketched, compared to viewing cooperatives as the means of changing the economic order, will be less exciting, but conclusions reached will be less debatable and more fundamental with respect to a private-property market system.

Orientation of This Study

The orientation of this study is not toward proposals for social reform but toward analysis of the performance of cooperatives and mutuals in a private-property market system. The emphasis is not on managerial problems, although much of the evidence and the conclusions derived from this study could be useful to those concerned with establishing or directing a patron-owned enterprise and to officials of rival investor-owned businesses. The conditions favoring one or the other of the two types of enterprises are merely evidence from which conclusions of an economic sort can be drawn. These include the significance of alternative and perhaps coexisting types of enterprise organization, and the ease with which one type can be established or grow relative to the other as market conditions warrant. The final and most significant economic consideration is the effect of each type on how well the markets in which they engage perform from the point of view of their patron-members, whether they are consumers, workers, or relatively small investor-owned enterprises.

The key to the economic analysis is the opportunity for and economic effects of entry by vertical integration carried out cooperatively by a substantial number of economic units. If entry by the cooperative succeeds, it and the remaining investor-owned ones may coexist in the same line of activity. Each serves as a check on the other. Members can cease to buy from or sell to the cooperative, or nonmembers of these enterprises can become patron-members.

Even where the market conditions are favorable, there remains the question as to whether the cooperative is an effective means of vertically integrating into that market. Some aspects of that issue will be explored in chapter 2 and tested in chapters 4-12, inclusive, which analyze patron-owned enterprises in various sectors of the economy. Conclusions on this fundamental point will be stated in chapters 13-15.

The literature of economics provides useful but not fully definitive criteria whereby one can predict the performance of a market from its organizational features alone. Generally, one can conclude that the ease of entry by new enterprises must have a socially beneficial effect on costs, prices, and the quality of product and service in the market. Hence, the role of cooperatives is as entrants except where they achieve a significant and enduring degree of monopoly power. Otherwise, the absence of cooperatives indicates effective competition in the market adjacent to the patrons, with one very important qualification. If there are high barriers to entry, or the cooperative is not an efficient form of enterprise to enter, continued noncompetitive performance is possible in the adjacent market.

2

The Cooperative in Economic Theory

Studying cooperatives as part of a market system leads one to pause, for in the economists' analysis of the coordination of economic activities through market transactions the business decision units are investor-owned firms. That theory is often called "the theory of the firm." But is the cooperative a firm in the economic sense? The answer will lead to an exploration of the problems of forming a cooperative, of its optimum size and volume rate, and of its reaction to the behavior of its members and of rivals. Conclusions on these points form the "theory of the cooperative" which will guide the analysis in subsequent chapters.

Is the Cooperative a Firm?

As the market system developed it was composed of investor-owned firms which employed workers and the savings of households to produce the commodities and services that households purchase and consume. Analysis of this system's operation rests on the assumption that each household and each firm selects among the alternatives open to it those expected to maximize its economic welfare. Workers choose the jobs that offer the preferred combination of wage rates and other advantages. Each household's welfare is maximized by making the best use of its income, whether to save or to spend. In spending it chooses among com-

13

modities and services in light of their relative prices and the household's preferences. As savers of part of their incomes, households choose among alternative uses of savings the preferred combination of income rate and safety and liquidity of principal.

Ordinarily, households are passive in all of these matters. They respond to offers of employment by profit-seeking business firms and to firms' offers of goods and services for sale. Firms anticipate households' wants, for production occurs in advance of consumption.

In the study of the operation of the market system the emphasis is on the active behavior of the firm regardless of the number of persons who own it. It is assumed to maximize economic profits, or net income, above what it could earn in the best alternative use of its capital. To succeed it must produce goods at the lowest cost and sell them at the best prices obtainable. By doing so it will obtain the largest profits. To perform in this fashion the firm must make commitments in advance and it may misjudge the prospects. If it predicts successfully and profits prove to be high, its superiority is temporary in a competitive market; imitation by others tends to wipe out any unusual advantage one firm uncovers. By these adjustment processes the whole system is brought into equilibrium by impersonal and nonpolitical market forces. The results are expected to be the best in the sense of maximizing the welfare of consumers, workers, and owners.

In working toward its optimum position each firm must be concerned with how its own costs behave when its operations are larger or smaller. Once the optimum size is reached there is no reason to alter it as long as the basic conditions are unchanged. The firm is then in equilibrium, as well as being part of an industry and of an economy that works toward a general equilibrium.

How does the cooperative or the mutual fit into this system? Does it tend to grow to a size determined by external opportunities and the behavior of its own costs? If it reaches that scale does it tend to remain there or is it unstable and tend either to gain volume beyond its efficient size, to lose volume, or even to disappear? What does it, or it and its members singly or together, try to maximize? The basic question is whether the cooperative is the maximizing unit as are investor-owned firms.

Answering these questions requires underscoring a feature of the cooperative that is assumed throughout this volume except when noted otherwise. Membership is voluntary in the sense that no individual or firm is forced to join or after joining required to remain as a patron or a member. It is not inconsistent with this assumption for each cooperative to set standards for membership or to have a short-period patronage contract with members, but limiting number of members other than temporarily raises additional questions, as will be seen.

The cooperative is an enterprise that carries out functions delegated by its members, but its objective is not to maximize its own net gain as such. Instead its function is to augment members' gains in the primary activity from which their patronage comes. The cooperative is an extension of that activity by at least one vertical step. Instead of vertical extension by a single household or a relatively small investor-owned firm the vertical integration is carried out cooperatively by a sizable group of patrons in order to achieve an efficient scale of operation. "Transactions" between the cooperative and members at "prices" are in principle equivalent to bookkeeping transfers between an investor-owned corporation and its departments or subsidiary corporations.

As an owned vertical step the cooperative has no net income conceptually, although net savings arise from its operations when its revenues exceed the cost of conducting the cooperatively owned activity. Such savings belong conceptually to the members in proportion to patronage, not in proportion to ownership. The savings may be used to adjust initial prices according to each member's patronage or part or even all of the savings may be withheld with the consent of the members to augment the cooperative's capital.

All of this leads to a basic issue; is the open membership cooperative a firm in the same sense as are its rival investor-owned enterprises?[1] Cooperatives do differ in that patron-members are all stockholders, a rare situation for investor-owned firms. Ordinarily, cooperatives cannot turn to the capital market as a basic source of funds. But they may borrow from commercial banks if their credit standing is good or from the banks for cooperatives in the case of agricultural cooperatives. Cooperatives in other fields do not have the latter aid. Clearly the typical cooperative differs in a number of regards from investor-owned firms. But these differences have not handicapped successful cooperatives.

Open membership is typical of most farmer cooperatives and is the practice of consumer cooperatives but not generally of cooperatives owned by urban businesses. Members may or may not be bound by patronage contracts. In the case of cooperatives made up of urban businesses new members who would compete with old members usually are not admitted. Farmer cooperatives are generally open to new members if the cooperative has sufficient capacity. These cooperatives may bind members by patronage contracts which go far to assure the cooperative a stable supply of the product handled. Except for consumer cooperatives the other types studied tend to operate as do their investor-owned rivals. This involves bases for assuring a stable volume of business. To cap this conclusion it should be noted that many states have incorporation laws for farmer cooperatives. Altogether cooperatives tend to operate much as do investor-owned firms, given similar market situations.

Thus the open-membership cooperative is an association of the "vertical extensions" of numerous members' primary activity, a characteristic that is most significant at the time of founding or in a later period of adversity.[2] Quite different is the closed-membership cooperative to be considered in a later section.

Entrepreneurship in the Cooperative

All organizations come into being because one or a few persons devote time and often money to the promotional or entrepreneurial task. The organizers of an investor-owned firm expect to receive income from their investment sufficiently above that obtainable elsewhere to more than compensate for the time and expenses incurred in developing the enterprise. In small enterprises much of the expected income may be in the form of a salary for a well-paid manager.

Compared to the financial reward expected by promoters of the typical investor-owned firm, the few of what is expected to be the far larger membership of a cooperative which takes on the entrepreneurial task cannot generally expect comparable monetary gain. Lucrative managerial positions for them are unlikely, in part because such sponsors' experience typically has been in the "earlier" or a "later" vertical step from which stems their interest in forming the cooperative. The pecuniary inducement to these organizers is limited to the absolute amount by which the expected net gain from patronage provides a higher return on investment in the cooperative than is obtainable elsewhere. In a cooperative with 1000 members, involving an average investment per member of $200, the economic profit or gain above the return the $200 could earn elsewhere would be very small for each member. But prospective profits earned on $200,000 could attract one or more stockholders to promote an investor-owned firm.

This bleak portrait of entrepreneurial rewards to sponsors of a cooperative may not have been painted with all of the appropriate "colors." Rewards for entrepreneurship are not always in money. Otherwise much that happens in society would not have occurred. Even the founder of an investor-owned firm takes pride in its success and the position he achieves in the community. Whether such nonpecuniary considerations weigh more heavily in the values of promoters of cooperatives and are more comparable to those obtained by leaders in religion, education, or in public life, cannot be judged definitively.[3] What does remain is the question whether persons who rank nonpecuniary rewards highly are also well qualified to appraise the opportunity for a cooperative, business-type operation and to promote the venture.

The need for entrepreneurship does not end with the founding of the cooperative. Operating decisions must be made continually, and at times problems of added investment or of new directions of activity of the cooperative enterprise must be dealt with. Not surprisingly leadership comes from a small group, perhaps a few members but often from the hired management.[4] The latter is not unusual in large cooperatives and is characteristic of large mutuals (as will be seen in chapters 10 and 12). The fact of managerial, not member, leadership of large established cooperatives does not mean that the basic decisions of members to patronize or not are made by top management. Nevertheless the more efficient the management the more the cooperative can attract and hold members' patronage.

The Optimum Volume Rate of the Open-End Cooperative

While each member of the open-end cooperative extended vertically to encompass his pro-rata share of the cooperative constitutes the maximizing unit, or firm in the economic sense, the cooperative is an enterprise owned collectively by many such "patron-firms." Its functions have to be selected and its horizontal scale determined. On the basis of those decisions it must choose the types and proportions of facilities and labor it will use. Thereby the level of the cooperative's average costs and the effect thereon of higher or lower volume will also have been determined. These costs compared to rivals' prices indicate what members gain as patrons of the cooperative. How all of this can be expected to work out may be seen most easily by comparison with the way an investor-owned firm deals with the same issues when selling in a market where it has no effect on the existing price, the situation faced by most cooperatives.

Consider first an investor-owned firm's short-period output decisions with a given scale of plant. Referring to figure 1, if the market price is Pr_1 the firm should produce quantity $0Q_1$ at which the average cost per unit (which includes the return on capital in its best alternative use) is least. More significantly, at that volume Pr_1 equals MC, or the added cost of producing the last or marginal unit added to make total volume $0Q_1$.

The significance of MC would be more evident if the market-determined price were Pr_2. Then revenues from additional output would exceed the additional cost of the added output, as portrayed by MC, up to volume $0Q_2$, which would then be the profit-maximizing volume. Producing more than $0Q_2$, say $0Q_3$, would involve marginal costs in excess of

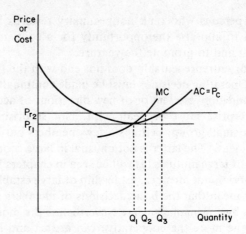

Figure 1. Equilibrium of a buying cooperative under simplified assumptions

Pr_2 and would be uneconomic, for profits would be reduced or an operating loss might even be incurred.

What is the optimal volume for a cooperative from whom members acquire goods, given that its rivals' price is Pr_1 or, alternatively, Pr_2? This question will be explored first for an open-end cooperative through which members acquire goods. In a later section the cooperative that limits membership will be considered.

Initial Simplified Assumptions

Consideration of the theory of the open-end cooperative will be aided by making three assumptions, each to be discarded later. First, assume that the cooperative acts as if its operations will not affect the price of rival investor-owned enterprises. Second, in order to identify the essence of the cost-volume problem faced, assume that members decide to join and be patrons solely on the basis of the cooperative's price, adjusted for net savings, compared to price offers of rival enterprises. Presumably each member will be a patron as long as the cooperative's net price is marginally better than that of the investor-owned firms. Finally assume that the net savings of the cooperative are known in advance by its members with certainty and whether paid in cash or not are viewed as having full cash equivalent value.

Volume Rate and Capacity

Again figure 1 can be used but curve AC now has a double meaning. In addition to portraying the relation between the cooperative's volume of output and its average cost per unit the AC curve is also the net price to members. It is a P_c curve for different volumes, the original "price" charged less each member's pro rata share of the cooperative's net savings.

At what point could one expect the cooperative's volume to settle? It should be noted first that if the rival investor-owned firm's price were Pr_1 there would be no economic gain from patronage of a cooperative even though the AC curve includes as a cost the return on investment members could earn from alternate use of the funds. The relevant question is the volume the cooperative could obtain were rivals' prices higher, say Pr_2. The answer will be found in the relation between Pr_2 and the relevant cost of the cooperative to members as represented by AC, because AC is also the cooperative's net price to members.

Three possibilities should be compared.

1. If the cooperative's volume were $0Q_1$ its average cost per unit and hence its net price to members would be lowest. As a buying cooperative it would then obtain the highest net savings per unit of volume. But this volume was shown earlier to be neither the most efficient use of the plant nor the profit-maximizing output for an investor-owned firm selling at Pr_2 because the added cost of added volume, or MC, would be less than the price. Would volume of an open-end cooperative also be above $0Q_1$ when the rival's price is Pr_2?

2. The answer is in the affirmative but for quite a different reason. The investor-owned firms would produce $0Q_2$ because up to that point the *added cost* per unit, or MC, would be less than the price per unit, Pr_2. Hence its aggregate profits would increase up to volume $0Q_2$. So would the aggregate net savings of the cooperative, but the net price *to each member* as measured by AC, the average cost per unit, would *rise* whenever the volume exceeds $0Q_1$.

3. An important point then becomes evident under the assumptions made thus far. If rivals' price is Pr_2, the cooperative's volume will not remain at $0Q_1$, *not even at* $0Q_2$, *because the decision makers in an open-end cooperative are the individual members, present and potentially added, each acting autonomously.* Even though the cooperative's net price per unit as measured by AC rises for volumes in excess of $0Q_1$, the aggregate net savings of the cooperative are maximum when its MC equals Pr_2. Under the assumptions as to member behavior, added volume will be induced as long as the net price to members, or AC, is below Pr_2, the investor-owned firms' price.

Old members would be made worse off because they would pay higher net prices as shown by the rising AC whenever the volume exceeds $0Q_1$. But given the independent decision-making by the members each new member as well as each old one would be a patron-member and purchase as large a volume as he desires as long as the cooperative's net price is below that of investor-owned firms. Consequently, under the assumptions stated above the volume could be expected to grow to where AC would nearly intersect Pr_2, or volume $0Q_3$. At that point costs per unit will have risen to about Pr_2 and the cooperative's net savings would approach zero! No longer would there be either significant monetary advantage or disadvantage to belonging to the cooperative. The cooperative's success in providing a better net price for patrons than offers of rivals would have attracted so much volume that the advantage of membership would have disappeared.

That need be only temporary, however. The cooperative could expand, particularly if it were to be at least as efficient at the larger scale. Its enlarged volume would put pressure on rivals to reduce their price. Under the assumptions used thus far it would appear likely that expansion of the cooperative (at constant costs per unit of volume) would force its rivals out of business. But this rarely happens except where the only grain elevator at a shipping point or milk processing plant in a locality is a cooperative. Otherwise there appear to be restraints on the cooperative's market share.

Restraints on the Cooperative's Growth and Its Equilibrium Scale

One or more of several influences affecting potential members' decisions may restrain the cooperative's growth. Potential members may disregard small price differences because of a preference for doing business with a cooperative or with an investor-owned enterprise. A more general and lasting influence affecting potential members' decisions may be the "package" or composite of quality and service offered by the rival types of enterprise. The appeal of cooperatives, at least at the time of founding, has been to potential patrons who do not need credit from buyers or sellers and want the best price for an acceptable but largely unadorned "product." Many buyers at retail prefer a chain store "package" made up of mechanized, impersonal service, cash and carry, and the lower prices made possible thereby. Others are willing to pay for credit and delivery service with emphasis on top quality merchandise. Some farmers in a locality sell to the X creamery and others to Y, both investor-owned firms, even though they would receive a higher price from a cooperative. Advances of credit without a specific interest charge by investor-owned firms is frequent, but not by cooperatives, which may affect the patronage decision. Finally potential members may be deterred from patronage of a cooperative when the full net savings are not reflected in the initial prices. The size of the year-end net savings is often uncertain. Also cooperatives often retain part or even all the net savings to finance expansion, and members may have different preferences for cash dividends versus an evidence of added investment in the cooperative.

These patronage attitudes of current and potential members can be portrayed in figure 2 as a demand curve, D_c, given a particular level of rivals' price. This curve assumes that any member of a selling cooperative who would be a patron at a higher price would also be a patron at a lower price and that more patron-members would be attracted at lower prices.

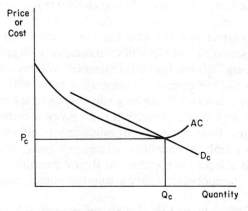

Figure 2. Equilibrium of a buying cooperative given rivals' price and members' preferences

Given the prospective demand for the cooperative's output, it can acquire a plant of the type and size for which the average cost curve, AC, is intersected at or near its lowest point by the demand curve, D_c. It is true also that a marginal cost curve would intersect the average cost curve at its lowest point. As long as neither the member-customers' preferences or rivals' prices are unchanged the equilibrium will be stable. Furthermore assume that over a fairly wide range of increase of size of the plant, or building of another plant, the cooperative will have similar costs. In either of these plausible events the long-run cost curve is constant over a wide range. As long as neither member-customers' preferences nor rivals' prices are changed the equilibrium will be stable.

As the cooperative's share of the market volume rises the prices of rival investor-owned enterprises must be affected. If the latters' prices reflect monopoly, that position will be more difficult to maintain as their volume shrinks. If the level of the rival firms' prices reflect inefficiency, their high-cost capacity would be eliminated and their prices forced down. Except to the degree that the second and third assumptions posited earlier are invalid and assuming constant costs in the long run over a wide range of capacity of the cooperative, the prices of surviving investor-owned enterprises should be forced toward the level of the cooperative's average cost per unit of volume.

Equilibrium of a Limited Membership Cooperative

Aside from investor-owned rivals' reactions a cooperative may not grow to the scale suggested above for other reasons. The restraint on growth other than temporarily because of inadequate capacity would reflect a conscious policy except in one circumstance. In some situations the prospective member is a rival of old members in their primary activity to such an extent that any gain the new member would obtain from membership would enhance its ability to compete with and thereby injure the old members. Second, the added members' volume may set in motion the tendency for the open-end cooperative to be inefficient, but that would be only temporary if the long-run cost curve is horizontal. Third, so many may join the cooperative that its investor-owned rivals will be forced to adjust their prices. If so, nonmembers obtain a costless gain while the old members' benefit is reduced relatively. But that is important only if it affects old members in their competition with nonmembers. Fourth, the cooperative may attempt to obtain monopoly gains for its members.

If membership is limited to obtaining monopoly gains, best illustrated by a "selling" cooperative, the rational policy is to set membership and

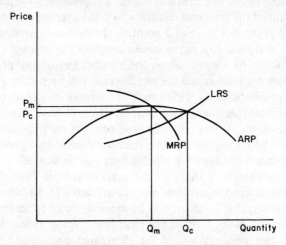

Figure 3. Monopoly versus competitive equilibrium of a selling cooperative

THE COOPERATIVE IN ECONOMIC THEORY

volume at the quantity at which the cooperative's aggregate net savings would be maximum. In order to illustrate a "selling" cooperative price the lines on figure 3 must be "upside down" compared to those in the preceding charts. Assume that the cooperative limits membership in order to maximize its patron-members' net incomes.[5] This goal would be obtained when its volume at the average price of the ARP curve is equal to additions to revenue, or MRP. The cooperative's volume would then be Q_m, and its price would be P_m. Had the cooperative been open, as was assumed for figure 2, its price would have been P_c and quantity Q_c, determined by the intersection of the ARP curve and the long-run supply curve, LRS, indicating the member volume attracted at various prices. The absolute distances on the chart are not significant or expressive of actual situations. It is the relative position of curves that is important.

Is the Worker Cooperative Unique?

Most readers think of cooperatives as handling commodities or providing services and carrying out these activities by employing workers for wages. But at various times in western countries, including the United States, and recently in developing countries, cooperatives of workers engaged in farming, manufacturing, or trade have been started.[6] Recently the Soviet Union, Yugoslavia, and other Communist countries have encouraged worker cooperatives.

The worker cooperative differs from the typical commodity handling cooperative in that members of the latter are patrons not active participants in the cooperative's activity. In the worker cooperative members constitute the work force of the enterprise. Consequently their shares of the cooperative's revenues above nonlabor costs constitute their entire incomes, not a marginal addition to income obtained by members of successful farmer, retailer-owned, or consumer cooperatives. Otherwise, does a worker cooperative differ analytically from other cooperatives?

For those formed voluntarily and without government restraints the answer is negative. In a voluntary work cooperative, members are in a "selling-of-labor" format. If membership is open presumably members will be faithful participants at least as long as the monetary return equals wages elsewhere. Their preferences for being a cooperative member or not are reflected in the labor supply curve, such as the LRS curve in figure 3. If the membership is closed and employment and output are such as to maximize the wage income of a limited number of members the volume of employment would be that at which ARP equals MRP in figure 3. Otherwise employment would be where the LRS curve intersects ARP.

Equilibrium Characteristics and Economic Analysis

The economic effect of cooperatives, whether open- or closed-end, is to aid each member individually in maximizing his economic welfare. Clearly where membership in an open-end cooperative is of positive advantage to its members the offers of the investor-owned firms must be less good than they would be if these firms were in competitive equilibrium. Consequently the opportunity members seize by organizing a cooperative for their own gain has the effect of pushing the cooperative's rivals toward the competitive equilibrium, the social optimum.

The conclusion does not hold for a closed-end cooperative by itself. If membership is restricted to the extent that rivals' prices are not forced to the level of necessary costs, the intent and effect is monopolistic. The benefits of the cooperative are obtained only by its limited membership. Full market adjustment is not forced. Actually cooperatives that limit total membership are quite rare.

Having demonstrated that a cooperative can reach an equilibrium position it is possible to use economic theory to analyze the effect of its entry on the performance of the market. Developing that theme is the task of chapter 3.

3

Entry by Cooperatives or Mutuals

Whether entry of new enterprises into a market is easy or difficult goes far to explain the economic performance of that market. Where entry is difficult, prices can exceed necessary costs, with the return on investment obtainable in alternate uses of capital included in cost. Where entry is easy, prices above necessary costs will attract new enterprises whose output will force prices down to the level of costs as just defined. But entry by a cooperative may be easier or more difficult than by an investor-owned firm.

The Theory of Entry

After the theory of entry provided in the literature of economics has been stated, it will be developed further and then adapted to the special case of entry by cooperative vertical integration. The modified theory leads to hypotheses with respect to conditions that favor or inhibit entry by cooperatives. These hypotheses provide the focus for the investigations in the following chapters of why cooperatives have entered and expanded in some markets and not in others.

The Static Theory of Entry

In popular usage there is confusion about what constitutes entry, a

25

term given a precise meaning in economic theory.[1] Entry consists of the establishment of a new participant in the market, but only if this enterprise simultaneously adds capacity. It is the added capacity that alters the condition of competition and thereby affects the economic performance of the market.

Types of Entry Barriers

A new participant that adds capacity in the market often must overcome one or more types of entry barriers.[2] A barrier is generally present when the established firms are few because the percentage an entrant of efficient size would add to the capacity would be high. The higher this percentage the more difficult is entry because of the effect of the new seller's volume on the postentry price and on the volume of both the established firms and the entrant. (Implicitly, the analysis is carried out as if the size of the market were not changing.)

If the entrant expects established firms to continue to sell their previous quantities, its addition to the market volume would force both its price and that of the established firms to drop, as governed by the elasticity of demand for the product. If demand is of unitary elasticity an entrant that would add 10 percent to the volume would expect the price after its entry to decline by that percentage. The expected postentry net income of the entrant would then be lower than the established firms had enjoyed and might be so low as to discourage the entry. Second, the potential entrant might expect that after his entry the established firms would declare war by such large price changes that a fledgling entrant could not survive. Third, the established enterprises' only reaction might be to reduce their volume enough to hold the price at the preentry level, and then they and the entrant would operate at less than capacity. If so, both their and the entrant's average cost per unit would rise and profits would fall, potentially so much that entry would not be attractive.

There is no definitive theory whereby the potential entrant can predict which of these outcomes will occur. It should be underscored that the entrant's effect on the postentry price is a function of the capacity it adds relative to the size of the market, not the entrant's absolute size.

Quite different is the barrier to entry when the entrant faces significant absolute cost disadvantages, such as high cost of capital or lack of access to patents or to raw materials. A frequent handicap when entry would require building a large plant is the difficulty of obtaining enough capital on favorable terms. If *absolutely* large size also means being large *relative* to the size of the market, the entry barriers are compounded.

Finally, entry may be made difficult if potential members prefer for nonmonetary reasons to do business with certain or all of the established firms. In that event the entrant would have to offer sufficiently better prices to woo patrons or incur the cost of persuading them by expensive advertising and selling efforts.

Even in a market where only a few firms of efficient scale can exist it is possible that the established firms will prefer to hold their prices at a level that will permit some entry. There may be an unusually advantaged potential entrant, such as the holder of a patent for a much more efficient process or the discoverer of a rich deposit of material. Established firms' profits might then be higher after the entry of such an enterprise than at prices that would have discouraged entry. Also, the process of successful entry may take so long that the present discounted value of expected profits over this interval from prices that permit entry would exceed the profits obtainable from prices low enough to discourage entry. These exceptions to the more general statement of the condition of entry indicate that the qualifications of the potential entrant are important.

Entry by a New or by an Established Enterprise

Entry need not be by a new enterprise,[3] a fact that could make entry much easier. The entrant may be an enterprise already established in the same activity in another geographic market or engaged in a quite different line of business. Of particular interest here is that an established enterprise may enter the market from which it previously bought or into which it sold by vertical integration.

Since entry by cooperative vertical integration is the central feature of all cooperatives except those that bargain only, the term should be explained. Few enterprises both produce raw materials and sell finished goods to consumers. A farmer's roadside stand which sells home-grown products may appear to be an exception, but even he purchases fertilizer and seeds. In contrast most finished goods are the result of several production and distribution steps. These begin with raw material production and go through various production and marketing operations before sale to consumers.

There is a time sequence to these operations and when viewed from operations at any one of the vertical processing steps can be referred to as "earlier" or "later." Alternatively the steps can be identified as "upstream" toward earlier operations or "downstream" toward consumers.

Compared to a newly formed cooperative an established enterprise has several advantages as an entrant. It has already developed its managerial personnel and policies. Its personnel have the specialized knowledge and skills needed for success in its added operations. It either has the capital required for successful entry or will be able to obtain the funds on more favorable terms than those which a newly formed enterprise must meet.

Easier still, it seems plausible, is entry by vertical integration on the part of an established enterprise. If it integrates into the market from which it previously bought it thereby becomes a self-supplier. If the integration is downstream the operation entered becomes the outlet for the goods from the enterprise's original activity. It must then develop its market connections for disposing of the output of the capacity it adds in the downstream operation.

It seems probable therefore that entry downstream is ordinarily the more difficult direction to integrate.[4] Except where standard commodities are sold in a large market by grades, as are butter and wheat, sellers usually take the initiative in persuading customers to buy. A major reason is that the seller is ordinarily more specialized in location, organization, and facilities and hence has fewer alternatives than do buyers. Compared to the variety of items usually offered by sellers, buyers other than consumers ordinarily use materials inputs that are more standardized and for which the markets are large.

Compared to either backstream or downstream integration an established enterprise that spreads into another geographic market or enters another type of business must develop both sources of supply and customers for the output of its new operation.

Potential Versus Actual Entry

In markets where each established firm accounts for a very small percentage of the volume, only actual entry affects performance. The rational behavior of each established firm is to get the best possible combination of price and volume in the present period. It cannot count on rivals doing otherwise nor can it inhibit entry when prices are attractive relative to costs.

The situation is quite different where participants in the market are very few. Each of the relatively large firms must realize that its decisions will have a significant effect on the price that will exist. To the extent that each acts on the basis of the mutual interest of the group of firms the price arrived at will not be as low as necessary costs (including a competitive return on capital) but at a more profitable level. By the same reasoning it would appear that each will be aware of the consequences of holding prices at a level that would invite entry.

The restraining effect of potential entry on the behavior of established firms in markets of few firms poses a difficult problem for this study. Some information is available about the barriers to entry in the various commodity, service, and financial markets to be examined in the next several chapters. But most of the direct evidence is about the actual entry or nonentry of cooperatives, about the survival and growth or failure of those formed, and about the effects of those that become well-established on investor-owned firms' prices or market shares.

Much of the entry by cooperative vertical integration analyzed in the next several chapters has occurred in local or even in larger markets where the established firms were few. Some of this entry could have been made by an especially advantaged potential entrant, an unlikely quality of cooperatives in light of their entrepreneurial problems (see chapter 2). A more general explanation of such observed entry is suggested by some limitations of the static theory of entry.

Some Nonstatic Elements of the Condition of Entry

It is important to understand the methodological character of the theory of entry stated above for its use may limit one's ability to predict entry. It is of the "long-run equilibrium" and "stationary" sort. In it the behavior of the established sellers and their estimates of the prospect of entry are appraised as if the market were in full adjustment given the number of participants and the forces of technology, cost and demand. But these forces are brought into full equilibrium only over a long period of time during which significant further changes frequently occur. This does not mean, necessarily, that such a period must have elapsed before these forces affect the condition of entry. Instead it is assumed that in a market of few firms each established seller, and each potential entrant, appraises the costs the entrant must achieve and the effect of his volume on the postentry price in terms of what can be expected in the longer-run future.

All of this estimating has to be done in a changing world in which technology, demand, and other important considerations do not stand still. Decision makers may not understand the full implication of current developments, and they know much less of those to come. Each established firm could have a quite different estimate of the height of the entry barriers and also of the prospective entrant's estimates of those barriers. Furthermore, with the scene subject to change and with any disparity between present and potential costs often requiring years to correct, established sellers may take a short view and prefer to earn the substantial near-term profits made possible by prices that risk entry.

Where there are several established sellers no one of them necessarily carries the burden of forestalling entry. Responsibility of the established firms for holding prices at the entry-barring level is divided and affected by different estimates of the level of prices at which entry would occur.

If the market is growing, actual entry need not affect prices for, were entry to occur, the established sellers could then expand less or not at all. In that event their "loss" would consist only of foregoing a higher than competitive level of return on added investment, not of lower profits on their preentry capital.

All of this can be summarized by saying that the typical market of few firms, whether sellers or buyers, is an imperfect arrangement for "agreeing" about the best policy on any matter. As the literature on the theory of oligopoly demonstrates the exigencies of rivalry among the few established firms makes more urgent "agreement" not to make war on each other. As a result the uncertain possibility of entry may become a subordinate consideration. If so, the price may be at a level that invites entry, and the additional sellers would then weaken the ability of the established enterprises to hold prices at a noncompetitive level.

The purpose of the comments just made is two-fold. One is to point out the difficulty of analyzing entry solely in the framework of long-term static equilibrium under stationary conditions. The second is to show the importance of study of actual entry into markets of few firms.

Fortunately, observation of what happens after entry can be instructive. If the established firms then revise their prices relative to costs (or the quality of their product or service) this is objective evidence of what entry forced. Of more general significance, such postentry developments indicate the degree to which the established sellers were not alert to, the entry limitation on their prices. Attainment of a significant market share by the cooperatives is further evidence on the same point, particularly where the investor-owned firms' volume then declines absolutely. A similar interpretation can be made in cases where cooperatives produce a disproportionate part of the added capacity in a growing market.

Entry by a Cooperative

It now appears that the characteristics of the cooperative require special consideration of its ability to seize an entry opportunity. Potentially it has the advantages that accrue to entry by vertical integration as outlined above. If the cooperative represents downstream integration its initial membership provides for a time an assured volume of the major input. If it constitutes upstream integration its members' patronage assures a certain volume of sales for its output. In either case the cooperative initially operates only at one vertically adjacent transaction step. There could still be serious problems in buying or in selling at the further vertical step where the cooperative itself does business with investor-owned firms.

On the other hand the cooperative faces unique problems in entry by vertical integration. In contrast to vertical integration by an established investor-owned firm the cooperative is a new enterprise. It has all the problems of initiation and development into an efficient operation that were suggested in chapters 2 and 3 and need not be repeated.

Another possible problem is conflict of interest among members because they are rivals in their primary activity. This would not hold where the members are in a "purely competitive" relationship to each other because they are numerous and the receipts or purchases of each member is a minute portion of the volume of a large market. Households, farmers, and many small urban enterprises as buyers of commodities or insurance or as investors of savings or as borrowers are not aware of being rivals. In manufacturing, the number of enterprises in a geographic market is usually much smaller, and the firms are conscious of being rivals in selling.

Finally, in contrast to vertical integration by an investor-owned firm, a cooperative need not add capacity initially in order to disturb the market. An investor-owned firm may elect to keep as profits savings obtained by vertical integration rather than to pass them on to patrons as better prices. But when a newly established, open-end cooperative is able to obtain better net prices for its members this fact becomes evident to rivals and to their patrons. More members will be attracted to the cooperative and the diversion of volume from the investor-owned firms will press them to improve their price offer. In a meaningful sense a cooperative can have the effect of an entrant even though it does not add capacity initially.

4

Cooperative Marketing of Farm Products

Most people in the United States think of cooperatives as marketing farm products. It was to their early struggles that allusion was made in the opening paragraphs of chapter 1. But farm cooperatives were firmly established long before the late 1970s, when their annual sales volume, excluding duplication, reached $25.8 billion. When this sum is adjusted to at-the-farm values by steps explained below, it represents about 29 percent of all farm receipts from sale of products and by far the largest share cooperatives enjoy in any broad area of commodity handling. Cooperatives market widely differing percentages of various farm products, as is shown in table 4.1. The conditions giving rise to changes in these percentages will be explored in this and the following chapters.

Farm Marketing Cooperatives in 1975–1976

Following the steps taken to measure accurately the percentage of farm output handled by cooperatives serves two purposes. One is to indicate why some of the percentages cited in the early 1950s, whether by enthusiastic supporters or by critics of cooperatives, erred by being too large. During the early postwar attack on the essentially exempt status of farmer cooperatives under the federal corporate income tax laws, opponents claimed cooperatives handled 30 percent of the volume farmers marketed.

That 30 percent figure erred in two regards. It was computed by use of the *gross* volume of all cooperatives whose principal business was marketing farm products. This total included transactions between federated cooperatives and their member-locals and also the substantial volume of farm supplies handled by marketing cooperatives. Beginning with the reports by the Farmer Cooperative Service for 1950–1951, these two items have been subtracted but are partially offset by adding the volume of farm products marketed by cooperatives engaged primarily in handling supplies. The resulting figures, presented in column 4 of table 4.1 for the 1975–1976 crop year, are the marketing cooperatives' share of each category of farm products.[1] Included are both the volume of products handled and the volume for which the cooperatives' primary role is bargaining with the processor or handlers. For comparison the 1950–1951 percentages are also presented.

Since 1950–1951 the cooperatives' shares advanced for all but four farm products: livestock and products, eggs and poultry, rice, and tobacco. The percentage more than doubled for cotton, but only reached 26 percent. For fruits and vegetables the percentage rose by a third and for the large volume milk and dairy products category by nearly a half. For most other major commodities the cooperatives' share advanced substantially, as for grains and for sugar products. For smaller volume products the cooperatives' shares also advanced, some by substantial percentages.

Such wide differences in cooperatives' shares of marketing farm products presumably reflect both the performance of investor-owned firms with whom farmers deal and the difficulty of the entry by cooperative vertical integration. Exploring these possible deterrences in farm product markets will be a major part of this and the following chapter.

One may question whether the percentages in table 4.1 overstate the cooperatives' share of products "marketed." This term connotes such packing or processing as is needed for shipment, varying amounts of storage (as of grains), and choosing among buyers' offers. Cooperatives do perform these functions for most of the products for which the volume is reported in table 4.1. For some the cooperatives' chief and sometimes only function is to bargain collectively with the investor-owned enterprises that do the processing or marketing.

Even though bargaining as such is not cooperative vertical integration it is not possible or desirable to exclude such collective activity from this study. Only in a few cases can the volume for which bargaining is the on-

Table 4.1. Estimated Percentages of Farm Products Marketed by Cooperatives, 1975-1976 and 1950-1951[a]

Commodity group	Cooperative net sales (in millions of dollars) 1	Less marketing margins 2	Farm value of products handled (in millions of dollars) 3	Cooperative shares	
				1975-1976 4	1950-1951 5
All milk and dairy products	$ 8,480	13%	$ 7,378	69%	48%
Grains, soybeans	10,634	6	9,996	40	31
Livestock products	2,806	5	2,666	9	14
Fruit, vegetables	2,861	27	2,089	27	18
Cotton products	960	20	786	26	12
Eggs, poultry	807	28	581	8	8
Sugar products	1,337	30	936	71	59[b]
Tobacco	291	2	285	13	15[a]
Rice	869	35	565	54	54[a]
Nuts	555	15	472	43	22[b]
Edible beans, peas	116	10	104	28	20[b]
All other	238	5	116	3	2[b]
Total	$29,954	12.6%	$25,944	29%	20%

[a]Except where stated otherwise the information was provided by the Farmer Cooperative Service of the Department of Agriculture.
[b]Computed by the author using data supplied by the Farmer Cooperative Service.

ly, or even the principal, activity be separated from the volume marketed in the full sense of that term. Also, many bargaining cooperatives do some handling or processing, and for some products bargaining is an alternative to engaging in steps in marketing prior to distribution to consumers.

The current status of marketing cooperatives suggests several questions. Why has not cooperative marketing of commodity output succeeded in nonfarm areas? The commodity-handling cooperatives owned by nonfarmers, to be reported in chapter 8, engage only in purchasing for their members. Second, why is not the marketing cooperatives' average market share well above 29 percent, or far less? Third, why do these cooperatives' market shares of various farm products range so widely? The first of these questions will not be explored here but presumably reflects basic differences between farm product and nonfarm product markets. Answering the last two questions is the task of this and the following chapter.

Developments in Agriculture and the Growth of Cooperative Marketing

The opportunities for cooperative vertical integration lead to the prediction that the growth or decline of these enterprises' shares in marketing various farm products can be explained by developments in agriculture and in the markets for particular farm products. These changes reflect technological advances in farming and off the farm as well.

Of particular interest is the degree to which agriculture has been commercialized at various times. By that is meant the extent to which farmers' welfare depended on cash costs and cash receipts from the sale of products rather than on family labor and on farm-produced production inputs and food for the family. In the five decades prior to 1960 the percentage of purchased to the total inputs used in farm production increased slowly, then shot up nearly two and a half times, and by 1971 represented about 82 percent of cash receipts from farm marketings. In 1910 about 20 percent of the gross farm output was used in direct farm home consumption and in farm production. This percentage did not change materially for decades but by 1949 had fallen to 7 and by 1969 was only 1! Accompanying farmers' increased reliance on the prices of purchased inputs compared to receipts from sales of products was the trend toward specialization on each farm in the production of one or at most a very few products. Unfortunately there is no comprehensive measure of such specialization. Finally, the number of nonfarm persons (at home and abroad) which the average farm worker supported in the sense of providing the raw materials of food and clothing advanced from four in 1820 and was only seven in 1900, but rose steadily to sixteen in 1959 and jumped sharply to forty-one by 1970.[2]

With the passing decades geographic markets for most farm products became progressively larger and many became national. The railroad network, completed by 1900, and later highway transport permitted commodities to be produced at great distances from consuming centers. Major raw and some processed products were sold in active broker markets. Most farmers continued to sell their output to the few buyers in a locality.

Decades ago local buyers were much more informed than were farmers about product demand and prices in the distant markets. Progressively this disadvantage disappeared as grades were established for many products and price information in both local and distant markets was disseminated by newspapers and radio.

These developments in agriculture and in markets for farm products provide insights into conditions favoring these cooperatives. A few were established in colonial days, but the number did not become large until after the Civil War. The Grange, or Patrons of Husbandry, then became active sponsors of local cooperatives, chiefly in the specialized grain and dairy farming areas of the Midwest. The mortality rate of cooperatives was high; by 1900 only 1200 survived of several times that number born in the preceding decades.[3]

After the turn of the century, cooperatives fared better in this period of rising prices. By 1913 they handled an estimated 6 percent of farm output,[4] a percentage that surged during the farm prosperity of World War I and in the years just after to 12 in 1921. A slow advance to 15 percent in 1929 followed. A temporary spurt then occurred during the Federal Farm Board's attempts to stimulate cooperative marketing, but that passed quickly. Doubtless the cooperatives would have fared badly in the 1930s had not moratoria on farmers' debts plus new loans from federal credit agencies enabled farmers to obtain short-term credit without turning to advances from buyers of farm products. Also the new banks for cooperatives were a source of credit to cooperatives (see chapter 11). During the late thirties and World War II the cooperatives' share oscillated between 15 and 18 percent. Because of farm prosperity just after World War II the share advanced slowly and then took the recent surge to 29 percent in 1975-1976.

In contrast to earlier experience the cooperative failure rate has been low in recent decades. While the number of separately organized cooperatives declined by a quarter in the last two decades this reflects primarily consolidations to gain more efficient size, often made possible by improved rural transportation. As a preliminary appraisal it seems probable that the recent low failure rate reflects in substantial part a clearer understanding by farmers, farm leaders, and public officials of the necessary conditions for cooperative integration into marketing.

The economic bases for such integration (or for collective action via bargaining) to be explored in this and the next chapter should explain both the widely different market shares of recent date and the recent changes in cooperatives' shares of various commodities reported in table 4.1.

Legal Aspects of Farmer Cooperatives

More than with respect to most other areas of the economy public policy has affected the characteristics, growth, and performance of farmer cooperatives. This is most evident with respect to farm marketing cooperatives compared to cooperatives handling farm supplies and equipment used in production. The latter have not given rise to serious policy issues and are considered in chapter 6.

Recognized quite early were the differences in structure and operations of cooperatives and of investor-owned enterprises. Section 6 of the federal Clayton Act of 1914 stated that "nothing contained in the antitrust laws shall be construed to forbid the existence and operation of—agricultural organizations, instituted for the purpose of mutual help, and not having capital stock or conducted for profit—nor shall such organizations be held or construed to be illegal combinations or conspiracies in restraint of trade under the antitrust laws."

Nevertheless the Department of Justice investigated the California Associated Raisin Growers in the decade ending in 1920 and held the cooperative to be a monopoly. This cooperative had term contracts with growers whose combined output represented about 80 percent of the annual crop, as I remember. In 1920 the Department of Justice sued the cooperative, accusing it of monopolizing the raisin market. The suit was settled by the cooperative's agreement to cancel the old membership contract and to substitute a contract which would allow members to withdraw at a specified time in each crop year. A high percentage of the growers signed this new contract.

That such a suit could be filed alarmed not only the raisin growers but also other farmer cooperatives and led to legislation that became law in 1922 as part of the Capper Volstead Act. Section 2 of this act provides that only in the event that the secretary of agriculture finds that a farmer cooperative "monopolizes or restrains trade or foreign commerce to such an extent that the price of any agricultural product is unduly enhanced by reason thereof" shall he take the legal action spelled out in the act. As far as I know, no secretary has made such a finding.

This does not mean that farmer cooperatives are immune from court decisions under laws affecting cooperatives' structures and practices. This will be seen from a number of court cases.

In *United States* v. *Borden* (308 U.S. 188 [1939]) the Borden cooperative was accused of combining and conspiring with noncooperative parties in violation of the Sherman Act, section 1. The district court ruled that the cooperative could so combine and conspire to restrain trade as long as prices were not "unduly enhanced," the phrase from the Capper Volstead Act. On appeal the Supreme Court held that the Capper Volstead Act provided only for the formation and existence of cooperatives, not for any combination or conspiracy with other persons in restraint of trade that these producers might see fit to devise. The cooperative had conspired with distributors, labor officials, municipal officials, and others to fix artificial prices. This, the Supreme Court held to be a violation of section 1 of the Capper Volstead Act.

In *Maryland and Virginia Milk Producers Assn.* v. *United States* (363 U.S. 458 [1960]) the Supreme Court confronted a civil case in which it was alleged that the cooperative had attempted to monopolize, and had monopolized, the interstate fluid milk market in Virginia, Maryland, and the District of Columbia in violation of section 2 of the Sherman Act. Through contracts and agreements the cooperative had forced an independent dairy to foreclose its competition in the market in violation of section 3 of the Sherman Act. Also, the cooperative had acquired the assets of this independent dairy, which lessened competition in violation of section 7 of the Clayton Act.

The district court upheld the right of the government to go to trial on the Sherman Act, section 3, and the Clayton Act, section 7, charges. But this court dismissed the Sherman Act, section 2, monopoly charge. The stand of the trial court stemmed from that court's view that cooperatives were entirely exempt from the antitrust laws.

The Supreme Court reversed the dismissal of the section 7 charges, saying that "we do not believe that Congress intended to immunize cooperatives engaged in competition stifling practices under the antimonopoly provisions of Section 2 of the Sherman Act." The remainder of the Court's decision extended elements of that principle. The following comment about this landmark decision emphasizes the full meaning of the decision.

The Maryland and Virginia decision is important for a number of reasons. First, the Court made it clear that cooperatives were subject to the antitrust laws even where they did not combine or conspire with unprotected persons. Cooperatives are subject to the antitrust laws beyond the *Borden* situation. Second, the Court clearly held that when cooperatives engage in unilateral predatory behavior, they are subject to the antitrust laws. Agricultural cooperatives hold no special exemption to engage in unfair trade practices. Third, agricultural cooperatives were liable to Section 2 of the Sherman Act monopolization charges. Fourth, the Court indicated that cooperatives could not lawfully engage in any practices not permitted corporations. The extent of their antitrust immunity was to be free to exist and operate as corporations operated.[5]

In the *Sunkist Growers* v. *Winkler and Smith Citrus Products Co.* (370 U.S. 19 [1962]) the Court considered whether a federated cooperative (Sunkist), and two affiliated cooperatives, all owned by the same group of growers and performing different economic functions, could be considered independent parties under the conspiracy provisions of the Sherman Act. The Court concluded that Sunkist and the two affiliated cooperatives were "in practical effect and contemplation of the statutes one 'organization' or 'association' even though they had formally organized themselves into three separate entities."

In *Case-Swayne Co.* v. *Sunkist Growers* (389 U.S. 384 [1967]) the issue was whether Sunkist was an association within the purview of the Capper Volstead Act, notwithstanding that some of its members were private, profit-seeking citrus packing plants, which were "engaged in the production of agricultural products" only in the extremely strained sense of buying fruit from growers for processing, if at all. The Court held that a Capper Volstead association must be composed exclusively of actual producers of agricultural products. It could again be argued that the Court treated Sunkist, a federated cooperative, as though it were a single centralized cooperative. Under the present state of the law, therefore, large agribusiness corporations may join agricultural cooperatives so long as they are producers of agricultural commodities.

In *North Texas Producers' Association* v. *Metzger Dairies* (348 F.2d 189, 194-196 [5th Circuit 1965], *cert. denied*, 382 U.S. 977 [1966]), an independent dairy charged that a milk producers' cooperative had violated section 2 of the Sherman Act by monopolizing the milk market in Dallas-Fort Worth by gaining control over the supply of milk, the transportation facilities, and other activities which prevented the complainant from obtaining an adequate supply of milk. The Court of Appeals held that the cooperative "acts as an entity with the same responsibility under Section 2 of the Sherman Act as if it were a private business corporation." The court upheld the jury's verdict in the trial court that the defendants had violated section 2 of the Sherman Act. The defendant cooperative appealed to the Supreme Court, but that Court refused to alter the lower court's verdict.

In *Treasure Valley Potato Bargaining Association, et al.* v. *Ore-Ida*

Foods, (497 F 2d 203 [9th circuit 1974] *cert.den.,* 491 US 999 [1974]) two bargaining cooperatives filed an antitrust suit against two of their buyers: Simplot and Ore-Ida. The case was tried in the Ninth Circuit Court. The defendants counterclaimed and established that the cooperatives colluded to achieve uniformly favorable price terms in their contracts with the defendants. The cooperatives argued that this behavior was immune from antitrust liability since they were cooperatives. This was the first appellate case that included bargaining cooperatives in the definition of Capper Volstead associations. The court said that the growers could have formed one legally distinct cooperative and that forming three to fulfill the same functions was only a *de minimas* difference when two groups of growers conspired to ask for one price.

A final argument in support of the court's interpretation of "marketing agencies in common" was provided for in the Cooperative Marketing Act of 1926. The Supreme Court refused to hear the case.

United States v. *National Broiler Marketing Association* (550 F. 2d. 1380 [5th Cir. 1977]) involved the issue of whether the broiler operation was actually conducted by the cooperative's members. The major part of the production process was performed by independent operators that hatched the eggs, grew the chicks, and continued on to process the poultry for market. The district court found that the cooperative's members maintained ownership of the broilers in all stages of the production process. In contrast the Federal Court of Appeals concluded that we cannot conceive that "the ordinary, popular sense of the word farmer would fit broiler integration companies." As was expected, the case was appealed to the Supreme Court, which refused to consider the case.

Dairy Cooperatives

Dairy cooperatives rank first in date of becoming firmly established and in share of output of large volume commodities marketed. In 1975-1976 cooperatives played some part in farmers' disposal of over two-thirds of all milk and cream sold off farms, as was shown in table 4.1.

The Status of Milk and Dairy Product Cooperatives

The role of cooperatives with respect to milk to be consumed in fluid form differs sharply from cooperative manufacturing of milk into storable products as is shown in estimates for 1964 in table 4.2. For over 70 percent of the milk distributed to consumers, the cooperatives' major function is to represent members in the formulation and administration of federal marketing orders or to bargain with distributors over price. An additional small percentage of milk is distributed by farmer cooperatives

Table 4.2. Cooperatives' Shares in the Marketing of Milk and in Manufacturing of Dairy Products, 1964[a]

Product	Cooperatives' shares (percentage)
All milk and cream sold off farms	67[b]%
All milk consumed in fluid form	
Bargaining and related activities	70–75
Distribution	10
Manufactured dairy products[c]	
Butter	65
Natural cheese	24
Nonfat dry milk	75
Ice cream	6
Cottage cheese	16

[a]The data apply to 1964 as reported by the National Commission on Food Marketing, "Organization and Competition in the Dairy Industry," *Technical Study No. 3* (June 1966): tables 12.1, 12.3, 16.39, 17.24, 18.15, and 19.33.

[b]This percentage is halfway between the percentages for 1960–1961 as reported in Farmer Cooperative Service, *Information* 87 (1973): 9, and the 1975–1976 percentage in table 4.1 above.

[c]Subtracting total cooperative volume of milk for which they bargained or distributed in fluid form leaves a residual of milk from which cooperatives manufactured products.

to consumers. In areas located at long distances from major cities both cooperatives and investor-owned plants manufacture milk into storable and easily transportable products such as cheese, butter, and nonfat milk powder, which are sold in national markets.

Dairy cooperatives engage in more extensive manufacturing than do cooperatives for any other farm product, but this varies by commodities. The latest available estimates are for 1964 (table 4.2). Their shares of the output of butter and of nonfat milk powder were 65 and 75, respectively. But cooperatives accounted for only a quarter of the natural cheese volume. Preliminary estimates for 1975-1976 by the Farmer Cooperative Service indicate little change in these percentages except an increase for cheese. Such wide differences must reflect the performance of the investor-owned enterprises in making various products compared to the difficulty of entry into the operation by cooperative vertical integration.

There are two distinct markets for milk. One is for milk to be manufactured into storable products. The other market, and now the largest by far, is for milk to be consumed in fluid form or to be made into such products as cottage cheese. Associated with this distinction is a difference in grade of milk as affected by the sanitary standards in production and handling. Milk to be distributed in fluid form must meet the strict quality standard set for Grade A and is denoted Class 1. Other milk acceptable for manufacturing, Grade B, is a shrinking percentage of the total. As will be seen, the amount of Grade A milk produced in recent years far exceeds fluid milk consumption. The excess supply of Grade A is diverted to plants that produce storable products.

Conditions of Entry into Manufacturing Dairy Products

Until recently, cost savings from substantial-size dairy product plants were not high, and the number and size of the plants were also affected by the conditions of rural transportation. It was not feasible to collect whole milk or farm-separated cream over a wide area. But with improvements in rural transportation enough whole milk can be collected to supply the present-day large and far more efficient milk processing plants to make cheese or nonfat powder, usually in conjunction wih the production of butter.[6] The net effect of these developments has been to reduce the number of plants that compete for a farmer's milk.

An overriding condition of milk production and marketing in recent years has been the slow growth or even decline of demand for the composite of milk and most of the products made from it. The per capita consumption of fluid milk has been slipping.[7] Among manufactured products, the consumption of butter has fallen by a third since the war, and evaporated and condensed milk have almost disappeared. In this period nonfat milk powder output has more than doubled. So has the consumption of cheese, which is booming, and the cooperatives' share in producing it has grown in recent decades.

Development of Dairy Product Cooperatives

Some dairy product cooperatives were started in the northeastern states before 1880, but the major movement came later in the north central states, where conditions are favorable for dairying. Because of the distance to major consuming markets the milk and cream were manufactured into storable products. Organizing cooperatives was aided by the large number of farmers who had emigrated from northern European countries, where cooperatives had been widespread.

The surge in forming local cheese manufacturing cooperatives (in Wisconsin and Minnesota primarily) before 1900 was in response to the tardy development of investor-owned enterprises.[8] Making cheese from whole milk where dairying was the principal type of farming but using skim milk as animal feed was not remunerative. Efficient cheese manufacture required more equipment and skill than the individual farmer possessed. Small groups of farmers early established cheese "rings," more or less cooperative in ownership.[9] By 1914 about 75 percent of Minnesota's natural cheese output was from cooperative plants, and nearly 40 percent of the Wisconsin cheese factories were farmer-owned.[10] An estimate for 1926 placed the cooperatives' share at a third of national volume. This share fell to a sixth by 1936 but rose to a fourth in 1964.[11]

Butter manufacture by cooperatives started slowly until the separator for removing cream from milk and the Babcock tester for gauging the butterfat content facilitated the sale of cream by farmers. Butter-making could then move from the farm to a local factory, but development of investor-owned butter-making plants lagged for some time. Where established, discontent with their buying practices was widespread; usually they paid a single price for all grades of cream.

There followed a rush to develop cooperative plants, many promoted by sellers of butter-making machinery. Not surprisingly, hundreds failed.[12] But a large portion survived, and cooperatives acquired a major role in butter-making before World War I, particularly in the north central states.[13] For the country as a whole they accounted for about 40 percent of butter output by 1936,[14] a percentage that surged to 65 by 1964 for reasons to be considered later.

Before 1914 many local butter and cheese cooperatives joined federated cooperatives to engage in terminal-market and even later-stage operations. The federated Challenge Cream and Butter Association operated in the far western states and the larger Land O'Lakes in the north central area,[15] establishing wholesale outlets in major consuming markets and by 1936 handling about half of the butter made in cooperative plants.[16] The two cooperatives marketed quality butter under their brands, but that advantage was soon eroded by chain store imitators whose presence, together with development of an active broker market in Chicago, restrained the second-step cooperative handling of butter. For cheese the Wisconsin Cheese Federation, established in 1931 and later joining Land O'Lakes, and the Tillamook County (Oregon) Creamery Association engaged in wholesale distribution. Today, most of the local cooperatives' output of both products is sold through brokers or other terminal market operators.

Conditions of Entry and Effect of Dairy Product Cooperatives

Dairy product cooperatives could be expected to achieve their highest percentages of volume in areas of concentrated production of milk for manufacturing. There farmers' cash receipts are chiefly from sales of milk or cream, and the investment in cows and equipment provides continuity of production and of producer interest in the cooperative. Density of dairy farming facilitates organization of farmer-owned processing enterprises.

The regional pattern of cooperative dairy product manufacturing bears out these predictions. By 1964 the two north central regions together produced 80 percent of the national output of butter, 77 percent of the cheddar cheese, and almost 74 percent of the nonfat milk powder. The cooperatives' share of east north central regional output of butter was 60 percent, of cheese 22 percent, and of nonfat milk powder 73 percent. In the west north central states the cooperatives' percentages of these products were, respectively, 75, 28, and 87.[17] Were these large regions broken down, one would find that cooperatives dominate in northeastern Iowa, eastern South Dakota, and in the southern counties of Wisconsin and Minnesota, where milk production per square mile is high.[18] West and south of these areas most production of milk was until recently a side-line activity of farms—which correlates with the cooperatives' lower shares.

The cooperatives' volume of some dairy products also reflects merchandising problems. Only to a limited degree are consumers responsive to persuasion to buy more of age-old, large volume, and quite standard products, such as butter and cheddar cheese, or to purchase a particular brand of them. Evaporated milk manufacturers had an uphill fight to gain the degree of consumer acceptance they were able to achieve.

Similar influences help to explain the decline of cooperatives' share of cheese production after the mid-twenties. The patented processed cheddar came on the market about that time and boomed in volume in the following decade. The new types of natural cheese that were put on the market after World War II involved new techniques of production and their producers encountered difficulties in persuading retailers to stock and consumers to buy them, activities in which large investor-owned companies have had successful experience.[19] The investor-owned firms' volume of cheese increased consistently until 1964, but the Farmer Cooperatives Service estimates an increase in the cooperatives' share more recently.

Quite different developments explain the cooperatives' dominance of nonfat dry milk output and the related upsurge in share of butter production. Powdered milk does not involve merchandising problems, for most of it is bought by industrial concerns as an ingredient in finished food products. Doubtless the continuing decline in total butter consumption discouraged investor-owned firms from making the large outlays necessary for them to engage in a modern butter-powder operation. But incomes of cooperatives' members are augmented by selling sweet whole milk hauled to factories by improved rural transport, compared to separating the cream at the farm and using the skim milk for animal feed.[20]

These facts encouraged cooperatives to build new and large buttermilk powder plants, at times with government aid. Some cooperatives merged to achieve the higher volume needed for efficiency in powder-making than producing butter from cream. Investor-owned firms generally did not follow this trend, and their absolute volume of butter fell by over half from 1936 to 1957 and, compared to the latter year, a third more by 1964. This trend reflected the diversion to manufacturing of Grade A milk delivered to urban markets in excess of consumption of fluid milk, as will be seen below.

Cooperatives have not lost in the share of any manufactured dairy product, except a slight percentage of cheese, and that has been more than offset by recent growth. Their percentage of butter output has advanced sharply and of nonfat milk powder is dominant. Investor-owned firms either were not alert to, or could not prevent, the entry and recent growth of the cooperatives.[21]

Farmers' Cooperative Activity in the Fluid Milk Channel

Of the half of all milk sold that reaches consumers in fluid form cooperatives play some part with respect to over two-thirds of the volume. Except for the limited cooperative distribution of milk their role is now so interrelated with federal market orders which set minimum prices to farmers that these two influences on milk markets must be considered together.

Development of Cooperative Action in the Fluid Milk Channel

The first strong stimulus to cooperatives' activities in fluid milk markets occurred during World War I[22] but for reasons quite different from those recounted above. Very few strong cooperatives existed in 1913, though attempts at cooperative bargaining with distributors and some cooperatively owned milk distribution had occurred in the 1800s. City distributors of milk were often able to woo farmers away from the cooperatives or to prevent producers whom they financed from joining. But the rapid rise of urban incomes and of dairymen's costs from 1914 to 1920, while prices for milk for fluid distribution lagged, set the stage for the establishment of enduring cooperative bargaining associations.[23] Of thirty-six milk bargaining cooperatives responding to a questionnaire in 1920 all but five had been formed after 1913.[24]

Further support for cooperatives and later for government action stemmed from the decline of prices paid farmers from 1920 to 1921 and again from 1929 to 1933. In both periods the price of milk at the farm dropped much more quickly and further than did retail prices.[25]

This indicated that price competition among distributors was weak; cooperative integration into milk distribution might appear to have been the logical move for producers. Some milk distribution cooperatives were formed in 1919-1923 and again in 1933-1935.[26] A number have been in operation in recent years, but handled only about 10 percent of the milk reaching consumers in fluid form. In most large markets producers now rely on cooperative bargaining with distributors, on government fixing of minimum prices in a market order, or on a combination of both.

The problem of entry differs sharply between a bargaining cooperative and one manufacturing milk. In both types of markets there are only a few buyers in each local market. The few buy from producers and distribute milk in a metropolitan area. By 1962, in nearly all except the very largest metropolitan markets, over 70 percent of the volume was in the hands of four distributors,[27] a situation that has not changed. Because the larger retail food chains from which most of the milk is now purchased by consumers could do their own milk purchasing and handling they are the most evident restraint on milk distributors' margins. Otherwise the inelastic consumer demand for milk,[28] together with the scarcity of distributors, could result in distribution margins well above the competitive level.

The problem of entry differs sharply between a bargaining cooperative and a cooperative that undertakes milk distribution. The former does not add capacity to the market. Nor does it have to obtain much capital for a plant except possibly to manufacture milk received in excess of fluid consumption. To be effective in bargaining the cooperative must sign up a high percentage of the eligible production in the milkshed. The earlier milk distributors' rigorous opposition to bargaining cooperatives has been weakened sharply by the producers' alternative of a government order setting minimum prices in consuming markets. On the other hand, were a cooperative to undertake to distribute milk it would have to persuade retailers and consumers to prefer its milk over that of established investor-owned distributors.

The marked seasonality in milk production while consumption is quite stable throughout the year poses a problem in the absence of some type of control program. Otherwise, given the inelastic demand for milk to be consumed in fluid form, prices received by farmers and paid by consumers would jump sharply in low production months, and the reverse would occur during the spring and summer flush output. Such behavior of farmers' prices would encourage some opposite adjustment of production by controlling the cow-freshening dates and by feeding practices. It does not appear that the maximum output adjustments that could occur would eliminate a substantial spring and early summer surplus and much lower production in the fall and winter.[29]

The Geography of Milk Production, Consumption, and Prices

The upper midwestern states, Wisconsin and Minnesota and parts of adjoining states, constitute the lowest cost producing area. There a vast amount of milk is produced in excess of local consumption. This area provides most of the Grade B milk used for manufacturing storable dairy products. It also is the largest source of Grade A milk eligible for Class 1 milk distribution for human consumption. Consequently the delivered prices of Grade A in most of the country tends to be the value of that grade in the center of the surplus-producing area plus truck transport costs.[30]

Because of this geographical pattern of milk production and of delivered prices, developments in the midwestern fluid milk market and the role of cooperatives there are very important. In this large area the average per farm milk production tripled between 1949 and 1964.[31] Farm specialization in dairying and the enlarged size of dairy herds provide most of the explanation. Between 1955 and 1965 the number of fluid milk cooperatives in this area fell by a third, chiefly as the result of mergers and the formation of federations.[32] During these years such groups of local cooperatives as Associated Milk Producers, Incorporated and Central Milk Producers Cooperative were formed. By 1971 there were six regional consolidations or federations of cooperatives in the Midwest.[33]

Cooperatives and Milk Market Orders

A solution to the problems stated above is the milk market orders authorized under the Agricultural Adjustment Act of 1937. These orders set for various markets the minimum prices that distributors must pay for Grade A milk delivered to these metropolitan markets. Almost 75 percent of the nation's population lives in metropolitan markets covered by these orders.[34]

The minimum price distributors in a federal order market must pay for delivered milk is computed monthly. The foundation price for each market order is the price of Grade B or manufacturing milk paid by processing plants in Wisconsin and Minnesota[35] plus a Grade A differential and truck transport costs to the particular consuming market. The Wisconsin-Minnesota price base for order prices extends over most of the United States east of the Rocky Mountains except at some points in the far southeastern states.

It should be noted that the cooperatives often succeed in bargaining with distributors for over-order prices in particular consuming markets. Such prices were paid for only 4 percent of order market volume in 1956 but for 65 percent by 1965.[36]

The Surplus Grade A Problem

In recent decades prices producers receive for Grade A milk have been sufficiently high to encourage a large number of Grade B producers to so change their facilities and practices that they could acquire Grade A status. The result has been the production of a substantial amount of Grade A milk in excess of consumer demand at the going price. Surplus Grade A is diverted to plants making storable milk products. For this milk producers are paid the Grade B price. By 1971 about 30 percent of Grade A milk produced was used to make milk products. Between 1955 and 1971 fluid milk consumption fell from 84 percent of Grade A milk supplies to 69 percent.[37]

There are at least two possible explanations for this development. If analyzed in a market order framework, the incentive for producers to become eligible for Class 1 would have to be that the Grade A differential over manufacturing milk prices used in computing market order prices is too high. Thus the price encouragement to quality for Grade A.

A more obvious explanation is the ability of cooperatives marketing Grade A milk to negotiate above-order prices from milk distributors in markets having market orders. This higher realization is reflected in higher prices to the cooperatives' members. Grade B producers are then attracted to qualify as Grade A producers and thereby add to the surplus of milk for fluid consumption.

This tendency has been most marked in large markets near to or in the low-cost production areas. In 1972 the Twin Cities market distributed as whole milk less than half of the fluid milk received, and in the Chicago market only 41 percent of delivery was so distributed.[38] The remainder was diverted to plants manufacturing storable products. Some was shipped to distant consuming markets.

The above-order prices for Grade A milk have contributed to two developments. One is an "unneeded surplus" of Grade A milk above the volume consumed as whole milk. This surplus is defined as the excess above the volume sold to consumers plus a 20 percent margin to offset irregularities in deliveries.[39] Also these above-order prices encourage consumers to substitute milk made from milk powder, the consumption of which is increasing.[40]

The outcome of the growth of the volume of Grade A milk relative to fluid consumption is not clear at this writing. Presumably the relative cost of producing and handling Grade A compared to Grade B milk will govern the relative prices of the two grades. The recent conversions of Grade B producers to Grade A indicates that the cost differential between producing and handling the two grades is less than the difference in prices of the respective grades.

Several regional fluid milk cooperatives that together cover most of the country have been under investigation by the Department of Justice to see if they have engaged in business practices in violation of the antitrust laws. The first such case involved Associated Milk Producers Incorporated. After a lengthy trial the case was settled in 1975 by a consent decree in which AMPI agreed to cease and desist certain practices. Several regional cooperatives are being investigated at this writing.

Cooperative Marketing of Grain and Soybeans

Cooperatives handling grains and soybeans rank first in dollar volume among farmer cooperatives, and their 40 percent of farmers' marketings places them first among cooperatives handling major field crops. One estimate reports that they handled and did some crushing of 35 percent of the soybean crop in 1963.[41] Here the focus will be on these cooperatives' grain operations, which was their original business. Grain volume consists of wheat plus a substantial fraction of the corn and soybean crops. A large percentage of the corn crop does not enter commercial channels but is either fed on the farm where produced or in a nearby area.

Condition of Entry into Grain Marketing

Production of grain and soybeans and their local market handling differ sharply from milk production and marketing. Grain and soybeans are produced in annual crops, are storable without refrigeration (although fungus growth and insect infestation must be guarded against), and can be handled and stored in bulk. Because these products do not deteriorate when dry and are highly transportable they are grown where the costs of their production are lower than the costs relative to the prices of alternative crops. For this reason, and because high-protein wheat from which high-quality bread flour is made grows only in semi-arid regions, 60 percent of the wheat is produced in the second tier of states west of the Mississippi River and in the northern Rocky Mountain plateaus, most on one-crop farms. The major corn and soybean acreage is further east.

Local cooperative warehouse or elevator enterprises engage in drying, when needed, and in storing and selling the grain delivered by farmers. (To varying degrees they also handle farm supplies, which adds to member loyalty.) The typical local elevator accepts a member's grain or soybeans on a grade basis and commingles it with other volume of that grade. The cooperative either buys the member's volume at the going price upon delivery or stores it for a charge and later sells that amount of grain or soybeans at the member's order.

Entry into the local market operation was quite easy, at least until recently. In 1935 the typical local cooperative elevator had assets of only $40,000, a figure that had advanced to $275,000 by 1954. Recent studies indicate that additional cost savings are not high for local elevators above 200,000 bushels capacity.[42] In 1970-1971 the Farmer Cooperative Service reported over 2000 local cooperatives handling grain and soybeans. Usually each competes with one or more local investor-owned elevators.

Selling grain in terminal markets by local cooperatives was difficult decades ago but not now. In the postwar years being able to ship the types or blends of wheats desired by a particular miller or to make shipments of several carloads have become more important. Such cases have encouraged more locals to become members of federated cooperatives, to merge, or to work out arrangements for joint shipment.

Development of Cooperative Marketing of Grains

Numerous cooperative elevators were established in the chief grain-producing states shortly after the Civil War, but the major movement came later.[43] Most early cooperatives failed, and by 1880 nearly all of the local warehouse business was back in the hands of their rivals. The farmers' interests were protected somewhat by the easy entry of "scoop buyers," or dealers without local storage facilities. But farmers complained about excess dockage for waste materials and downgrading by those dealers. Sometimes competition among local buyers led them to agree to pay more than was warranted by terminal market prices, with resultant bankruptcy and the farmers' loss. At other times the local elevator had a monopoly, aided on occasion by collusion with the railroad which placed impediments to loading and shipping by scoop buyers. Often buyers could play on the farmers' lack of knowledge of grain grades and terminal market prices. There is scattered evidence, although not for a representative sample of transactions, of dealer margins twice the cooperatives' operating costs.[44]

The strong and lasting cooperative elevator movement was in response to collusion in the grain trade. Local investor-owned elevators had trouble with dishonest terminal market commission agents, and agreement among central market purchasers was alleged. State associations of local dealers corrected that situation, but once formed they boycotted terminal market commission houses that represented either scoop buyers or cooperatives.

The permanent growth of the cooperatives came as a reaction to the monopoly position achieved by the line warehouse companies. Each of these owned many, sometimes several hundred, local warehouses. They grew rapidly in the 1860s by buying out or by forcing out of business a large portion of the local warehouses whether owned by farmers or not. Favorable treatment by the railroads in rates and availability of cars helped these line companies. They soon dominated the state grain dealer association and either by-passed the terminal market commission men or had them at their beck and call. Collusion on prices paid for grain was widespread.[45]

Farmers reacted by forming local cooperatives, but these faced two hurdles. The line warehouse companies could pick off a cooperative easily by overpaying for grain in its locality, a short-term gain which few members could resist. The successful countermeasure was the penalty clause for nondelivery inserted in the contract between a cooperative and its members, first used in 1889 by a Rockwell (Iowa) cooperative. Second, as this membership clause and continued farmer discontent with prices strengthened the cooperative movement dealer associations attempted to block cooperatives' access to terminal markets. But some commission houses elected to represent local cooperatives and even to sponsor their development. Also, groups of cooperatives formed terminal marketing agencies, of which there were twenty-nine by 1937-1938. Faced by such competition, investor-owned commission houses switched to active handling of the cooperatives' business. Cooperatives now face no handicap in selling in terminal markets.

Following the general adoption of the penalty clause about 1900,[46] local grain cooperatives grew rapidly. There were about 4000 in 1920, one at "practically every shipping point throughout the Grain Belt."[47] Of the 2614 existing in 1936 about 60 percent had been formed before World War I.[48]

A corresponding growth occurred in the share of grain handled locally by cooperatives. By 1913 they marketed 11 percent, a share that mounted during the period of rising prices that followed. The advance continued to 38 percent in 1925 even though prices were lower. The percentage jumped to about 50 in 1930 when grain cooperatives particularly were aided by the Federal Farm Board, in part by financing vertical elevators, which facilitated a rapid shift from sack-handling to bulk-handling of grain.[49] After the demise of the ill-conceived Farm Board, the cooperatives' share dropped sharply but recovered to 30 percent by 1940.[50]

What has happened since World War II is not entirely clear, for recent data combine the cooperatives' volume of grain and the rapidly growing volume of soybeans and soybean products. The cooperatives' composite share in 1975-1976 was 40 percent.

Attempts at Monopoly Pooling

The account of cooperation in grain marketing would not be complete without reporting the attempt to operate a monopoly pool. The rapid rise of grain prices during World War I enabled farmers to provide capital for local and even terminal facilities which contributed to the sharp growth of cooperative marketing of grain. Because of the rising wheat prices within several of the July-to-June crop years from 1914 through 1919 members of cooperatives operating crop-year pools[51] got higher average prices than did farmers who sold at harvest time. This may explain why the National Wheat Growers Association, formed in 1920, adopted the crop-year pool practice.

This organization was founded at a most inopportune time, for deflation was just starting and extending through most of 1921. By then the wheat price at harvest was well above the average for the crop year. Nevertheless, the pool idea stuck during the early 1920s and grew as several regional pools were formed. An attempt to form a national pool to encompass most of the wheat production failed. In part these plans were designed to carry out the prosaic task of lower-cost marketing, but whether they accomplished that is debatable.[52]

There was more than an overtone of the idea that the pool management could outguess the market or could even influence the market price in favor of the farmers. This hope was not borne out, and even obtaining the average price for the year became doubtful.[53] Pooling got its death sentence after 1928 when the downward trend of grain prices reduced the season's average price below the prices at harvest time.[54] Grain cooperatives now usually pool only the operating expenses of handling members' products.

Currently farmers appear to place primary confidence in governmental programs to affect the general level of grain prices and to mitigate their fluctuations. That leaves for the cooperative the area of demonstrated success, that of cleaning, storing, and merchandising grain on a margin equal to costs, with a competitive return on capital included.

Entry and Performance of Grain Cooperatives

The record has been recounted above, but some summary points are relevant. The most successful development of grain cooperatives has been in farming areas devoted primarily to production of one or two field crops. This characterizes most of the grain production in the north west central, west south central, northern Rocky Mountain, and sections of the Pacific Northwest states that together supply the overwhelming percentage of the wheat and much of the corn and soybeans entering commercial channels. These states account for 80 percent of the cooperative volume of grain and a substantial percentage of soybeans.

Even in areas of one-crop grain farming cooperatives appear not to have driven out investor-owned elevators from most shipping points, although the evidence is sketchy and somewhat conflicting. In Nebraska in the mid-1930s about 80 percent of the cooperative elevators were located where there was no other elevator.[55] But in 1927-1928, of fourteen representative cooperative elevators in Montana, all but two were located where they had to compete with two or more investor-owned elevators.[56] More recently Kansas cooperative elevators faced three local competitors on the average, and the larger cooperatives five.[57] Yet there is clear evidence of substantial economies enjoyed by larger elevators than many cooperatives own, some of which operate at a loss.[58] Many went back to horse and wagon days, but most, I have been informed, have been replaced by large units in the last two decades. There are added economies when a local cooperative owns more than one elevator.[59] Member loyalty may be influenced now by the fact that cooperatives may carry out, as agents for members, the involved arrangements for federal price support loans on stored grain, a role barred to investor-owned handlers.[60]

Local cooperatives may sell grain or soybeans, usually on order of members, to millers or bean crushers or to large elevator-sales companies, particularly regional cooperatives. In contrast to the attempts by regional cooperatives in the interwar years to influence the price of grains the present-day regionals provide vast elevators at critical locations. They buy the grain (or soybeans) from locals[61] and undertake to be efficient merchandisers by providing the quantities and the particular type of grain wanted by millers or exporters. But the regionals are dependent on being able to buy from locals the volume for efficient operations. In 1974-1975 it was reported to me that the farmers' and local cooperatives' expectations of rising prices inhibited the regionals' ability to perform as grain merchandisers.

A major postwar development has been the rebirth of regional cooperatives but with a different concept of their "mission." Now the emphasis is on providing supplemental storage of grain at strategic points and effective "merchandising" of the grain. By that is meant being able to supply the volume and type of grain or soybeans wanted by processors or buyers for export. Some gigantic storage elevators have been built, such as those at Hutchinson, Kansas, and Enid, Oklahoma. Sizeable elevators have been built also at a few salt water ports and on inland waterways. Smaller elevators have been built at numerous points in the grain- and soybean-producing areas.[62]

Many grain cooperatives have obtained substantial net savings for their members. In the nation as a whole they earned 9 percent on members' equity in 1936,[63] a quite satisfactory return in those years. Postwar data for three major producing states show substantially higher net savings rates,[64] in large part traceable to the potentially temporary earnings from storing government-owned grain under the support program.[65] Aside from that the recent upward movement of the composites of local and regional grain cooperatives have done well.

In 1973 primary regional cooperatives (not federations of regionals) handled 1671 million bushels of grain, including soybeans. In addition, federations of regionals handled 25 million bushels.

Export sales by primary regional cooperatives accounted for 850 million bushels, to which should be added 323 million bushels handled by federations of regionals. Altogether, cooperatives are a major influence on the grain trade.[66]

5

Cooperative Marketing of Other Farm Products

The remaining farm products will be considered in the order of the co-operatives' current market shares. To reduce detail, sugar products (for which much of the cooperative activity is bargaining), beans and dry peas, rice, and wool and mohair will be omitted although data for them were presented in table 4.1. Of the major commodity groups to be examined here fruits and vegetables rank second in volume but first in the cooperatives' market share with about one-fourth. Cooperative marketing of nuts will be referred to only briefly. Then follow cooperatives' shares of one-fourth of cotton and cottonseed, one-eighth of tobacco, and one-tenth of livestock and products and also of eggs and poultry.

As reported in table 4.1, over the two decades ending in 1975-1976, the cooperatives' shares of marketing of nuts and of cotton and cottonseed approximately doubled, while the share of tobacco declined. The share of fruits and vegetables advanced by a third, but their share of livestock fell by that ratio. Shares for other products can be seen in the table.

Cooperative Marketing of Fruits, Vegetables, and Nuts

Cooperatives' experience in marketing various fruits, vegetables, and nuts has differed widely, as is shown in table 5.1 for 1964, the latest year for which comprehensive data for particular products are available.

Leaders of many cooperatives have envied and, at times, tried to imitate the price and volume gains from merchandising some specialty fruits and nuts. Few other commodities offer opportunity for such programs.

Plans for supporting prices, either by financing carryovers or by diverting part of the output to lower priced and more price-elastic uses, have worked for a time. Often price-propping discouraged needed reductions in capacity to produce or even encouraged expansion. In several such cases the cooperative was rescued, if at all, either by rising demand or by government control of the quantity marketed. But for most large-volume vegetables and for some fruits that reach consumers unprocessed, cooperatives have not gained a lasting and substantial market share.

Varied Conditions of Entry

The widely differing shares of various fruits, vegetables, and nuts cooperatives market, portrayed in table 5.1, must reflect diversity of conditions of production and of handling or of processing these products.[1] Also, important differences exist in the location of production of various of these products vis-à-vis consuming markets and in the alternatives open to producers.[2]

Most fruits and vegetables shipped in fresh form, with the notable exception of apples and potatoes, are now grown in the western and the southern states where the soil and climate are well adapted to their production. These perishable goods are shipped to the major consuming areas to the north and east, which augments problems of adjusting volume shipped to demand in total and by destination. Less of these difficulties affect marketing such storable products as nuts, dried fruits, and processed fruits and vegetables. In between are apples, citrus fruits, and potatoes, for which sales can be staggered over many months.

The conditions of production determine the degree to which farmers have a continuing interest in one product. Potatoes and most vegetables to be processed are grown where farmers can adjust the use of their land among various crops. These products may be sold in the fresh vegetable market or sold for processing.

Entering the freezing or canning business is most difficult. While the size of plant required for efficiency is not absolutely large, often it is substantial relative to the raw material supply of the local market.[3] An added plant could start a bidding contest for the raw material and reduce processors' profits. Much more capital is required for an efficient processing plant than for a produce packing shed and also to pay growers at harvest time at least part of the going price for the raw material, while the processed goods are sold throughout the year. Part of the needed funds can be borrowed at favorable terms to finance stocks of standard

Table 5.1. Cooperatives' Shares of Farm Marketings of Fruits,
Vegetables, and Nuts (varying dates, from 1964 to 1975-1976)

Commodity	Percentage marketed by all cooperatives	Percentage of cooperatives' share marketed by Pacific states' cooperatives
All fruits and vegetables	27%[a]	
Fruits (no composite estimate available)		
Fresh (circa 1964)		
Oranges	56	77%
Grapefruit	34	48
Cranberries	85	Nominal
Apples	21	47
Peaches	7	11
Cherries	19	25
Pears	59	65
Dried	46	100
Figs	58	
Prunes	63	
Raisins	34	
Canned deciduous fruits and juices	31	
Frozen deciduous fruits and juices	18	
Processed citrus fruit and juices	42	
Nuts		
Walnuts	55	100
Almonds	55	100
Pecans	25	
Peanuts	Nominal	
Vegetables (no composite estimate available)		
Fresh		
Potatoes (processed included)	10	
Other fresh	Nominal	
Processed[b]		
Canned vegetables and juices	9	
Frozen vegetables	9	

Sources: The percentages for all fruits and vegetables are from table 4.1. All other percentages are from, or computed from, tables in National Food Marketing Commission, "Organization and Competition in the Fruit and Vegetable Industry," *Technical Study No. 4* (Washington, D.C.: U.S. Government Printing Office, 1966). Estimates for particular types of nuts were provided by the Farmer Cooperative Service and apply to 1959-1960.

[a]This is also the estimated overall fruit and vegetable percentage for 1975-1976 (see table 4.1).

[b]Bargaining cooperative volume is omitted because reliable estimates are not available.

goods. Selling under the cooperative's brand is difficult, for large investor-owned enterprises have built up considerable consumer preference. While selling goods to chain stores to be distributed under their brands avoids this problem, price competition is keen for this business.

Where a fruit or a vegetable can be sold in either the fresh produce channel or for processing the price in one use is restricted by the price obtainable in the alternative use. This situation exists for most fruits but not for many vegetables because their production for processing and for shipping as fresh produce are largely in different areas.

Development and Current Status of Fruit and Vegetable Cooperatives

While there were scattered but largely unsuccessful cooperatives marketing fruits in the last century, strong growth began with citrus fruits in California before World War I. Some cooperative marketing of more perishable fruits also started then. The strong surge of cooperative handling of dried fruits occurred after 1910, stimulated by low prices blamed on the local buyers or on terminal market commission agents. Actually the prices primarily reflected the more rapid growth of dried fruit output than of demand.[4]

Continuous success of citrus cooperatives dates from the formation of the local "exchanges," which later formed a federation. An exchange pools its members' fruit by type and grade and pays the pool price realized from sales for a period, less a marketing margin. By 1906 local exchanges shipped over half of the California citrus crop through the federated cooperative, now called Sunkist Growers, Inc., widely held to be the model of cooperative operation and efficient merchandising.[5] Citrus cooperatives now exist in all producing areas, and their composite shares are shown in table 5.1.

Attempts at cooperative marketing of apples also date back to the last century. But only three cooperatives established prior to 1900 were still in operation in 1945. As apple growing came to be concentrated in areas well adapted to commercial production, such as the Pacific Northwest, cooperatives there acquired market shares twice the national average reported in table 5.1. Attempts at a nationwide cooperative have been short lived.[6]

Cooperative marketing of highly perishable fruits and vegetables bought by consumers unprocessed has had a checkered career. While the California Fruit Growers Exchange, established in 1901, did handle an estimated 22 percent of the state's deciduous tree fruits years ago,[7] the percentage was only 10 in the early 1950s,[8] although much higher by 1964 for most fruits (see table 5.1). Cooperatives handle only nominal percentages of fresh vegetables now.

Outstanding success in some cases has been achieved for processed fruits produced principally in one or very few localities. Cranberries is an extreme example, with the cooperative share being 85 percent, although much of that is sold unprocessed. Cooperatives gained a major role in processed citrus items and also a substantial share of processed deciduous fruits through the efforts of the North Pacific Canners and Packers and the recently formed California Canners and Growers. The latter entered and expanded largely by acquiring established plants. Co-operatives now produce some wine, and one cooperative markets most of the grape juice consumed, a position achieved by purchasing the well-known Welch Company. How long this cooperative can add to members' incomes more than interest on the capital invested in acquired plants is yet to be determined for it cannot control output in the long run. Dried fruit cooperatives boomed after 1910 and by 1920 handled very high percentages of several fruits but, for reasons detailed below, their shares are now at the lower but still substantial levels reported in table 5.1. Over half of the walnut and almond crops are marketed by a Cali-fornia-Oregon cooperative.

Overall the cooperatives' share of farm marketings of all fruits and vegetables has grown slowly from the 10 percent level in 1921, when their volume consisted primarily of California citrus and dried deciduous fruits. For other products there was little advance until after World War II, when their composite share of all fruits and vegetables moved by 1975-1976 to the 27 percent cited in table 4.1. For years cooperatives' percentages of output marketed have been quite uniformly highest in the Pacific states, from which most of the volume is shipped to eastern markets.[9]

Fruit and Vegetable Bargaining Associations

In 1964 there were forty-three fruit and vegetable associations engaged in formal bargaining with buyers with respect to prices and grading of the raw materials.[10] These associations' composite dollar volume was triple that of 1958 although farmers' total receipts from fruits and vegetables had risen by only half. Many of the associations have represented such a small percentage of the supply that they are not very effective and their casualty rate has often been high—except for those formed by producers of some fruits for processing.[11]

Because cooperative bargaining with buyers of milk for fluid use was analyzed in chapter 4, only significant differences applicable to fruit and vegetables will be considered here. On the buying side of the local market for raw materials, say green peas or cling peaches for canning, there are a varying number of processors. On the producing side, most vegetables for processing are grown as annual crops in areas where there are several alternative uses of the farm land. Consequently, the processors and each producer usually agree on the price of a particular vegetable before planting time. As a general rule the contract price cannot yield net incomes below what unorganized producers could expect from the best alternative use of their land. Since producers' costs and yields differ, a monopoly buyer's profits might be higher if he sets a price below that which would emerge if there were many buyers, even if the acreage he could contract would be reduced thereby. Higher cost producers, or those with better alternatives than producing the particular vegetable at the set price, would grow other crops.

This is not the complete setting; local processors must be concerned about the character of the market for the processed goods. Each processor has established customers whose business he would like to hold while meeting the offers of sellers of the processed foods in a large regional or the national market. Consequently, processors are to varying degrees oligopsonists as buyers in a particular area but often to a high degree competitive sellers of the processed foods.[12]

To the extent that processors' monopoly power as buyers is checked by these influences a bargaining association whose members could provide a high proportion of the raw material output would be in a strong position. Clearly they should obtain at least a price and volume approximating that which would exist in a fully competitive buyer-processor market, and even more temporarily if the processors have no alternative use for their local facilities. But attempts by the cooperative to obtain monopoly levels of prices in the longer run will be restrained by the entry of additional acreage, perhaps in other areas. Quite different conditions face bargaining associations where the farmers have no year-to-year alternative uses of their land, such as in production of most fruits.

Bargaining with canners of cling peaches in California is an extreme example of the latter.[13] The output in other states is nominal, and there is no close alternative use of this type of peach. Members of the California Canning Peach Association produce about 80 percent of the one-half of the California crop that is not produced by or under contract to canners. Each year the association's officials study the prospective carryover, the production, and the demand for peaches for canning and arrive at a price with which to start bargaining with one of the larger canning companies. Other contract terms, such as the grading of farmers' products, are bargained also. The terms that emerge from the bargaining with one canner are not binding on the others but they usually follow.

The association cannot make an effective all-or-nothing demand even for the half of the crop that is not under control of canners. The members have no alternative use for their fruit, or for their land. In the short period the growers' land is planted in fruit trees or vines. It might seem that the few canner-buyers could force the price below the level covering costs of producing a significant portion of the fruit but this does not occur.

Does this mean that the canners do not have oligopsonist power or that they take the long-run view of the prices necessary to maintain the desired peach orchard capacity? Or is the association's position strengthened by disagreement among the buyers who are barred by law from colluding? Or is the cooperative's hand strengthened where producers can petition for a government order that limits the quantity, perhaps by specifying the level of product quality that may be put on the market?[14]

How a state order provides support for a cooperative bargaining is seen in the California Pro-rate Act under which a cling peach order has been in effect since 1937.[15] Each year the state director of agriculture makes a finding as to the price that will yield a "reasonable return to growers." If a surplus in that sense is expected orchardists will be required to knock the green fruit off enough trees to reduce expected output to the target level. If the volume at harvest still exceeds the target the excess is diverted to other uses or destroyed.

Bargaining cooperatives have also been effective in areas where vegetables for processing are grown. Farmers have alternatives for the use of land. Hence contracts to growers are signed before planting time. The cooperatives can be effective in bargaining because the processors need to be assured of supplies.

For a substantial portion of fruits and a lesser portion of vegetables marketed in fresh form the major function of many cooperatives is to represent their members' interests in the formulation of federal or state marketing orders. Most of these orders specify grade, minimum quality, size, maturity, and/or quality of goods that may be shipped and sometimes vary those standards or directly limit the quantity. Some orders provide for controlling quantity. Altogether there were ninety marketing orders in effect in 1966, a high percentage of which were in California.[16]

Finally, cooperatives can or freeze substantial percentages of fruits and citrus juices but only small percentages of vegetables, as is shown in table 5.1. (This table does not, however, include the volume of cooperative bargaining, a topic dealt with separately below.)

In 1964 there were forty-three active cooperative bargaining associations, of which half were in the Pacific coast states. The number was about evenly divided between fruit and vegetable associations. Total cooperative bargaining volume was $120 million. The Farmer Cooperative Service estimates that the number and volume of cooperative bargaining associations has increased and accounts for 4 percentage points of the higher cooperative market share in 1974-1975.

Table 5.2. The Organizational Structure, Membership Policy, and Market Shares of Fruit and Nut Cooperatives with Varying Degrees of Market Power

	Membership structure	Membership policy	Market share		Barriers to entry[a]
			Cooperatives	Largest four marketers	
Cooperative					
Ocean Spray Cranberries	Centralized	Open	85%	98%	2.5
National Grape Co-op	Centralized	Restricted	50	75	2.5
Sunkist Growers	Federated	Open	70	90	1.5
Diamond Walnut Growers	Centralized	Restricted	55	90	2.0
Sun-Maid Raisin Growers	Centralized	Restricted	41	80	2.5
Sunsweet Growers	Federated	Open	50	85	2.0

Source: Adapted from James G. Youde and Peter G. Helmberger, "Marketing Cooperatives in the U.S.: Membership Policies, Market Power, and Antitrust Policy," *Journal of Farm Economics* 48 (August 1966): tables 1, 2.

[a]Key: 1.0 = low; 2.0 = moderate; and 3.0 = high.

62

Cooperatives' Merchandising and Market Control Programs

More than for any other commodity, some fruit and nut handling cooperatives have undertaken to enlarge the demand for their members' product. Presumably no one investor-owned processor undertakes market development expenditures for the commodity because, if successful, obtaining more raw products from producers in competition with other processors would force the passing to producers of possibly all of added revenue arising from the enlarged consumer demand. But added income for its members is the objective of the cooperative as the sales agent for its members. The high market shares currently enjoyed by cooperatives that aggressively merchandise products are shown in table 5.2.

A high share was acquired early by Sunkist and is now enjoyed also by several other fruit and nut cooperatives. The citrus industry would have remained much smaller for some time had not consumers been persuaded, by Sunkist first, of the dietary value of citrus fruits. Rising consumer incomes would eventually have expanded demand, but the merchandising activity of the cooperative, including having its own agents in terminal markets, undoubtedly pushed ahead the date. Demand rose and both the quantity bought and the price increased.[17] Soon the benefits were lessened by the expanded citrus production in California, Arizona, Florida, and Texas, invited by the high returns. When demand fell sharply in the thirties, prices collapsed and the cooperatives diverted the surplus to other channels or even destroyed it. But not enough could be disposed of this way, and California growers were rescued by the prorate system described above[18] and after 1945 by the frozen juice surge that removed most of the Florida output from the fresh market.

In imitation of Sunkist's success an ill-fated attempt was made just after World War I by cooperatives handling dried fruits to combine market development with control of very high percentages of the output. Sun-Maid raisins, for example, became a well-known brand. At no time did the dried fruit programs approximate the success achieved and still enjoyed by Sunkist.

This is not definitive proof that dried fruit merchandising was ill-founded. The high prices during and just after World War I stimulated the planting of trees and vines which started to bear fruit after several years. But after an early postwar fillip of export shipments the demand for dried fruits fell sharply and remained at about the lower level for two decades. Aggressive sales efforts by the cooperatives were of little avail, in part in the near term because they attempted to apply the "commodity theory" attributed to Aaron Sapiro, the exercise of monopoly power by withholding from the market the volume that could not be sold at a target price. This price was above the market-clearing level, and large inventories accumulated, which depressed prices further. Consequently dried fruit prices were very low relative to producers' costs from 1921 until World War II.[19]

Cooperative marketing of pecans has had a history similar to that just recounted, but the almond and walnut cooperatives were rescued by the upward trend of demand even before the war.[20]

The present market shares of several fruit and nut marketing cooperatives are shown in table 5.2. Each is produced only in a single area or in two or three states. The cooperatives' shares range from 41 to 85 percent, and for each commodity 75 percent or more is sold by four enterprises, the cooperative and three investor-owned firms. Added to this concentration in marketing is the height of the entry barrier a new marketer would face, which the economists making the study assumed was measured by the ratio of the established marketers' advertising expenditures to sales. The results are the degrees of control of supply enjoyed by four handlers, of which the cooperative is the largest in each case.[21] The shares enjoyed by these cooperatives are impressive and have been quite durable. Members seem satisfied compared to the marketing alternatives available to them.

Another test, suggested in chapter 2 and used by the authors of table 5.2, is the extent to which these are open-membership cooperatives. A federated cooperative is owned by and subject to the membership policies of a substantial number of local cooperatives. Each of them usually welcomes more members. In a centralized cooperative each grower is directly a member of the cooperative. All but one of the centralized cooperatives named in table 5.2 restricts membership. Each is located in a relatively small area(s) adapted to a single type of agriculture—as are several more not reported in table 5.2.

Open membership restrains a cooperative's ability to obtain monopoly returns, except temporarily. Similar to the lemon case above, a merchandising program that adds to members' net incomes will stimulate added output from them and from new members. The cooperative must then intensify its sales effort, probably with diminished marginal effectiveness, or reduce its selling price. At the same time the expansion of consumer demand will induce the noncooperative handlers to increase prices to growers and thereby reduce the gain from membership in the cooperative. The probable and potentially damaging consequence of higher prices would be the expansion of producing capacity, but with the consequences lagged several years, as was recited above.

Performance of Fruit and Vegetable Cooperatives

Cooperatives handle or engage in bargaining for large percentages of the less perishable fruits and vegetables produced in concentrated areas, typically on farms that specialize in one or a very few products. Usually these are products of trees or vines in which the farmer has a long-term investment. Cooperatives have not had large-scale and sustained success in marketing highly perishable fruits or vegetables or, except for some fruits, in processing them.

Given these observations it is not surprising that cooperatives in the Pacific states not only market high percentages of these states' output of products of the sort just referred to, but also account for 55 percent of cooperatives' national volume of all fruits and vegetables marketed, even though these states produce only 40 percent of national output. They do produce nearly all the almonds, walnuts, and dried fruits.[22] Presumably these cooperatives' net savings accounted for most of the average net savings rate of 16 percent of net worth obtained by fruits and vegetable cooperatives in 1936, a high rate of return for those years.[23]

Whether in the Pacific states or elsewhere, the position of bargaining cooperatives is strengthened where producers can turn to federal or state programs that restrict the volume produced or marketed when prices would be depressed otherwise.

Cooperative Marketing of Cotton and Cotton Products

Cooperative marketing of cotton was unsuccessful for decades even though the local markets were not effectively competitive. Buyers often took advantage of their greater knowledge of cotton quality and terminal market conditions. Prices received by farmers for cotton of identical quality differed widely in the same general area on the same day. Grade differentials in local markets were much narrower than on organized exchanges, and the prices of higher grades in some areas were below prices of lower grades elsewhere.[24]

Cotton fibers and seeds must be separated locally by ginning to facilitate the long-distance transport of cotton. Economies of plant size limit to very few the number of gins that can exist in the area within which the loose cotton with seeds can be transported economically. Once separated, both fibers and seeds are highly marketable under established grades. But prior to World War I neither grading nor other conditions provided easy access to distant markets by producers.

Unique handicaps to the formation of cooperatives have existed in the South. Farmer's reliance on merchant credit was more widespread there than in most other areas. Such credit was expensive, hidden usually in the high prices charged the farmer for his supplies, and at harvest time he was not a free agent.[25] Much of the failure of members to deliver cotton to the cooperatives in the 1920s was traceable to opposition of the farmers' landlords or other creditors.[26] Substantial percentages of contracted cotton were not delivered to the cooperatives.[27]

Sporadic attempts at cooperative marketing of cotton were made as far back as the 1870s, but no lasting movement got underway until after World War I. The expanded acreage and the prospect (and after mid-1920 the actuality) of drastically lower prices for cotton led to attempts to use cooperatives to avert the price decline. Newly formed state or regional organizations undertook to become large overnight by forming locals "from the top down." They could not have been started at a worse time nor have adopted more impossible policies. The American Cotton Association campaigned for acreage reduction, but this brought a speculative advance in the price of cotton that encouraged expansion instead!

Unfortunately, the persuasive Aaron Sapiro also convinced most state cooperatives, and such overhead organizations as the American Cotton Association, that they should not only operate on the pool principle but could outguess the market and even exercise monopoly power. But never was more than 17 percent of the crop delivered to the cooperative, and returns to members were not clearly better than to nonmembers. Even though members signed seven-year contracts, the cooperatives had difficulty in holding their low share of the market during the late 1920s. When prices plunged downward after 1929 the cooperatives found that even the price rivals paid to members at harvest time could not be realized from the cooperatives' sales over the crop year. Widespread bankruptcy was averted by government purchases by the new Federal Farm Board, but all who owned cotton benefited whether cooperative members or not.

Several inhibitions on the growth of cooperative marketing of baled cotton have been removed. The federally sponsored production credit associations established in 1934 (see chapter 11) enabled many cotton producers to cut loose from merchant credit. In 1936 the net gain of cooperative gins was 13 percent of net worth, but cooperatives engaged only in marketing experienced an overall loss.[28] The rapid mechanization of cotton growing, with a marked increase in the size of farms, largely operated as well as owned by whites, and the greater concentration of cotton production in the Mississippi Delta and California all aided the growth of cooperatives.

Far from avid interest in cooperative membership in recent decades reflects contrary influences. With the price of cotton in past decades (but not currently) held up by government action at a level above what would be the open market price, the floor price could be netted back to the local shipping point for a given trade. To a farmer not tied to a lender the full local price of cotton is evident. It is not surprising that much of the gain from cooperative membership consists of lower net charges for ginning.[29] Also, in years past when a large part of the cotton went under government loan the cooperatives could act as members' agents in making the arrangements, while noncooperative handlers could not.

The cooperatives' share of marketing cotton and cotton products advanced from 15 percent before World War II to 26 percent in 1975-1976. (This volume does not include the bulk of the cooperative ginning operation; it is reported separately as a "service related to marketing.") With cotton acreage lower in recent decades the increase of the cooperatives' share of output held the investor-owned marketing enterprises' absolute volume at about the pre-World War I level.

Cooperative Marketing of Tobacco

Cooperative marketing of tobacco has had an erratic and at times stormy history. Before 1914 cooperative selling of tobacco was attempted in order to fight the American Tobacco Company, which, prior to its dissolution into four large and several small companies, purchased about 80 percent of the crop. In 1905 and 1906 the Burley Tobacco Association and the Planters Protective Association obtained control of a substantial part of the crop. But the tobacco monopoly was able to meet its needs from other sources. In 1908 the association members agreed not to grow a crop, and many nonmembers were persuaded to do likewise by use of terroristic methods, including destruction of crops. The Tobacco Trust capitulated and paid a high price, but this one success was the end of effective tobacco cooperatives for decades.[30] Perhaps the farmers expected competitive buying of their crops because of the earlier dissolution of the American Tobacco Company, but this proved to be illusory.[31]

Unlike the marketing of many other commodities, cooperative marketing of tobacco did not surge during World War I but did so immediately thereafter. Acreage then expanded sharply and prices tumbled for the 1920 crop. Region-wide associations were formed in every important tobacco-producing section and signed up 44 percent of the crop in 1923. But when members' five-year contracts expired most did not rejoin.[32] By 1930 the cooperatives' share was back to about the pre-World War I level of 3 percent.[33] After World War II the percentage rose to a modest 15 percent by 1950-1951 and was only 13 percent in 1975-1976 (reported in table 4.1).

The recent advance of the cooperatives' share cannot be explained by low prices for tobacco leaf. Under the federal agricultural program the acreage of tobacco has been the most continuously and tightly restricted of any farm crop. The high level of leaf prices aided by government price support created values for the *right to grow* an acre of tobacco (above the value of an acre for other uses) that have ranged from $900 to $1500 according to year and locality.[34]

This does not mean that farmers have been selling in a fully competitive market. In its 1946 decision the Supreme Court concluded that there had been a significant degree of at least tacit collusion among the large buyers of leaf at local auctions.[35] No significant change in the number of buyers has occurred since that date. It is quite possible that the cooperatives have forced more competitive handling of tobacco leaf and thereby added to prices farmers would otherwise receive as the result of the acreage restrictions. The result of the cooperatives' surge has been to hold the investor-owned marketers' absolute volume approximately constant.

Cooperative Marketing of Livestock and Products

While cooperatives that market and in small amounts process livestock rank third in dollar volume, they account for only a tenth of the value of all livestock sold by farmers (table 4.1). These cooperatives' marketing margin is extremely small, for most of them merely act as commission agents at local or terminal markets. While a larger gross margin is obtained for the fractions of 1 percent of all livestock slaughtered by cooperatively owned plants, that margin has frequently not covered operating costs, as the failure record has shown.

Cooperative Marketing of Livestock

Even after railroads became the means of transporting livestock to meat packing centers the local shipping point markets did not function satisfactorily for the producers. A single producer often did not have enough animals of a given species and quality ready at one time for him to by-pass the local market by shipping a carload. Mixed carloads involved special shipment problems and were not looked upon with favor by terminal market buyers. Local buyers sprang up to assemble unmixed carloads to ship to terminal markets, but these buyers were few in a locality and had more information about the market situation than did farmers. These dealers' margins were thought by farmers to be far above costs.[36]

In the fourth quarter of the last century farmers began to form local cooperatives to ship livestock to terminal markets. There were about 600 locals in 1916, most of them in the north central states. During and after World War I associations were formed rapidly, mostly by small producers. Up to that time large-scale ranchers and feeders were discouraged from forming cooperatives by their dependence on credit from investor-owned commission houses or banks associated with them. This situation was eased after 1923 by the formation of the intermediate credit banks which loaned to livestock credit corporations, and after 1932 by other new farm credit agencies.[37]

Around World War I there was much producer dissatisfaction with the practices of the large packers and the commission agencies through which individual producers or local cooperatives sold in terminal markets. A few large packers owned the terminal stockyards, dominated the newspapers reporting market receipts and prices, and slaughtered about three-quarters of the livstock received in those markets. Local cooperatives held that commission rates were unnecessarily high. Passage of the Packers and Stock Yards Act gave the Department of Agriculture jurisdiction over commission agent practices and rates, but with little effect on operating practices for some time. Even before that date some cooperative terminal market commission houses had been formed, and their number grew in subsequent years. From 1922 to 1926 eighteen terminal marketing associations earned net savings equal to one-third of the going commission rates allowed under the law. But this amounted at most to 1 or 2 percent of the price of cattle.[38]

Cooperatives have never handled a high percentage of the livestock marketed. In 1922 their share was only 4 percent of terminal market receipts, a figure which advanced to about 12 in 1926 and to 14 in 1936.[39] It was only 9 percent in 1975-1976, and much of the volume consists of cooperative auctions in areas of limited livestock output.

Since 1920, and at a more rapid pace since World War II, four important developments have made competition in the sale or purchase of livestock more effective. Truck-hauling directly from the farm to the packing plant and of meat in refrigerated trucks to consumer areas facilitated geographical decentralization of meat packing from such centers as Chicago and St. Louis. Packing plants are now dotted throughout the major areas of surplus output of livestock ready for slaughter. Second, most producers can now reach several differently located packing houses with their own trucks or by contract truckers who collect small lots from a number of producers. Third, radio broadcasting of market news provides the farmer with up-to-date information on prices in alternative markets. Finally, packers have turned to field buying which, together with direct delivery by farmers to nearby packing houses, has reduced sharply the role of terminal stockyards.

The Chicago stockyards have been dismantled, and the percentage of packers' total purchases of cattle acquired at all terminal markets fell from 88 in 1930 to 37 by 1964 and of hogs from 60 to 24 percent. By 1964 direct buying by packers from producers or country dealers accounted for 45 percent of their purchases of cattle and 63 percent of hogs, and these trends have continued. Much of the remaining percentage of live-stock changed hands at local auctions in the producing areas, usually for shipment to more distant plants.[40] How long the large auctions of live-stock—"block marketing"—will endure remains to be seen.

The measurable direct savings to the members from cooperative selling are miniscule compared to the charges of investor-owned organizations. Where the cooperative is a substantial seller in a market its presence as-sures active competition among commission agents, and all producers selling there benefit. Direct savings to members from lower net commis-sion charges in 1936 were about one-fifth of 1.5 percent commission margin charged, or less than 0.3 of 1 percent of the value of the livestock sold. By use of the profit-and-loss statements for a number of regional cooperatives I found that the associations' net savings varied from about 0.4 percent of the value of livestock handled in 1940 to about 0.8 in 1950 and then fell to only 0.2 in 1955!

Cooperative managements assert that if the farmer follows the guidance of the cooperative and produces the proper standard of quality and uni-formity for the market, the cooperative obtains a significantly higher price. That most producers, who are propagandized by packers' repre-sentatives, local buyers, and cooperatives' personnel, have not been per-suaded is indicated by the constancy of the cooperatives' share for the last thirty-five years.

Cooperative Meat Packing Plants

Cooperative meat packing plants have had the most dismal record of all attempts by farmers to carry out cooperative integration downstream. Of the thirty cooperative plants established between 1914 and 1944, only five survived at the latter date. Of the thirteen started between 1914 and 1920 all but one had failed by 1923. Few further attempts at cooperative meat packing were made until after 1931 when eighteen were founded, but only four were operating in 1961, two quite successfully.[41]

The ventures rarely have had a promising foundation. In several in-stances farmers were misled by promoters. In not a few cases the cooper-ative was a desperation move by producers because the only local pack-ing plant was failing. Often the plant was inefficient, badly located, or poorly managed when the cooperative took over. Hanging over all the cases was inadequate capital to provide modern facilities. But the more basic explanation lies in the structure and performance of the livestock markets, particularly in recent years.

In the modern history of the industry the return on capital obtained even by the giant enterprises has been among the lowest in all manufacturing. One wonders how farmers could have been led to believe that there often is an opportunity for cooperatives in this field. In the major producing areas and in the terminal markets entry into meat packing is easy, particularly into the fresh meat phase of the industry. Competition is effective and profits low.[42] Were the latter not true the large chain food stores would have entered meat packing as they have other supplying activities. The only promising opportunity for farmer-owned plants is in localities where little livestock is shipped to a terminal market and the local supply will not support several slaughtering plants.

Cooperative Marketing of Poultry and Eggs

The first enduring egg and poultry cooperatives were formed in the Pacific states and Utah just before World War I. At that time these were the only areas where egg production had become the major activity on a substantial number of farms. In Washington State, for example, when a burdensome surplus of eggs was produced but shipment to eastern markets was costly, the Washington Co-op (as it was then called) was formed. It undertook rigorous grading of eggs and advertising the cooperative's brand in eastern markets.[43] The program paid off, and by the mid-1920s its eggs sold at a premium in eastern markets. But, cooperatives and other marketers in East Coast states imitated these practices, and the premium disappeared.

Cooperative marketing of eggs (and poultry also) continues strongest in the Far West. There cooperatives handled nearly 20 percent of farmers' output in 1967-1968, but the percentage had been 40 in the early postwar years! In the north central regions, which together long produced nearly half the poultry and egg supply of the country, largely as a sideline to other farm operations, egg and poultry cooperatives handle only a nominal percentage.[44]

The poultry (as distinct from egg) cooperatives have not fared well recently as broiler and turkey production have become factory-like operations. This involves integration of on-the-farm activities with either the feed suppliers or the slaughterers.[45] The farmer owns neither the birds nor the feed but operates on a margin. The poultry is marketed by the nonfarm owners or is so tied up with the financing that the farmers are not free agents. While cooperatives were already engaged in poultry slaughtering and handling, they have participated only to a limited degree in this integrated operation because of the large amount of capital and the risk involved. The percentage of broilers that reach the market not tied by contract to slaughterers or providers of feed declined from 60 percent of the volume of thirty-seven slaughterers reporting in the early postwar years to only 29 percent of the receipts of sixty-five slaughterers reporting in 1964-1965.[46] Nevertheless some cooperatives engage in poultry processing on a large scale.

The cooperatives' share of poultry and egg marketing together has remained constant since World War II at about 8 percent, while total volume of these products increased sharply. Consequently the absolute volume of the investor-owned firms grew substantially. Only in a few locations do cooperatives now find conditions in this industry to be favorable for them.

Conclusion

The widely different degrees to which farmers have cooperatively integrated into marketing various products reflects primarily the organization and performance of the particular local markets in which they would otherwise sell. For some products these market characteristics have changed over time, usually in the direction of improved performance, and often stimulated by the entry and growth of cooperatives. The consequent competition restrained the growth of the cooperatives' market shares. In markets for milk for fluid consumption, sugar crops, and some fruits and vegetables for processing, recent growth in market shares has primarily taken the form of cooperative bargaining. Where the goods are handled, including processing by the local cooperatives, integration into terminal market handling occurred successfully where these more distant markets were not effectively competitive. But little added vertical integration has occurred for several decades. Another form of further cooperative vertical extension has been the not always markedly successful merchandizing programs for fruit specialties. Some have achieved high market shares but few have held that position. Except in fluid milk and some fruit specialties, continued and substantial monopoly via a cooperative has rarely been held for long.

Aside from the character of the markets for farm products several features of the farming operation itself condition the interest in marketing cooperatives. A general and logical condition is that the product account for a substantial share of the farmers' sales and that their commitment to this product be more than temporary. Cooperative marketing has developed most vigorously where farmers specialize in one or a few products and have substantial investment that cannot be diverted to other uses. Some bargaining cooperatives, for example, in sugar beets, are an exception.

In addition five conditions have aided the formation and continued success of marketing cooperatives. One is the concentration of output of a product (that meets the tests just stated) in a small geographical area, which facilitates organizing the cooperative. Second, cultural homogeneity in the local community, as among farmers of Scandinavian descent, aids information of cooperatives. The opposite, the white-black problem in the South, long inhibited cooperative activity. A third condition is the financial position of the farmers. More important than their ability to provide the limited equity capital of the cooperative is their financial independence of local buyers of their output or of banks tied up with these buyers. Development of the special agricultural credit agencies in the 1930s (see chapter 11) reduced farmers' reliance on merchant credit or even loans from local banks. The banks for cooperatives provide both operating loans and capital funds for farmer cooperatives. The generally prosperous state of agriculture since 1940 has increased the financial independence of farmers. Finally, and important for many products, are government marketing orders and the role of cooperatives in developing these orders and influencing their administration.

But successful cooperative marketing is selective, not uniformly the best marketing instrument. The basis for that conclusion stands out in the widely differing market shares cooperatives have attained for various farm products sections. Assuming that the local buying market offers the opportunity, successful cooperative by-passing of that market rests usually on the degree and persistence of potential gain to the individual farmers, the commonness of interests among them, and their freedom financially to choose the outlet for their products. Beyond these points they must be able to organize and finance the enterprise. By no means is cooperative marketing generally advantageous, and clearly it is not a device for rescuing farmers from adversity due to higher output than the market demand at prices covering producers' costs.

For some commodities, notably fluid milk and fruits and vegetables, the cooperative's major function is to represent their members' interests in the formation and operation of government marketing orders.

A final point that aids farmer-owned cooperatives is their ability to borrow from the bank for cooperatives of their district. Such funds may be used to acquire facilities or to carry inventories of goods in the process of marketing.

6

Farm Supply Cooperatives

Through cooperatives farmers purchased from one-fifth to nearly one-third of various types of supplies used in production by 1975-1976, as shown by table 6.1.[1] But farmers purchased only a nominal amount of farm equipment from cooperatives. There was, however, a significant increase between 1950-1951 and 1975-1976 in cooperatives' usage of fertilizer, petroleum used in products, and pesticides, as will be seen.

Cooperative purchasing of animal feeds and of fertilizers are treated intensively in this chapter, followed by a brief consideration of the cooperatives' limited role in handling durable goods used in farm production. The uniquely successful petroleum product cooperatives owned by farmers are the subject of the following chapter.

Status of Farm Supply Cooperatives

Three categories to be studied in this and the following chapter, feed, fertilizer and lime, and petroleum products, account for almost three-fourths of the total cooperative farm supply volume (table 6.1). Most supply cooperatives were established to handle one of these commodities but nearly all now sell a variety of supplies, some farm equipment, and occasionally consumer goods.

Farm supply cooperatives differ widely in form of organization and in

74

horizontal and vertical scope. In a few cases farmers of a whole state or a larger area are organized directly into one centralized supply cooperative, as in the Grange League Federation Exchange, which has retail outlets throughout New York State and parts of adjacent states and performs wholesale and some manufacturing functions. In the 1960s GLF and parts or all of several other cooperatives merged to form AGWAY, which does business over the vast area east of central Ohio and north of Virginia. But most regional cooperatives are of the federated type, owned by locals for whom the regional acts as wholesaler and, to varying degrees, as manufacturer of supplies. In contrast to nearly all marketing cooperatives most regional supply cooperatives were established by and are associated with statewide farm organizations founded for other purposes.

Conditions Affecting Entry and Growth of Farm Supply Cooperatives

The technological advances in farming and in availability and quality of supplies and equipment used in farming demonstrated the cost savings from use of more purchased and of less farm-produced supplies, and of more equipment and less labor. Forming cooperatives to obtain supplies and equipment must have reflected farmers' dissatisfaction with the performance of the markets in which they had been buying. But farmers' ability to purchase, and particularly to become self-suppliers via cooperatives they own, depended also on their net incomes and the availability and cost of credit.

Rather than documenting the first of these points further, attention is called to the slow changes in farm output and use of purchased inputs prior to 1940 (as shown in table 6.2) compared to the dramatic developments since. With farm real estate changing but little, output rose by three-quarters in the three decades after 1940, while farm labor fell by two-thirds. All of this was made possible by a four-fold increase in the use of selected seeds and of fertilizer and by a four-fold rise in the use of purchased feeds and development of power farming. But a strong start of supply cooperatives had come earlier, which suggests that the roots were in the performance of supplying markets.

The conditions under which farmers purchase supplies are similar to those under which they sell their output—with one major difference. While there are usually very few dealers in supplies in a farming community, this fact is overshadowed by the relatively few manufacturers making important types of supplies and equipment and their relations with their dealers. Each manufacturer merchandises its brand aggressively by advertising and usually selects one dealer to handle his brand in

Table 6.1. Dollar Volume and Percentages of Farmers' Purchases of Farm Supplies and Equipment Used in Farm Production Obtained from Cooperatives, 1975–1976 Compared to 1950–1951[a]

Purchases	Total purchases by farmers for production use, 1975–1976 (millions of dollars)	The percentage of farmers' purchases from cooperatives	
		1975–1976	1950–1951
Feed	$2,471	19%	19%
Seed	358	15	17
Fertilizer and lime	2,261	36	15
Petroleum products	944	28	18
Pesticides	622	33	11
Building materials, etc.	227	6	2
Containers	113	[b]	10
Miscellaneous supplies	697	[c]	[c]
Farm machinery and motor vehicles	267	2.0	2
	$7,960		

[a]Data for 1975–1976 and estimates for 1950–1951 supplied by the Farmer Cooperative Service.
[b]Not calculated because some sales were made to marketing cooperatives.
[c]Omitted because unknown percentages of purchases are not used in farm production.

Table 6.2. Indexes of Farm Output and of Major Categories of Farm Production Inputs, Selected Periods from 1910–1914 to 1970 (1957–1959 = 100)

	Farm total output	Farm real estate	Farm labor	Mechanical power and machinery	Fertilizer and lime	Feed seed and livestock purchased
1910–1914	52	88	209	20	12	16
1920–1924	59	90	222	32	16	23
1930–1934	61	91	212	33	21	26
1940	70	92	192	42	28	45
1950	86	97	142	86	68	72
1960	106	101	92	104	111	109
1970	120	106	62	115	115	151

Source: "Changes in Farm Production and Efficiency: A Summary Report," USDA, *Statistical Bulletin No. 233* (rev., 1970): tables 21, 22; and USDA *Agricultural Statistics* (1971): 465, 466.

a locality. The business of each dealer is identified with that brand, and he functions as the last step in the manufacturer's merchandising program of building preference for his brand so as to minimize price competition.

In recent decades the farmers' financial position at various times can be related also to the growth of supply cooperatives. The unprecedented farm prosperity from 1914 to 1920 did little to stimulate cooperative purchasing. Only 2 percent of farmers' purchases of supplies at the end of this period were obtained through cooperatives even though about half of the supply and marketing cooperatives surveyed in 1936 had been established before 1920.[2] Farmers had been prosperous in the preceding decade; cost savings were not critical. Also, purchased supplies were not yet a high percentage of total farm inputs nor was the volume yet concentrated in one or two commodities.

After 1920 the price-cost squeeze provided incentive for economizing when buying farm supplies, and by 1930 farmers acquired 8 percent through cooperatives. Many of the major farm supply cooperatives of today got their start in those years. Doubtless this was facilitated after 1933 by the greater availability of credit to farmers and to cooperatives, supplied by the new federally sponsored credit agencies (see chapter 11). The cooperatives' share of farmer purchases of supplies advanced by 1936 to 11 percent, a level maintained until after World War II.[3] While the war years brought great farm prosperity it was also a period of shortage (at controlled prices) of most supplies. Newly established enterprises were not welcome customers of manufacturers.

Such handicaps eased rapidly after 1945, in part by integration of many regional cooperatives into manufacturing. This fact, plus the sharp turn of farmers to purchased inputs (table 6.2), facilitated the marked advance of the percentage of all farm supplies obtained through cooperatives to 11 percent by 1950-1951 and on to 18 percent in 1975-1976.

Cooperative Supplying of Livestock Feeds

Animal feeds rank first in dollar volume but only fourth in percentage of farmer purchases of the major categories of farm supplies obtained through cooperatives (table 6.1). The overwhelming proportion of these feeds are of the mixed type, often referred to as commercial feeds. They include ground grains, supplements such as soybean meal to add protein, and other ingredients to provide mineral and vitamin content. The most intensive use of these feeds is in the diets of poultry and dairy cattle, but increasingly they are fed in fattening beef cattle and in some hog production.

Entry and Growth of Cooperative Supplying of Feeds

Two developments in the production of livestock have contributed to use of purchased rather than of home-grown feeds. One is the large proportion of milk for fluid consumption and of poultry and eggs now produced in areas where it is not equally advantageous to grow grain and other feed materials of agricultural origin. Second, advances in knowledge of animal nutrition have shown the advantage of including ingredients that are by-products from a variety of industrial operations. The volume of feed concentrates consumed per animal unit rose only slowly from 1910 until after World War II and then advanced 20 percent by 1968.[4] The output of livestock and livestock products (including poultry, eggs, and milk) and the use of total commercial feeds increased at about the same rate from 1910 to 1950, after which the advance in use of these feeds was at double the increase of the output of livestock and products.[5] Expenditures for feed were 15 percent of farmers' receipts from livestock and products before World War I, then advanced to 20 percent in 1940, and on to 33 percent by 1969.[6]

Unsatisfactory performance of feed manufacturers and distributors stimulated interest in purchasing through cooperatives. Sketchy information indicates that the margins of the investor-owned retailers were well above necessary costs through at least part of the 1920s.[7] A more important stimulus to forming cooperatives was the generally low quality of formula feeds, whose ingredients were often unknown; the industry was "largely in patent medicine stage."[8] Farmers had no way of knowing the make-up of egg mash, for example, and frequently poor quality hid behind brands.[9]

This led to the "open formula" movement, or the identification of ingredients on a tag attached to each bag of feed.[10] Agricultural Extension workers publicized research findings about the productivity gains from various ingredients, and cooperatives joined the campaign for buying feed on the formula basis.[11]

Such indirect government aid facilitated entry of feed supply cooperatives but the path was not always smooth. While little capital or experience was required to operate a feed warehouse and to follow Extension Service recommendations, groups of investor-owned retailers forced manufacturers to refuse to supply the cooperatives. Backed by farm organizations, cooperatives then made long-term contracts with feed makers who did not have well-developed distribution. Later, regional cooperatives undertook the grinding and mixing of feeds.[12]

By 1936 cooperatives engaged principally in the feed business, nearly half of which had been established for ten or more years, handled 15 percent of farmers' purchases.[13] The percentage did not advance during the war. By 1950-1951 the cooperatives' share had risen to 19 percent, a level just held since then (table 6.1).

Cooperative Vertical Integration into Feed Manufacture

To an unusual degree the feed supply cooperatives have integrated into wholesaling and feed grinding and mixing. By 1959 90 percent of the formula feeds distributed by locals was obtained from cooperative manufacturing plants, the highest percentage of self-manufacturing in any phase of cooperative purchasing. A feed mill of small size is not disadvantageous, particularly if it can save in-bound freight on locally produced ingredients, engage in custom grinding of grain and blending in of other materials, and deliver these and other formula feeds directly to the members' farms, often in bulk. Of the 1054 cooperative plants in 1959 two-thirds had a capacity of five or less tons of formula feed per hour and are described as "manufacturing and retailing" operations. But over 90 percent of all of the output of cooperative mills has been provided by larger plants.[14]

Performance of Cooperatives Supplying Mixed Feeds

Recent comprehensive data on net savings obtained by cooperatives' supplying of mixed feeds are not available, but what these cooperatives have accomplished is quite clear. In 1936 the net savings were 22 percent of feed cooperatives' net worth.[15] Now most feed is handled by multiline supply or marketing cooperatives, which inhibits measurement of gain from any one product line. Because the cooperatives' share of farmers' feed purchases has not risen in recent years their net savings rate is probably below that of 1936. Presumably their rivals have become much more competitive in price and quality.

The performance of cooperatives is indicated also by their share of farmers' purchases of feeds by regions in 1964.[16] In the New England and Middle Atlantic regions the cooperatives' share of national cooperative volume was twice those regions' percentages of national use of these feeds. Approximately the opposite was true of the mountain states and southern regions. The regional percentages were about equal in the Pacific states, but the cooperatives' shares were somewhat higher in the north central regions. Again the low development of cooperatives in the South is evident, partly for the reasons advanced in chapter 5 and also because of the limited growth of dairy cooperatives, the logical suppliers of feed for their members.

For the country as a whole the cooperative supplying of commercial feeds has been restrained, but by no means stopped, by the growth of the investor-owned firms' volume. The 80 percent increase in farmer use of these feeds from 1936 to 1950 and another 40 percent from 1950 to 1969-1970 facilitated the entry and expansion of cooperatives.[17] Their added volume since 1950-1951 has not forced a significant reduction of the investor-owned firms' market share or volume on a national basis (see table 6.1). This indicates that their rivals' terms to farmers, in quality of feeds as well as in price, must have improved to the extent that the two types of supplying enterprises are at or are approaching an equilibrium relationship.

Cooperative Distribution and Manufacture of Fertilizer

Commercial fertilizer ranks second in dollar volume but first in percentage of farm supplies obtained through cooperatives. The development and present status of this phase of the cooperative business has much in common with the record for feeds, with one important difference. The active ingredients in commercial, or "chemical," fertilizers are of non agricultural origin, a fact that at times has limited cooperatives' access to supplies of these ingredients or of those already mixed with inert materials.

Entry and Growth of Cooperatives Supplying Fertilizer

In the more than half-century from 1910 to 1973-1974 use of all fertilizers increased by ten times, but crop production only slightly more than doubled. Most of this contrast developed after 1950 and is explained in large part by the relatively low price of these fertilizers compared to the prices of other inputs and of farm products.

The value of added output made possible by the use of fertilizer rose much faster than did its price.[18] With farm wage rates doubled since World War II, more fertilizer to obtain higher yields has reduced the labor cost per unit of output. Undoubtedly these developments plus improvements in types of fertilizers, including high analysis and liquid forms of plant food, favored added fertilizer consumption.

Decades ago the price and often the uncertain quality of commercial fertilizers sold by investor-owned companies stimulated cooperative activity by farmers. The quality issue parallels that already portrayed for mixed feeds. Early in this century fertilizer was identified only by brands; what it contained was a mystery. Yet different crops and different soil conditions require different combinations of active ingredients. Without knowledge of the contents, farmers could not relate a fertilizer to their experience or to the recommendations of the Agricultural Extension Service. Out of this situation came another "open formula" campaign. By 1916 all states where commercial fertilizer was sold in large volume required that the percentage of each active ingredient be listed on, or on a tag attached to, the bag of fertilizer.[19]

But that did not solve fully the farmers' problem of the price of the fertilizer. The price of the typical mixed fertilizer, about 80 percent of which was inert material (and still is for much of the volume), actually exceeded by a substantial but apparently declining margin the retail cost to the farmer of the active ingredients. Farmers were urged to mix their own fertilizer or to buy a "high analysis" type, but it was not widely available. Either practice would have reduced sharply the freight costs on inert materials. Oddly, the distributive margins of manufacturers were lower on active fertilizer ingredients than on mixed fertilizers.[20]

Not all of this situation represented unfettered competition among manufacturers of the ingredients or among those who mixed fertilizers. Few industries in the United States have been investigated as often concerning the participation of large companies in both domestic and international price and sales territory agreements. On a number of occasions, the manufacturers have been indicted and in some cases convicted. In others they signed consent orders agreeing to cease noncompetitive practices.[21]

Clearly farmers could gain from cooperative supplying of fertilizers but faced difficulties in doing so. Cooperative distribution of fertilizer could be entered easily provided supplies of the desired qualities could be bought from manufacturers at competitive prices. Once retailing was successful further integration into mixing did not require a heavy investment or unusual knowhow. But success in that step would in turn depend on ability to buy the active ingredients at competitive prices, a topic to be considered in a moment.

While some cooperative purchasing of fertilizer appears to have taken place before World War I the movement got its major start in the early 1920s. In 1916 the Federal Trade Commission referred to the rapid development of cooperative buying clubs in areas of heavy fertilizer use.[22] The commission recounted the reaction of the investor-owned companies and some of the methods proposed or used to resist the growth of the cooperatives. Nevertheless cooperatives became quite active, particularly in the south Atlantic and south central states and in Indiana and Ohio, first in distributing and then in mixing fertilizers.

The record of cooperatives supplying fertilizers is one of continued advance. By 1936 they provided 9 percent of farmers' purchases.[23] By 1950-1951 their share was 15 percent and by 1975-1976 had boomed to the 36 percent shown in table 6.1, coinciding with the phenomenal rise in fertilizer use shown in table 6.2.

Access to Materials and Vertical Integration by Cooperatives

For some time cooperatives were able to find fertilizer mixers who had excess capacity and welcomed the cooperatives' business, but this was not a long-run solution. A number of the largest manufacturers preferred to sell only under their own brands. At times manufacturers either would not sell as much as the cooperatives could distribute or on terms equal to those offered other large buyers.[24]

With scale requirements not high in fertilizer mixing the cooperatives undertook this operation early in the twenties. A significant portion of the supply of active ingredients could then be obtained from companies not engaged in mixing fertilizers. These ingredients could be shipped at bulk rates to the farming localities and the inert materials added there. The cooperative could deliver by truck from the mixing plant to outlets in several counties or even directly to farms.

Until after World War II the cooperatively owned plants had usually been able to obtain the ingredients they needed. They were the preferred customers for TVA's output of nitrogen and phosphates. During the 1930s the restraints on competition among suppliers of fertilizer ingredients were offset by the excess capacity situation in all phases of the industry. Use of commercial fertilizers fell by one-fourth to nearly one-half in various of those years of very low farm prices.

After World War II the sharp increase in use of fertilizers brought an acute shortage of active materials, and cooperative mixing plants had supply problems. Producers of ingredients that also mixed and marketed fertilizer gave priority to their own needs, as could be expected.

Large regional cooperatives individually or jointly undertook production of the raw materials for certain of the active ingredients. Not all of
these ventures were successful, in part because by the 1960s the North
American capacity for producing phosphate and potash grew faster than
the amount used. Cooperatives also built plants to manufacture from
natural gas a new fertilizer, anhydrous ammonia.

The *Census of Manufactures* for 1963 reports that plants owned by cooperatives accounted for 11 percent of the fertilizer production, which
includes an undetermined proportion of output of active ingredients and
of these mixed with inert materials. In addition cooperatives provided 13
percent of the output of plants devoted to mixing fertilizers from purchased ingredients.

Five large regional cooperatives led in the "buy-from-formula" movement and developed facilities for some manufacture of ingredients. They
bought other ingredients and sold mixed fertilizers adapted to particular
soils through local cooperatives. The result has been that the cooperatives' share of farmer-used fertilizers more than doubled between 1950-
1951 and 1975-1976 (table 6.1).

Pioneering by the Cooperatives

Four recent developments in fertilizer technology and in the distribution and use of these plant foods have been seized upon by the cooperatives. One is to make high analysis fertilizers available for distribution.
As early as 1949 cooperatives in the north central states distributed a
higher percentage of their fertilizer volume in the high analysis category
than did investor-owned companies, which provided substantial savings
to farmers per unit of plant nutrient.[25] Second, cooperatives pioneered in
mixing fertilizer to the formula desired by the farmer. Third, they were
among the first to handle mixed fertilizers in bulk all the way to the farm.
Accompanying this operation and the sale of high analysis fertilizers is
often the application of the fertilizer to the land by special equipment
owned by the seller. Fourth, cooperatives moved early into the distribution and even into production of new types of fertilizers, gaseous anhydrous ammonia and liquid nitrogen solutions.

Cooperative Performance in Supplying Fertilizers

The information base for a market for fertilizer that works well was
lacking until recent decades. Many farmers bought fertilizer by gross
weight not by pounds of active ingredients. Surveys by investor-owned
manufacturers had shown that a large proportion of farmers did not
want high analysis fertilizers,[26] although the cost savings from their use

have been amply demonstrated. Reinforced by the recommendations of the Agricultural Extension Service it appears that cooperatives have influenced farmers to buy more of the types of fertilizer adapted to the requirements of various crops and soils.

The cooperatives' effects on their rivals' prices, and possibly on their product quality, are suggested by changes in market shares and in absolute volumes. Of the fifteen-million-ton increase in commercial fertilizer consumption between 1936 and 1950-1951, cooperatives obtained only 6 percent of the increase. But of the twenty-eight-million-ton increase in farm use from the latter date to 1970-1971 the cooperatives' share doubled. Clearly cooperatives have been a powerful restraining influence on their rivals.

As was found for commercial feeds cooperatives supplied widely differing percentages of the fertilizer used in various regions. In the south Atlantic region the cooperatives' percentage of national cooperative volume was only half that region's percentage of total national use of fertilizer. Surprisingly the same contrast held for the Pacific region. But the reverse was true (and markedly so) for the north central and the west south central regions.[27] The latter region and Mississippi now have efficient cooperative plants to make fertilizers from natural gas.

For the nation as a whole the continued rise in the cooperatives' share of fertilizer suggests that an equilibrium had not been reached by 1973-1974 between their volume and net prices compared to those of investor-owned firms.

In addition farmers not members of a cooperative at times establish informal local groups which order one or more carloads of fertilizer of given specifications. To the best manufacturer's price the group can negotiate is added incoming freight. The farmer members pay cash with the order or upon delivery.

Cooperatives' Minor Role in Supplying Durable Goods

Farmers purchase through cooperatives very small percentages of more durable supplies and of equipment used in farm production. The reasons for this can be as instructive as were the conditions favoring cooperative vertical integration into supplying nondurable materials.

The continuing small cooperative volume of building materials and miscellaneous hard goods, omitting equipment, appears logical. Materials for repair of farm buildings by farmers themselves, supplies of which cooperatives handle substantial shares, are bought infrequently. This contrasts with repetitive purchase of such "hard goods" supplies as tires, batteries, small farm tools, fencing, hardware, and paint handled by cooperatives, usually under a cooperative brand. But development in investor-owned distribution of these goods has largely replaced the expensive two-step distribution of independent wholesalers to retailers appropriate for an earlier era. Outlets of the integrated retail-wholesale (with much manufacturing) of the original mail order and of other mass distributors blanket the country and forced the reorganization of hardware distribution described in chapter 8 below.[28]

To succeed in competition with such distributive arrangements the supply cooperative must obtain the members' confidence in its skill as a buyer, with emphasis on quality, and be able to purchase (as do mass distributors) at a price that covers only the manufacturers' factory costs plus a small margin. Attempting to solve this problem, several regional supply companies formed National Cooperatives, Inc., and United Cooperatives, Inc., to buy according to specifications and make available under the "Co-op" brand tires, some hardware items, a few types of machinery, and even household appliances. Their volume has been very small compared to farmers' purchases of these goods.

Farmers use the same automobiles and trucks as do other purchasers. Several established dealers handle each of these articles in every sizable town, but in small trading centers there may be only one or two dealers. Buyers often shop over a wide territory for purchases that are made infrequently and involve substantial outlays. For that reason, and because automobile and truck manufacturers press dealers to move a large volume, price competition at retail is keen. It takes the form of the size of the allowance for the used vehicle traded in by the purchaser, which often exceeds the sum of the reconditioning costs and money from the resale of the vehicle. The effect is to reduce by a third or more the (unnecessarily large) margin provided by the retail prices suggested by the factory. One-fifth of that shrunken margin consists of advertising and salesman expenses and nearly one-third of "other salaries." New car selling, as distinct from selling accessories and repair services, leaves little, if any, net income.[29]

Cooperatives face four barriers that effectively bar them from retail distribution of new motor vehicles. Providing repair services, mandatory during the early warranty life of a new car and generally expected by purchasers continuously, is an added and different kind of business from that in which cooperatives have demonstrated special competence. Second, the overwhelming portion of these vehicles are purchased on the installment plan, a difficult operation for cooperatives, with their limited capital.[30] Third, most sales involve accepting a used vehicle as partial payment, which is doubly difficult for a cooperative. Its employees must bargain about used vehicle allowance with, in a sense, their own employers, the members of the cooperative. A similar problem arises in disposing of the used vehicle; "blue book" values do not provide a valid guide to actual selling prices, which result from the bargaining.

Fourth, inability to buy new vehicles completely stops cooperatives from distributing automobiles and trucks made by the few large manufacturers. The four domestic manufacturers of automobiles, with over 90 percent of the output in the hands of three, have franchised retail outlets which function as a nonowned extension of the manufacturer's business, a role contrary to the buyer-orientation of cooperatives. Almost the same situation exists for trucks. Even buying automobiles or trucks with a large cooperative's name on it, as is done to a small degree in farm machinery, is unlikely unless one of the manufacturers were to become sufficiently desperate for volume. Sears, Roebuck and Company, which already had hundreds of outlets and an outstanding record in selling "hard goods," made such an arrangement about 1950 (with Kaiser-Frazer) but did not succeed in the venture.

For the reasons just considered cooperatives have not achieved a significant role in farm machinery. Some local associations do handle farm machinery, usually along with other commodities, under one of two arrangements.[31] For several decades a limited number of associations handled machinery as dealer representatives of manufacturers. But the manufacturers' investor-owned dealers objected strenuously, and in addition manufacturers have not found cooperatives to be aggressive retailers. When competition was intensified during the 1930s, along with the use of more liberal credit terms to farmers as a selling device, local cooperatives gave up most of these dealerships. Before the war several regional cooperatives joined to form the National Farm Machinery Cooperative, which purchased and distributed machinery under the "Co-op" brand. In one or two cases a local association, and beginning in 1941 the National Cooperative itself, undertook a limited amount of manufacturing of components and assembling of the "Co-op" tractors, a line since dropped.

Compared to handling gasoline or feed, success in distributing a high-unit-value, technologically unstandardized and changing commodity line such as farm machinery is a difficult and uncertain business. Up-to-date quality is important, and selling involves the unique problems referred to with respect to automobiles and trucks. The local cooperative must have enough volume so that it can, without incurring too large an expense, carry an inventory of parts and provide prompt repair service. Some cooperatives have not performed well in these regards.

Even if the cooperatives could solve these problems, they would still have to develop a source of supply for advanced models of machinery of large unit value. For large tractors and much of the tilling and harvesting machinery it is unlikely that any one of the four or five manufacturers that account for most of the output would be willing to supply the cooperatives for sale under the latters' brand. This would be aiding a major competitor, and there is always the possibility that word would get to farmers that the machinery handled by the cooperative was the same as that sold under the large manufacturer's brand.

The barriers to entering manufacturing of the latter types of farm machinery are overwhelming.[32] The capital needed to be efficient is very large. Even if that could be overcome entry at an efficient scale would add such a large percentage to volume that prices of rivals could be expected to decline and the cooperative's net savings would be reduced correspondingly. The problems of being up-to-date in design are serious.

No wonder handling, let alone manufacturing, machinery has not been an attractive venture for cooperatives. Significantly even the giant mail order and chain store companies now sell only a token amount of large-unit-value farm machinery.

7

Farmer-Owned Petroleum Cooperatives

Farmer-owned petroleum cooperatives warrant intensive analysis for several reasons. The production of crude oil, and more so its refining and long-distance transportation, are capital intensive. Not surprisingly much of crude production and most refining and long-distance transportation of petroleum and refined products are carried out by a few giant vertically integrated corporations. Most of these companies also distribute refined fuels through owned bulk stations. When one considers that all of these steps except product distribution are capital intensive, the difficulty of entry by cooperatives into refining and transportation is evident. While bulk stations do not require much capital, entry into that step depends on ability to purchase refined products delivered to the cooperative outlets. To obtain the needed volume, cooperative bulk stations to a substantial degree obtain supplies from investor-owned refining companies whose output exceeds the volume their bulk stations distribute.

The alternative of a cooperatively owned refinery faces several hurdles. The economies of plant size in petroleum refining are high, and the investment in a plant of efficient size runs into many tens of millions of dollars. Whether located near crude production or in the consuming area, the plant must have access to a crude oil, to a refined product pipeline, or to low-cost water transportation.

Status of Farmer-Owned Petroleum Cooperatives

Through cooperative vertical integration into petroleum-product distribution farmers obtain over one-fourth of the petroleum products they use in farming and in family living (see table 6.1). Most of the volume moves through 3392 cooperatively owned bulk stations scattered over nearly all states. About half of these stations' supplies are bought from investor-owned refineries. The remainder is obtained from eight refineries owned singly or jointly by regional cooperatives.[1] These cooperatives in turn own oil wells that supply 87 percent of the crude refined oil, a sharp increase from 31 percent in 1957.[2] The cooperatives own crude oil pipelines through which most of the oil from owned wells is transported to the cooperatives' refineries. While cooperatives own a thousand miles of pipelines to transport refined products, by no means is all hauled to consuming areas in these lines. Much moves in common carrier lines owned by others, by barge on the Mississippi River system, and by tanker from the Gulf Coast to the East Coast.

Development of petroleum cooperatives has been quite unequal among regions. Note in table 7.1 that the north central regions account for the highest percentages of cooperative volume and also the highest percentages of petroleum products used in farming. The obverse relationship holds to a marked degree for the southern regions, which parallels the limited role there of cooperative marketing, as considered earlier. More directly relevant to petroleum cooperatives is the geographic distribution of crude oil production and of refining, to be portrayed in the next section.

Most of the following analysis centers on the west north central region plus Illinois and the three northern Rocky Mountain states. By 1970-1971 cooperatives in these regions distributed one-third of the petroleum products used in farm production, plus a substantial volume for farm family use and sales to nonmembers.

Conditions Affecting Entry and Early Growth of Petroleum Cooperatives

The background to the development of petroleum cooperatives includes the phenomenal change from animal to mechanical power in farming and the organization and price behavior of the petroleum refining and distributing industries. Additional influences in the area studied here are developments in transportation of refined products.

Except for the northern Rocky Mountain states that are self-sufficient in petroleum the geographic pattern of refining and product distribution

Table 7.1. Regional Percentages of Total Farmer Cooperative Volume of Petroleum Products, and of Use of Petroleum Products, 1970–1971, and of Use of Petroleum Products in Farm Operations, 1964.

| | Regional Percentages of National Totals | |
Region	Petroleum cooperatives' volume, 1970–1971	Petroleum products used in farming, 1964
New England and Middle Atlantic	13%	6%
East North Central	25	19
West North Central	43	29
South Atlantic	4	10
East South Central	3	6
West South Central	3	14
Rocky Mountain	5	8
Pacific	4	8
Total	100%	100%

Sources: Computed from data in the *Census of Agriculture* (Washington, D.C.: The census, 1964), vol. 2, chap. 7, "Farm Facilities, Farm Equipment, Farm Expenditures, Farm Labor, and Cash Rent"; and unpublished Farmer Cooperative Service data for 1970–1971.

is built around the northward flow of crude oil and of refined products from the midcontinent area of Oklahoma, Kansas, and northern Texas. Crude oil moves by pipeline to refineries in the St. Louis, Chicago, and Ohio areas. Until after World War II over half of the gasoline consumed north of Oklahoma and of the Ohio River was shipped in by tank car.[3]

In the area of surplus crude production, small refineries sprang up and sold their products to investor-owned jobbers for resale under their brands. Small and some large refineries competed avidly in price for these jobbers' business, and the jobbers in turn were price competitors. There was little opportunity for cooperatives in these locations.

The situation was quite different in areas that imported from the midcontinent a substantial part of the refined products consumed, as did north central states. There, but varying in degree by periods, prices were significantly above the Oklahoma price, called the "Group 3" price,[4] plus the sum of the rail freight rate and the distribution margin necessary to cover costs and provide competitive returns on capital. This price structure was made possible by the organization of the refining and distributing phases of the industry.

The north central states were supplied with refined products by two types of companies that differed in size, location of plants, and role in product distribution. Several large companies with refineries located chiefly in the north central states obtained crude oil by pipeline at half the rail rates on refined products from Group 3 origins.[5] These refineries were not forced to reflect this saving in prices for refined products because a substantial portion of the area's consumption was still shipped in by tank car. These refiners' shipments were distributed to farmers and other business buyers and to service stations through thousands of owned wholesale or bulk stations or through nonowned outlets handling only one refiner's brand.[6] Rivalry centered on advertising and other sales efforts which stressed product superiority.

Much of the remaining shipped-in supply came by tank car from small refiners located in the midcontinent crude-producing area. Because of their small size and the distance to their markets few of these refiners developed their own brand distribution. They sold in the "tank car" market, directly or through brokers, to large refiners whose distribution volume exceeded their refining capacity, to industrial users, and to jobbers and cooperatives who resold under their brands.

With such a supply source all that a local cooperative needed was a vertical bulk tank, a small tank truck for deliveries, and an inventory of products. In 1936 the average net worth of local petroleum cooperatives was only $16,000.[7]

Early Petroleum Cooperatives and Their Record

Cooperatives organized to supply petroleum products had made a strong start by 1925. Of the 1057 whose primary business was petroleum products in 1936, half had been in business for more than five years.[8] The typical cooperative was organized by farmers of a locality, many as the cooperative counterpart of the county farm bureaus.[9]

Most early locals were highly successful, and their net savings rates were high.[10] But some experienced the vicissitudes of inept management or were victims of price wars, whether aimed at these farmer-owned bulk stations or not.[11]

Buying gasoline through brokers was not always satisfactory, and before 1930 several wholesale cooperatives owned by locals of a state or region were formed. Some were founded by general agricultural organizations. Of the four major regionals operating in the area being studied, Midland dates back to 1926, the Farmer Union Central Exchange and the Illinois Farm Supply Services (now joined with the Iowa Farm Supply Company to form FS Services) to 1927, and Farmland Industries (formerly Consumers Cooperative Association) to 1929. Their further integration into refining, some crude production, and pipeline and other transportation occurred later.

Petroleum Cooperatives in the 1930-1957 Period

While many petroleum cooperatives had become firmly established by 1930, their rapid growth and integration into refining occurred in the following three decades. In recent years, when needed, the cooperatives could borrow from the banks for cooperatives.

Developments Affecting Petroleum Product Markets After 1929

Between 1930 and World War II several developments disturbed the organization of refining and product distribution which enlarged the opportunity for cooperatives. Vast new crude discoveries, crowned by development of the rich East Texas field in 1931, brought a collapse of crude oil prices. Small refineries adjacent to this field sprang up by the score to profit from the extraordinary spread between the price of crude oil and the prices of refined products in northern markets where large refiners' selling prices did not reflect fully the distress prices of crude. Simultaneously the critical condition of agriculture, as prices farmers received fell by more than half after 1929 while the use of tractor power continued to grow, pressured farmers to buy gasoline at the lowest possible price. This spurred interest in cooperatives.

Of more enduring effect were developments in the transportation of refined products. Product pipelines built in the early 1930s could haul gasoline from Oklahoma to northern markets at half the rail rates,[12] but this savings was not reflected in pipeline rates until 1941. Even if their rates had been reduced earlier their capacity plus the output of the refineries in the north central region that received crude oil by pipeline was less than consumption in the area. A substantial part of the gasoline was still shipped in by tank car from the midcontinent refineries. By about 1938 the completion of clear barge channels on the Mississippi River and some of its tributaries allowed the geographic price differential to drop in areas near the waterways. As early as 1938 prices in Chicago, and by 1941 in Minneapolis, declined a cent a gallon below the price in Oklahoma plus the rail freight rate.[13]

Before these developments could have their full effect wartime demand for petroleum products dominated the scene. Excess demand at prevailing prices, unrestrained by rationing, continued for over two years after the cessation of hostilities. Obtaining supplies on as favorable a basis as previously was the problem of nonintegrated distributors such as cooperatives. This led them to integrate extensively into refining.

By about 1950 the vast wartime and early postwar building of both crude and products pipelines, together with water shipment on the Mississippi system, so expanded capacity that the import requirement of the north central region could be transported by low-cost modes. Tank wagon prices in northern areas relative to Oklahoma prices sagged and by 1953 did not even reflect pipeline rates in some markets (see table 7.2).

To varying degrees during different years in the 1930-1957 period farmer cooperatives could obtain net savings for their members when one or more of the following situations obtained:

1. When the going price to farmers charged by outlets selling large refiners' brands exceeded the sum of the margin on which these jobbers operated and the tank car price in the midcontinent plus the railroad rate. Later the lower pipeline rate became relevant. A local rail or truck haul to some destinations was necessary also.
2. When the regional cooperative was able to take advantage of lower cost means of transportation than that reflected in northern market prices of large refiners, or when they acquired or produced refined products in the midcontinent area at prices below those published.
3. When local cooperatives were able to distribute products to members at costs below the jobber margins of the bulk stations representing large refiners.
4. When the cooperatives were able to obtain patronage without incurring advertising and selling expenses comparable to those of large refiners and their distributive outlets, a point that cannot be appraised quantitatively.

Opportunity Provided by Geographic Price Spreads

The extent to which geographic price spreads in the large refiner-marketers' price structure was, or was not, in excess of transport costs is indicated in part by table 7.2. From the posted bulk station prices for sales to farmers is subtracted the going jobber margin at various dates. The residual is then compared with the landed cost of gasoline bought at the "low of the range" of prices in Oklahoma plus rail rates. By 1952 and more so by 1957 the added capacity of the pipelines and their low rates reduced the geographic price spread.

There followed also reductions in the margins of jobbers distributing to farmers. Note the sharp decline in this margin from 1929 to 1940, shown in table 7.3. The strongest proof is that in 1934 the leading refining-marketer not only adopted a policy of reflecting in its transfer price to jobbers the landed cost of gasoline as if purchased in Oklahoma, but also reduced the jobber margin of its owned and operated bulk station by two cents below that implicit in the price spreads of the years just earlier.[14]

Table 7.2. Average Differential Between Landed Cost and Tank Wagon Price of Gasoline to Farmers in Five Northern Markets,[a] Selected Years, 1930–1957 (cents per gallon)

Type of shipment	Form of transportation							
	Rail 1930	Rail 1936	Rail 1940	Rail 1949	Rail 1952	Rail 1957	Pipe line[b] 1952	Pipe line[b] 1957
Gross differential	5.9¢	3.9¢	3.7¢	4.3¢	3.7¢	2.7¢	5.6¢[c]	4.4¢[c]
Going margin jobber	n.a.	3.5	4.0	4.3	4.3	4.5	4.3	4.5
Net differential	n.a.	0.4	0.2	0.3	-0.6	-1.8	1.3[c]	-0.1[c]

Source: Prices at refineries in Oklahoma and prices to farmers in various northern destinations from the annual issues of *Platt's Oil Price Handbook* and from prices posted in bulk stations. Pipeline and railroad rates are those approved by the Interstate Commerce Commission. Barge rates from an industry source.

[a]The markets are Decatur and Peoria, Illinois; Mason City, Iowa; Mankato, Minnesota; and Fargo, North Dakota.
[b]Plus rail rate from St. Louis in the case of Decatur or the barge rate from St. Louis to Peoria.
[c]Without Peoria (where receipts by barge had driven down prices), the average for the four remaining markets was about 0.4 cent higher in each of these years.

It is not surprising that the potential savings cooperatives could obtain solely from the geographic price spread were not large in 1936 and 1940, as shown in the bottom row of table 7.2.

Table 7.3. The Jobber Margin on Gasoline for Sales to Farmers and the Average Gross Margins, Operating Expenses, and Net Operating Savings of Local Cooperative Members of Four Regional Cooperatives, Selected Years, 1929–1957 (cents per gallon)

Year	Jobber margin	Gross margin of locals	Operating expenses	Local cooperatives' net savings
		Average	Average	Average
1929	5.9¢	5.2¢	3.2¢	2.0¢
1936	3.5	3.4	2.4	1.0
1940	3.5	3.4	2.5	.9
1949	4.0	4.4	3.0	1.4
1954	4.5	4.3	3.4	.9
1957	4.7	4.7	3.5	1.2

Sources: Only averages are reported in order not to identify the particular regional cooperatives whose own data and that of its locals were supplied to me. In all cases supplementary figures, and for two regionals all data for 1949 and later years, were taken from reports of the auditing services associated with the regionals or were supplied directly by the regional to the author. Wherever possible, and quite generally for prewar years, only data for locals engaged almost exclusively in the petroleum business were used. Data supplied as percentages of dollar sales were converted to cents-per-gallon equivalents by multiplying by the posted price of the leading refiner-marketer. The jobber margin implicit in the leading refiner marketer's price structure was obtained from informed persons in the trade.

There are other reasons for doubting whether cooperatives paid the quoted Group 3 prices plus rail rates for most of the years after about 1937 except during the war and early postwar shortage. For other years the author has learned from unpublished sources that the published "low of the range" of Group 3 prices were usually the maximum prices for sizable purchases. Prices for most transactions were significantly lower. This became more evident as the refineries shipping by rail faced increasing competition from plants that could ship north by barge in 1938 and 1940 and by means of product pipeline after the wartime shortage disappeared.

In the years just before the war, transportation savings arose chiefly where products could be shipped by water. This opportunity was open for the large area near the Mississippi system and was seized with great success by the Illinois Farm Supply Company and some other statewide cooperatives that acquired fleets of transport trucks. Midland Cooperatives could gain in the parts of its market to which the low barge rates on the Mississippi plus local rail or truck charges were less than the all-rail rate from Oklahoma. Even Farmers Union Central Exchange could do similarly in its distribution near Minneapolis. But during the wartime shortage there was little opportunity to buy or transport advantageously.

The regional cooperatives in this large area and elsewhere responded by integrating into refining. Between early 1941 and the end of 1949 they bought ten small refineries. One had been acquired earlier and seven were bought subsequently to bring the total to eighteen. Many of the refineries were poorly located and lacked the size and modern facilities for efficiency. Most of these have been sold or closed, and with one added later the number operated in 1968 was only eight, each far larger.

It is not possible to measure precisely the net gain attributable to the regional cooperatives' activities. The basis on which they transfer petroleum products to locals has varied from time to time. Often the transfer price reflected most of the gain from the successful operation of the regionals. Then savings reported in the regionals' income statements stemmed from economies in long-distance transportation and refining rather than from buying products.

The net savings attributable to the locals' own operations consists of the difference between their operating costs and the margins of jobbers handling refiner-brand products. Table 7.3 shows that those savings varied from about one to two cents per gallon, not insignificant percentages of prices of gasoline (excluding fuel taxes) prior to and even after the war.

This table does not report the total net savings, for it excludes the locals' "other income," shown in table 7.4, which consists primarily of the patronage dividends of the regionals. These are included in the locals' income whether received in cash or in added equity in the regional. The

Table 7.4. Estimated Regional, Local, and Total Net Savings of Petroleum Cooperatives, Selected Years, 1936–1957 (cents per gallon)

Year	Other income of locals		Operating savings		Total net savings	
	Average	Range	Average	Range	Average	Range
1936	.2¢	.2– .3¢	1.0¢	.8–1.2¢	1.2¢	1.0–1.4¢
1940	.3	.3– .5	.9	.5–1.7	1.2	.8–1.8
1949	.6	.5–2.0	1.4	.6–1.7	3.0	.9–3.2
1954	.7	.1–1.4	.9	.8–1.8	1.6	.9–3.5
1957	.8	.2–1.8	1.2	.8–1.6	2.0	1.1–3.3

Sources: Other income of locals obtained from the same sources as the data for table 7.3. Operating savings are also from that table.

total net savings of the locals, thus computed, are shown in the last column. For reasons advanced in the next section it is not possible to present comparable data on gains since 1957. But the further increase in the cooperatives' market shares must be in response to members' gain from patronage.

The Petroleum Cooperatives' Record

More than for any other group of farmer-owned cooperatives studied it is possible to measure the savings from engaging in the petroleum business. Net savings of the locals of the four regionals were about 9 percent of net sales in the 1936-1940 periods (see table 7.5) and averaged 7 percent for all petroleum cooperatives in the country in 1936.[15] These savings included dividends in cash or added equity in the regionals as well as savings from the locals' operations.[16] After the postwar shortage the net savings rate returned to the prewar level. Such evidence as I have obtained indicates probably lower but still substantial results in the 1960s.

More meaningful are net savings as percentages of members' equity in the cooperatives over and above what members' equity could have earned elsewhere.[17] In 1936 net savings of all petroleum cooperatives in the country were 24 percent of members' equity,[18] a very high rate for those depressed years. In the 1936-1940 period the net savings of locals of the four regionals studied here averaged 34 percent of equity, almost six

Table 7.5. Estimated Net Savings of Regional Petroleum Cooperatives in the West Central States, Selected Years, 1936-1957

Year	Net savings as percentage of net sales		Net savings as percentage of members' equity	
	Average	Range	Average	Range
1936	8.6%	6.9-12.6%	34%[a]	24-55%[c]
1940	8.4	5.7-13.6		
1949	11.0	4.8-15.8	[d]	
1954	7.5	3.6-11.9	17[c]	13-24[c]
1957	8.1	6.3-10.6[b]		

Sources: Data on net sales, members' equity, and assets of locals used in calculating the percentages were obtained from the same sources as for the basic figures in table 7.3.

[a]Of necessity this is the percentage of overall net savings of locals primarily engaged in distributing petroleum products, but most of which also distribute other farm supplies.

[b]Average for locals of three regionals only.

[c]Data on members' equity in locals of the regionals are for various years from 1936 to 1940 and from various years from 1954 to 1957. Hence, an average return on equity is provided for 1930 and 1940 and likewise for 1954 and 1957.

[d]Members' equity not available.

times the rate obtained by the large investor-owned refining companies. After the postwar shortage the cooperatives' earning rate on members' investment fell to half the prewar level but was still about one and a half times that of large refining companies.[19]

Over the period studied here a sharply increasing percentage of locals' assets consisted of investments, primarily their equity in the regionals. The latter had been financed largely out of net savings of the regionals withheld to finance integration into refining, transportation facilities, and crude production.

The value to locals of this investment by regionals can be appraised by considering the operating situation they would have faced had they been dependent on purchases from investor-owned refiners. Then they would have had only the savings obtainable from their own distribution from bulk stations at best. In the early postwar period the locals' net savings would have been still lower because of inability to buy products advantageously. Consequently the fact that some of the refineries purchased were later sold for less than the net investment does not indicate that the investment had been unwise.

Most of the time since the 1950s buying petroleum fuels at favorable prices has not been difficult. The future at this writing is less clear for the number of investor-owned refineries located to supply the north central states that do not have their own brand distribution continues to decline. Few of these refiners are connected to product pipelines running north. The modernization and expansion of the remaining and much larger cooperative-owned refineries serves in part at least as a hedge against future supply difficulties.

Indirect Gains: Effect on Competitive Adjustments

Beyond savings reflected directly in the cooperatives' accounts both members and nonmembers have benefited substantially by the pressure that the cooperatives' rising share of farmers' purchase of petroleum products has put on the prices of investor-owned rivals. As shown earlier the cooperatives were a major force in forcing down prices outside the large cities when the marginal supply of the north central states came by rail. This is the implication of the belated adjustment of the geographic differentials shown in table 7.2.

Pressures were at work on distributive margins also. Both comments of officials of investor-owned companies and claims of cooperatives indicate that the petroleum fuels handled by both are of equivalent quality. Cooperatives' members do not now have to be convinced by expensive advertising. When, after a long period of stability, investor-owned refiners' jobber margins began to increase in 1949 the margin on sales to farmers advanced by a smaller percentage than for sales to service stations. The clear success of the average local cooperative in carrying on the bulk station operation at a cost (excluding return on investment) from 25 to 30 percent below the jobbers' margin (table 7.2) was a strong restraining influence on that margin. But the cooperatives' expenses were creeping up and had not some advance in the rival jobbers' margin occurred, by 1954 there would have been no net savings from the local distributive operation. In the 1960s cooperatives' managers indicated quite widespread selling of refiners' branded products at prices that anticipated at least part of the cooperatives' patronage dividends to members. Altogether the cooperatives and the investor-owned outlets have become checks on each other, but the former forces the latter to bow to the force of necessary costs.

Recent Developments

In 1972-1973 the Near East countries' embargo on oil exports brought a crisis in the domestic refining industry. The cooperative refineries were in a vulnerable position because they produced only a small percentage of the crude oil they refined. Affected similarly were the fourteen regional cooperatives that had no refining capacity and bought products from investor-owned plants.[20]

The situation was eased by a government allocation plan that required crude producers to treat refinery buyers in proportion to their previous rates of purchase and refineries to treat the purchasers of refined products likewise. Nevertheless some refineries operated below capacity and even shut down for short periods. They generally emphasized producing the fuels used in farm production as distinct from family living. The shortage ended when the Near East embargo was lifted.

Recognizing their vulnerable situation the cooperative refineries have taken three steps to insure that the situation just described will not recur. They expanded their exploration for crude oil domestically. They also formed a consortium to explore for oil overseas. To be certain that imported oil would be available to them several of the refining cooperatives, together with some investor-owned refiners, planned a crude oil pipeline from the Texas coast to Oklahoma, where there have been several cooperative refineries.[21]

By 1973-1974 the emergency passed. By that date the cooperatives supplied 35 percent of farmers' purchasing petroleum fuels, twice their 1950-1951 percentage.

8
Cooperatives Owned by Urban Businesses

Although not widely known the cooperative form of enterprise is found in parts of the nonfarm business world. Not surprisingly in light of the argument in chapter 2, nearly all of these cooperatives represent downstream integration carried out by groups of investor-owned firms, each of which is small compared to the size required for success in the operation into which the integration is to be made. Members of some of these cooperatives are absolutely large investor-owned corporations. No instance has been found of cooperative vertical integration downstream by a substantial number of nonfarm businesses. On occasion joint ventures by two, or at most a very few, large corporations are formed to carry out downstream vertical integration, but they are not studied here.

Retailer-Owned Wholesale Cooperatives

Wholesaling establishments owned cooperatively by retailers exist in a significant number of commodity lines. The *Census of Business* for 1967 reports the number and volume of cooperatives identified as a legal form of organization distinct from investor-owned corporations. Additional operating data were collected by mail questionnaires and interviews and may be incomplete, particularly about small enterprises. Of necessity data from the 1967 *Census* will be used here except where additional information has been uncovered. The 1972 *Census* includes the cooperatives' volume in a catch-all category of "other forms of legal organization."[1]

In the commodity categories listed in table 8.1 wholesale cooperatives' shares ranged from one-half of one percent to almost a quarter of the volume. Only three of the categories will be studied here because adequate information about cooperatives owned by retail drug stores was not obtainable.

Table 8.1. Retailer-Owned Wholesale Cooperatives' Market Share in Selected Lines

Commodity group	Cooperatives' percentage of total dollar volume
Groceries and related products (1972)	22.7%[a]
Hardware (1972)	7.1[b]
Drug and drug sundries (1967)	1.1
Construction materials (1967)	0.5

[a]This figure was computed by dividing the volume of the association of independent retailers (provided by their trade association) by the 1972 *Census* report of the total volume of groceries and related products.

[b]Computed as explained in note a except that the major hardware cooperative's volume is divided by census total volume of hardware plus the volume of other cooperatives as reported in the 1967 *Census*.

Except for the grocery field the retailer-owned wholesale cooperative enterprises' market shares are small. But a study of the condition that led to their establishment and their current influence adds to understanding of the cooperative form of enterprise. Some of that influence is suggested by the fact that the average cooperatively owned wholesale establishment in the commodity areas listed in table 8.1 accounts for a much larger percentage of wholesale volume than of establishments. The general-line grocery wholesaling cooperatives' share of volume was four times their percentage of establishments in 1967.

Retailer-Owned Grocery Wholesale Cooperatives

Growth of grocery cooperative wholesale enterprises was part of an almost complete transformation of the food distribution process that began even before 1920. The new arrangement was made possible by technological advances in food processing, communication, and transportation, developments which facilitated the emergence of chain food stores and the later almost complete shift to cash-and-carry retailing.

Simplification of the Transfer Process:
Redundancy of the Old Wholesaler

Until about 1914 the wholesalers performed very different economic functions from their role today. They were expert buyers of food, often in bulk and often shipped to the retailers in bulk containers; the cracker barrel was a fact in retail stores. Some packaging and branding was done by wholesalers, and their brands were widely accepted by consumers. Aggressive brand advertising by manufacturers had hardly started.

Communication and local transportation were so slow that retailers could not count on a finely timed flow of deliveries. Of necessity they carried far larger inventories relative to sales than is the practice today. Wholesalers carried large inventories (compared to present practice) that also turned over slowly.

Beginning before 1920, and at an accelerated pace thereafter, important technological developments altered these food distribution arrangements. New preserving processes and mass production methods in food manufacturing and packaging allowed the bottling, canning, or other packaging of foods to be done economically. Quality control facilitated transactions between manufacturers and large distributive buyers on the basis of commercial grades. Manufacturers were able to standardize the quality packaged under a brand, a prerequisite to successful large-scale advertising. Mass appeal was aided by such new media as the radio, which helped standardize consumer's tastes. Manufacturers were able to popularize their brands over large geographical areas or even the entire nation.

These and other changes upset the traditional wholesaling industry. Shipment to retailers by motor truck made closely spaced wholesalers redundant. The surviving wholesalers lost their unique buying and grading functions; quality of a product was apparent to the retailer with a glance at the manufacturers' label and without the wholesaler's mediation. As consumers' brand and package preferences became strongly entrenched through manufacturers' advertising the retailer's job became largely one of physical handling of packaged groceries.

With the wholesaler's job thus simplified it became possible to split much of his traditional function between the manufacturer and the retailer. The former took over most of the merchandising job; what was left for most wholesalers was the ordering, warehousing, and delivery operations. Creative merchandising at the wholesale level almost disappeared.

Investor-owned wholesalers could have gone far to adapt to this new situation, and a portion did so belatedly. They would have had to adopt mail or telephone order-taking, sale for cash, and possibly charge for delivery. But few wholesalers took these steps until their survival was threatened by the independent retailer obituary column. To add to the wholesalers' plight, when a retail chain had enough outlets in a market area it took on the purchasing-warehouse function. Some independent retailers met this situation by forming cooperatively owned warehouses.

Developments Directly Affecting Retailing

The developments just sketched contributed to major changes in retailing. With more and more goods packaged and manufacturers' advertising training consumers to purchase by brands the door to self-service retailing was opened. The housewife came to the store, and "cash and carry" selling rather than delivery became possible, particularly with the spread of automobile transportation. Urbanization of the economy and the rapid growth of wage-earning and salaried groups with periodic cash income made selling for cash feasible and paved the way for the rapid growth of chain food stores.

These developments presaged a radical decline in retailing costs. In the usually labor-intensive distributive trades, only in food distribution of all major categories of nondurable consumer goods did the manufacturer-to-consumer percentage margin decline as wage rates advanced sharply over the last century.[2]

There proved to be economies in some phases of multiple-outlet retailing. A single newspaper advertisement could serve all of the chain's outlets in a locality. Specialists on the chain's staff designed efficient store layouts, methods of systematic control of inventory at the retail level, and improved accounting procedures.

Except for these economies nothing in the developments directly affecting retail operations required their exploitation by chain stores. In fact self-help and cash-and-carry retailing whereby customers took over work previously done by store employees was pioneered by individual retailers. So was the "supermarket," which combines groceries, meat, and produce in one large outlet. Later the chains adopted these practices so rapidly that the public has come to associate them with the chain stores.[3] The advantages of multiple-outlet retailing have not proved to be overwhelming, as is shown by the persistence of a few store and single-outlet retailers who benefit from the low margins of the cooperative wholesalers and of the "voluntary" wholesalers to be considered later.

Entry and Growth of
Retailer-Owned Wholesale Grocery Cooperatives

Although some sort of an adjustment was necessary at all levels of distribution, retailers bore the initial impact of competition with the chains before wholesalers recognized their own plight. They were more remote from the revolution in distribution than were the retailers squeezed in the 1920s between the wholesalers' high prices and the nearby chain stores' low retail prices. The consequent independent retailer obituary column brought the shock to wholesalers, to which was added by the late 1920s the chains' shift to direct buying from manufacturers. Increasingly also, independent retailers were turning to the growing cash-and-carry investor-owned wholesalers.

Many cooperative wholesalers started as very simple operations. In some cases the retailer-members merely pooled their purchases of a few large-volume items to be delivered to one member's store or a railroad siding, where each member picked up his portion.[4] In 1929 the average stock purchase or deposit required of the members was nominal,[5] but they had to pay cash upon receipt of the goods. The small market shares of these cooperatives did not then disturb rivals.

Soon successful cooperatives accumulated sufficient capital from savings to own or rent a warehouse and to enlarge the list of goods handled. Their volume began to pinch other wholesalers, who pressed manufacturers not to sell to the cooperatives, but with little success.

The cooperatively owned wholesaler movement grew rapidly after the end of World War I, and by 1927 there were ninety-six in operation. Even though absence of selling and credit expenses reduced their total costs by four percentage points below those of investor-owned wholesalers, the cooperatives attained only 5 percent of wholesale grocery volume by the above date,[6] a small amount compared to 22.7 percent in 1972.

The Investor-Owned Wholesalers Form Voluntaries

Another form of adaptation was the voluntary, an arrangement between an investor-owned wholesaler and retailers of a city or region that enabled such wholesalers to be strong rivals of the cooperatives.[7] Typically a local wholesaler became a licensee of IGA or of Red and White, for example, enterprises which merely developed a voluntary plan and were not themselves wholesalers. IGA, for example, licenses one wholesaler to develop a voluntary in its market area by associating with it under contract a substantial number of retailers, each to be identified as an IGA store. Recently a number of regional wholesalers have developed their individual designations and formed their respective voluntaries. The voluntary's retailer-members are owners of single or few-store operations, but they do not own stock in the wholesaler nor, ordinarily, does the wholesaler have more than an occasional temporary financial interest in retail outlets.

The relative shares of all grocery wholesaling by cooperatively owned and by voluntary group wholesalers have varied from decade to decade, but both now overshadow the remaining full-service, nonvoluntary investor-owned wholesalers. By 1935 voluntaries accounted for 30 percent of the grocery volume, while retailer-owned cooperatives (as identified by the *Census*) had only 7 percent, shares that had not changed much by 1948. By 1958 the cooperatives' share had jumped to 18 percent and then on to 26 percent in 1967, at which date the voluntaries' percentage had advanced to 49.[8]

Organization and Operation of the Cooperative Wholesalers

The retailer-owned cooperatives originally concentrated on purchasing and warehousing the large-volume dry groceries, but since World War II they have enlarged the lines handled even beyond a full line of groceries. Purchasing is facilitated by three regional buying organizations owned by the cooperative wholesalers of the respective regions. This is particularly useful as a means of acquiring goods to carry the private, or distributor, labels and for merchandising these price-competitive commodities. Private-brand merchandise accounts for 12 percent of the packaged goods handled by the warehouses surveyed in the 1950s and was still below 25 percent of the retail volume of the groceries of most member retailers in 1965, as was true also for members of voluntaries.[9]

By agreement among members expensive operating methods are avoided by the wholesale cooperatives. If the warehouse handles only groceries orders are accepted only once a week except from very large stores but more often if the cooperative also handles perishable goods. Some cooperatives charge also a flat weekly fee which becomes a progressively smaller charge per unit as more volume is ordered. Ordinarily cash must be paid for goods ordered.

Operating margins used to set invoice prices to members vary widely among warehouses and among commodities. Initial margins on highly competitive items reflect expected savings and thereby provide members with invoice costs similar to those of chain stores. Some cooperatives attempt to return large patronage dividends at the end of the year and thus have somewhat higher initial wholesale margins, while others do the reverse.

Cost Savings and Competitive Position of the Cooperatives

The early cooperatives addressed themselves almost entirely to removing the first of the chains' advantages over the independents, the low cost of inventory to the retail outlet. This was made possible by zero sales and credit expense and by the 1950s by the general use of "preprint" forms on which members mail in their orders. A strong inverse relationship was discernible between both the percentage of preprint order business and the average size of members' orders and the height of the warehouse's margins.

Other cost savings were important. Even by the early 1950s about 75 percent of retail-owned cooperatives' warehouses were of new one-story design and mechanized to assemble shipments, a process aided by the infrequency and relatively large size of members' orders. In 1967 the cooperative establishments on the average were still far larger than the average size of all grocery wholesaler establishments. Except for such a notable example as Certified Grocers of California, which distributes over a wide area but charges for deliveries to more distant zones, a cooperative usually does business only in a city and nearby areas—the practice of chain store warehouses—with consequent low delivery costs.

Because of these operating practices the cooperatives' membership is selective in that it can be used most effectively by larger, financially strong retailers. Much, if not the bulk, of the volume is obtained from small groups of stores in common ownership. Having to pay cash for goods on delivery (or to settle very soon thereafter) adds to members' capital requirements. Ability to anticipate needs and to order infrequently without running out of many items is more likely to corollate with size of store, an application of the well-known principle of massing of reserves. Consequently the larger the volume the smaller the percentage of its capital a retail store must tie up in inventory.

A final aspect of selectivity of the cooperative's membership is the identification of the retailer-members, often by a large insignia. This lessens the opportunity for stores near each other to be members of the same cooperative.

All of these features of the cooperative warehouses (and of their members to the extent that their success is affected by the landed cost of goods bought) contribute to their operating expense record compared to other types of wholesalers (as shown in table 8.2). Operating expenses as percentages of sales of all types of grocery wholesalers, reported in *Census* surveys over three decades, show a downward trend, with the expenses of the voluntaries falling most sharply. In earlier years both the cooperatives' and the cash-and-carry investor-owned wholesalers' costs were clearly lower than those of rivals. In 1935 the average expense rate of the voluntaries had tumbled and was only about 1.5 percentage points above the cooperatives'. The persistently low expenses of the cooperatives and the radical decline of the voluntaries' costs are correlated with their growing shares of all grocery wholesaling (omitting chain store purchasing-warehouse operations) to 26 and 49 percent, respectively, in 1967.

Table 8.2. Average Operating Expense as Percentage of Sales of Various Types of Grocery
Wholesalers, Selected Years, 1935–1967

Type of grocery wholesaler	Operating expenses as percentage of sales				
	1935	1939	1948	1963	1967
All general line wholesalers	8.9%	9.5%	8.1%	6.7%	6.4%
Investor-owned wholesalers					
Voluntary wholesalers	10.1	10.6	8.3	6.2	6.1
Cash-and-carry	5.2	5.2	4.9	n.a.	n.a.
Other	8.9	9.6	8.7	9.2	9.0
Cooperative wholesalers	5.2	5.2	4.6	4.5	4.4

Sources: Computed from data in *Census of Business* 1935, "Special Report: Voluntary
Grocers and Cooperative Wholesalers" (Washington, D.C.: The census, 1935), p. 21; *Census of Business* 1939, vol. 2, *Wholesale Trade*, p. 50, 1948, vol. 5, p. 0.10, 1963, vol. 5, pp.
1-11, 1967, vol. 4, pp. 1-15. Comparable data not available from the 1972 *Census*.

Other evidence indicates that the gross margins, as distinct from expense
rates, of wholesale cooperatives and of voluntaries are now very similar.[10]
Now the cooperatives usually pay 20 percent of net savings as patronage
dividend, and the remainder is distributed to members in the form of
short-period (ten-year) interest-bearing evidences of indebtedness, practices encouraged by the provisions of the federal income tax law. To the
extent that the net savings of the cooperatives exceed the rate of return
members could earn on alternative uses of their investment in the cooperative, this amounts to a reduction in prices of goods ordered.

Equally important is a comparison of these wholesalers' expense rates
with those of chain stores performing similar functions. The average expense rate of cooperative warehouses in 1955 as found in the survey was
about 3.5 percent, or lower than the rates shown in table 8.2, but almost
identical with the average chain store's expense rate of 3.4 percent for
carrying out the purchasing, warehousing, and delivery functions in the
1950s. The chains' expenses for these functions in 1967-1968 were reported as between 3 and 4 percent, depending on the source of information,[11] compared to the 4.4 percent for cooperative wholesalers in 1967,
reported in table 8.2. These differences are small, and variance around
the averages affects particular wholesalers and retailers. Not unimportant is that small chains—mostly with less than eleven outlets—frequently
are members of wholesale cooperatives. One such cooperative has been
referred to as the "mother" of these groups during their early growth.[12]

Cooperatives Owned by Chain Food Stores

To round out this account of types of organizational adjustments in
the food trades brief reference will be made to cooperatives owned by

food chains of modest size. While these chains are large enough for efficient buying of most commodities and for advertising, they found that large-volume contracting with manufacturers for private-brand merchandise requires volume above that of any member. Because the large and small chains sell in full competition the latter need comparable merchandise obtained at comparable invoice cost. Such are the functions of the largest of these chain-store-owned cooperatives, TOPCO Associates.

In 1976 Topco's membership consisted of thirty-two corporate chains whose combined retail sales run into billions of dollars.[13] It is organized as a cooperative under Wisconsin law, and the capital structure conforms to the policy explained in chapter 2. Nondividend capital stock is issued to members on the basis of their total retail volume. While the quarterly service charge is slightly advantageous to larger members, net savings are returned in proportion to their patronage. A unique activity is acting on occasion as a middleman between banks and a member chain.

TOPCO has its own brands placed on large-volume groceries' lines that take up about the same proportion of members' shelf space allotted to a food as do the private brands of the average large chain. Retail prices on these brands are set by the member companies, but it is important to note that TOPCO has brands for different price niches: low quality brands are competitive brands, while highest quality labels sell for slightly less than do the top manufacturers' brands.

Savings to members in cost of goods are impressive, and the member chain store companies' retail margins on TOPCO brands average several percentage points above those obtained on competing manufacturers' brands.[14]

Results of the Adjustments

Out of the reorganization of food distribution portrayed in the preceding sections has emerged a continuum of arrangements for conducting the purchasing-warehousing function, together with varying degrees of independence of retailers. At one end are the independent and usually relatively small retailers not affiliated with wholesalers who often provide credit and delivery services. Then come the independent retailers served by autonomous cash-and-carry wholesalers, a disappearing type. They incur neither bad debt losses nor delivery costs, savings that competition forces them to reflect in prices to the retailers, who then must have more capital and pay transport costs. The voluntaries follow next, for the members of such groups contract away (to the investor-owned wholesaler) some of their freedom of decision-making in buying and in some phases of operations. Apparently they rate the prices, services, and private brand of the supplier worthwhile. Then comes the retailer-owned wholesale cooperative, whose members' freedom is not reduced for they may order from other sources when advantageous. Gain from membership is measured not only by lower prices of goods ordered but also from cooperative advertising and the wholesaler's private-brand program. Next are the small chains who use varying combinations of direct buying from manufacturers and from investor-owned or cooperatively owned wholesale sources. Finally, the large chains represent complete vertical integration of wholesaling and retailing and as much manufacturing as is of advantage to them.

Wholesale Cooperatives Owned by Nonfood Retailers

Wholesaling and other primary-market buying organizations cooperatively owned by retailers are found in most important nondurable consumer goods lines and for some durable products. Usually the cooperative's members are small single-outlet retailing enterprises, but some are owned by large retail organizations, such as metropolitan department stores or even small chains of them. In no one of these commodity areas are the cooperatives' market shares as large as for grocery lines, as was reported in table 8.1.

Retailer-Owned Building Materials Wholesale Cooperatives

Often using the descriptive term "reserve supply company" retailers of building materials in a number of localities have established cooperative wholesale enterprises. The 1967 *Census* reports thirty-three establishments, of which eighteen were engaged primarily in handling lumber. The remaining fifteen were engaged in the operation to be examined here, wholesaling primarily of small-volume, specialized construction materials. The thirty-three cooperative wholesale enterprises accounted for only one-half of one percent of the total volume in 1967, only half of their percentage in 1963.[15]

That large retailers often receive direct shipments from manufacturers "reserve supply" connotes the existence of a warehouse on which the members can call when they need materials in smaller quantities or more promptly than could be obtained directly from manufacturers. At times reserve supply companies arrange for carload shipments from manufacturers to retailer members.

After 1920 the variety of building materials, such as new types of roofing, wall board, and building hardware, grew markedly, and large retailers were dissatisfied with the conditions under which they bought these articles. In some localities the wholesalers carried limited stocks of these items. More frequently the retailers' dissatisfaction was with buying terms. Large retailers were not permitted to purchase at prices wholesalers paid to manufacturers even when equivalent quantities were ordered. Manufacturers also refused to sell even to the "line" or multioutlet retailers. The manufacturers' purpose was to encourage wholesalers to push the sales of new types of building materials by providing a wide margin for wholesalers. That margin far exceeded what large retailers thought were and later proved to be the necessary costs of performing the essential warehousing and delivery functions.

Manufacturers and investor-owned wholesalers often sold directly to building contractors, orders large retailers thought should come to them, or at least should be routed through them, and a small margin earned. Dealers' associations brought pressure on manufacturers to cease this practice, but the Department of Justice forced a federation of dealers to drop this effort.[16]

The first reserve supply company, established in St. Paul in 1926, has been imitated in a number of other metropolitan markets. Initially these cooperatives could not qualify to buy as wholesalers even though they maintained wholesale stocks of building materials. The other requirement, the maintenance of a sales force, was contrary to the cooperatives' purpose of low-cost operations. Later, by employing a token sales force, they were able to overcome this obstacle.

A detailed study of two of the larger reserve supply companies plus responses of others to a mail questionnaire provides a picture of the operations of these dealer-owned cooperatives as of about 1960.[17] They are essentially open-end membership cooperatives, but that creates no problems, for the cooperatives do not have their own brands on merchandise and the members are not identified as such on their store fronts or in advertising. These practices lessen old members' concern that nearby rivals might gain from membership in the reserve supply company. Without private brands the gain from membership is limited to cost savings from reducing the wholesaling function to a purchasing, warehousing, and record-keeping operation with no selling or credit costs.

Net savings reduce significantly the invoice costs of member retail dealers. Eight of the companies responding in the survey had been established for several years, and their net savings (above interest received on stock in the cooperative) ranged from 3.5 to over 8 percent of initial billing prices. One large company's average savings over a long period was 7 percent of the prices initially charged to members, and about half the gross margin.

Despite these successful cases no cooperative reserve supply companies exist in large parts of the country, and those in business do not form a pattern. The further growth of these supply cooperatives has been inhibited by major changes in the building material manufacturers' terms to retailers.

Buying Organizations Owned Cooperatively by Department Stores

Several cooperatively owned enterprises provide buying and other services for large department stores. Most of them were founded and grew to substantial size as investor-owned enterprises and included such old names as Cavendish, Frederick Atkins, and Mutual. As these firms' role as purchasing agencies came to overshadow other services that ranged from accounting analyses to advertising aids, groups of their customers took them over, in most cases since 1945.[18] The largest one, the Associated Merchandising Corporation, has been a cooperative since its founding.

Now known as AMC, it grew out of the Retail Research Association formed in 1916 at the suggestion of Lincoln Filene, the Boston merchant, to develop a standard accounting system so that each store could compare its margins and expense rates with the averages for the group. RRA's functions soon expanded to include buying of some types of goods for members, and it became AMC in 1918. In 1966 twenty-four department store companies, some with a number of outlets, were members. Each is a leading store in its community but is not located so as to compete with another AMC member.

Patronage of AMC is encouraged by the method of financing it. Before a fiscal year begins AMC estimates its operating costs and obtains deposits from each member approximately in proportion to its total retail sales not its purchases through AMC.

To provide the desired market coverage and merchandising service AMC maintains a large staff in its main office in New York, supplemented by offices in other domestic and foreign cities. Apart from current buying to meet members' requirements the staff canvases markets to find desirable merchandise and to develop new sources. Close relations are maintained with suppliers to assure manufacturing and delivery schedules, to collaborate with manufacturers in the development of special products, and to study and appraise fashion and merchandising trends—all to provide information to members to aid them in competing at retail.

Generally AMC contracts with manufacturers for the goods members have requested. Members then place orders directly with suppliers based on the information about merchandise and prices circulated by AMC. The manufacturer ships to and bills the member. In the case of medium-priced dresses, for which a wide variety of styles must be carried by the stores, AMC does purchase and warehouse the merchandise and fills orders from members.

For some commodities, such as appliances, AMC maintains an active private-brand program on goods made to its specifications. Different brand names are used for different commodities and also for different price lines. This enables the member retailers to stock the variety of separately identified goods needed to compete with both nationally branded merchandise and the brands of mass distributors.

The critical question is whether members of AMC, as autonomous retailers aided by AMC's buying and technical services, can match the large chains. Using the test of survival and growth there is no evidence thus far that the chain system is a superior arrangement for distribution of the medium to higher price lines handled by AMC's members. AMC and other similar organizations appear to have matched the buying and specialist services of chains handling similar goods, while the members' job is to match rivals' efficiency at the retailing step.

Cooperative Buying by Hardware Retailers

A major reorganization of the distribution of hardware has occurred, of which retailer-owned wholesale enterprises are only a small part. They sprang up for reasons analogous to those recounted earlier in this chapter. As in the grocery trade the voluntary form is also widely used. Setting this arrangement aside the *Census* of 1967 reports only twenty-one cooperative hardware wholesaling establishments whose individual volume was 2 percent of total wholesale hardware sales (see table 8.1). But the oldest and largest of these cooperatives (which by 1974 had eight regional warehouses) alone had volume in 1967 nearly one and a half times that the *Census* reported as the composite volume of the group. The data in table 8.1 were adjusted for this omission and for the largest cooperative's growth since 1967.

The operating methods of this cooperative apply in varying degrees to all of them. No member is admitted that is a close competitor of an old member, a logical practice since members' stores are usually identified by the insignia and handle goods with the cooperative's brand. Applicants must have a specified minimum volume and physical facilities and merchandising policies comparable to the other members. The applicants subscribe in cash to the capital of the wholesale (or forego patronage dividends until the stock has been paid for) and pay cash for deliveries within a week.

Members are expected to cooperate with the merchandising program of the cooperative and to do a substantial portion of their buying from it. Repetitive buying of goods the cooperative handles from other sources is not viewed favorably. The cooperative handles products representing about a third of the typical hardware store volume. It puts its brand on only a few large-volume products, such as paint, for which substantial savings can be obtained.

The criteria for billing members reflect the character of competition for various products and the delivery arrangement. For highly competitive items for which brands are unimportant the billing prices are substantially below that charged by investor-owned wholesalers. This enables members to match the retail prices of mass distributors. When direct shipments from the manufacturer to the retailer are arranged the margin is nominal. On items for which manufacturers suggest wholesale prices which represent most of the wholesale volume, the members are billed at those prices. Given the wide margin on these goods and the cooperative's low-cost operating practices most of its net savings to pay year-end patronage dividends are earned on these commodities.

The large cooperative studied intensively, and to a lesser degree the others, have reduced costs through efficient operating practices. Although the cooperative incurs some costs properly denoted "selling expenses," there are no salesmen and orders are mailed in on checklists. Because members pay the cost of delivery from the wholesale warehouse, frequent shipments are penalized. No credit is extended.

The savings from patronage compared to average costs of investor-owned wholesalers (reported in a survey I have seen) amounted in the early 1960s to 4 percent of billing prices of the average noncooperative wholesalers. Ten years later the savings were twice that amount for members of the largest cooperative wholesaler. But in the earlier years some other cooperatives' expense rates were as high as the average for the investor-owned wholesalers. Either there has been little or no gain from membership in such cooperatives or they are in competition with noncooperative wholesalers with gross margins well above the average for the latter.

Both hardware retailing and wholesaling have been affected strongly by two developments not stressed thus far. One is the widespread and efficient retail stores of the mass distributors with hardware departments. The other is the development by noncooperative wholesalers of arrangements with retailers that to varying degrees are similar to the voluntaries in food distribution but are not reported separately by the *Census*. Indeed the parallel with developments in the grocery trades is quite close.

Cooperative Purchasing by Manufacturers

Only to a small degree have manufacturers formed cooperatives to purchase materials or equipment. Because the *Census* classifies newspaper publishing as manufacturing, the Associated Press, a cooperative which provides the major part of the nonlocal news "ingredient" to its members, will be considered here. Also the development of cooperatives owned by relatively small wholesale baking companies will be portrayed. No other comparable cooperative development has been found.

Cooperative Purchasing Organizations Owned by Baking Companies

A substantial portion of the relatively small wholesale baking enterprises, each usually selling in only one metropolitan market, belongs to one of the sixteen or so cooperative buying organizations. Most if not all of them grew out of investor-owned companies which sold auditing and technical services to one-plant and some larger baking companies and then undertook buying of supplies for their customers. After World War II most of these service-buying companies adopted the cooperative form, a move that had been made earlier by the Quality Bakers of America, whose management provided the information used in this subsection. QBA has 130 members, few of which own more than one plant. Their combined volume equals that of the largest company in the industry, the Continental Baking Company.

Financial requirements for membership in QBA are not onerous but are such as to attract the financially strong bakers. In addition to a nominal purchase of common stock each member contributes annually in proportion to its preceding year's tonnage to a fund to meet the estimated expenses of QBA. Members must pay for purchases within ten days after receipt of the goods. No member company has failed since the cooperative was formed, and only one had sold out by 1966.

QBA buys and resells to members all types of equipment and of supplies except flour and sugar. It will place orders for direct shipment of those high-volume items bought in carload or larger quantities.

For other goods the member is billed at the price, adjusted for quantity discounts, that he would have paid on direct order from the manufacturer. Year-end patronage dividends are paid equal to the difference between the billing prices to the individual member and the prices the cooperative paid suppliers plus its buying costs.

The cooperative provides a number of managerial and merchandising services for its members. It sponsors the use of a common brand by the members (94 of the 130 members were using it by 1960) so that other than local advertising media can be employed and economies obtained in printing wrapping paper and containers. QBA makes available auditing and other services that range from advertising copy through product testing, personnel service, and plant design and equipment. Members are billed for such services at estimated cost.

A comparison of Quality Bakers Association, together with its members, with a large baking company will bring out several highlights. QBA is large enough that it can potentially provide to members purchasing

skill and technical and advisory services comparable to those a large baking company's central office renders to its local plants. There was not until very recently concentration on merchandising the common brand
"Sunbeam" comparable to that of the very large baking companies.
Each member of QBA makes all operating decisions and stands on his
own feet financially. In contrast the large baking company is a single
pool of funds which relieves local managers of financial problems. But
even under an extremely decentralized plan of administration the local
manager would not have the autonomy enjoyed by the member of QBA.
This is a local market business, and unless handicapped by diversities of
views among members or by lack of entrepreneurship by QBA this buy-
ing-service cooperative goes far to assist its members in having the costs
and merchandising skill comparable to the large baking companies.

Associated Press

All news media must obtain news from all over the world, but that
service could be provided by investor-owned enterprises, several of which
have existed in the United States. Only two have been in business in recent years, the United Press and the International News Service, and they
merged in 1958. The largest and best-known service, the Associated
Press, whose name has become synonymous with worldwide news coverage, is a cooperative owned by about 1750 newspapers and about 2000
radio and television stations.

Citywide or regional cooperatively owned news services sprang up in
the last century in several parts of the country. The oldest was established
in New York in 1848 for the purpose of reducing the cost of obtaining
news by telegraph. News from more distant places was bought from the
United Press of New York (not the organization using that name in recent years), which was the agent of the famed Reuters of England. But
the demands of United led in 1893 to a union of several regional associations to form the Associated Press.[19] Within a few decades AP became so
effective in news gathering that most daily newspapers sought to become
members, although some were barred.

Prior to 1942 the members of a certain type in a locality, say morning
papers, could veto the application of a rival for membership, but that
veto could be overridden by a four-fifths vote of the entire membership.
If approved an applicant would have to pay to the old member(s) affected
by his entry a sum equal to three times what they had paid to the AP in
assessments from 1900 to the date of admission. Following the institution of antimonopoly action against the AP these rules were modified in
1942 so that only a simple majority of all members had to approve the
application, and the payment was reduced to 10 percent of the past as-

sessments of local member(s) by AP. But the federal district court held that the established competitors still had a "conditional veto," and AP was required to further modify its policy.[20]

There is a two-way flow of news between AP and its members. AP has 7500 staff members in the 150 offices maintained in this country and abroad. Each member is also a source of news to AP, so that the news collecting staff is actually multiplied several times.

Members supply news to AP free, while the latter charges for its services, although not on a per-item basis. Each year AP estimates its expenses for the coming year and levies an assessment on the members in each area, typically a city and its nearby suburbs, according to circulation. By adjustments in the assessment rate AP avoids having either net income or losses.

Newspapers and radio and television stations can choose between a cooperatively owned and an investor-owned news service. Every major newspaper in the country, with the exception of a few Scripps-Howard newspapers, is a member of the Associated Press. Over eight hundred daily newspapers depend exclusively on AP, while less than five hundred obtain their news only from UPI (United Press International). Nearly four hundred use both services. Radio and TV stations use one or both services. Editors receiving the wire reports of both AP and UPI take such factors as fullness of coverage, quality of writing, speed of delivery, and price into consideration in selecting stories to be published.

Cooperatives Providing Transport Service

As a means of providing better and sometimes cheaper transportation in particular situations groups of investor-owned enterprises have established cooperatives to provide certain specialized services. The larger cooperatives owned at various times by investor-owned transport companies performed a service which an individual company could not provide efficiently. All but one of these has either disappeared or become an investor-owned corporation. Both the reasons for founding as cooperatives and either their disappearance or reorganization are instructive for a time at least to solve particular transport problems.

In two types of cases the transport cooperative is owned by the shippers. Those that are farmer-owned are included with miscellaneous services connected with marketing and supply cooperatives. But the recent growth of shopper-owned freight-forwarding cooperatives as distinct from those earlier railroad-owned will be considered briefly.

Freight-Forwarding Cooperatives

In the early history of long-distance rail movement of commodities, when railroad lines were quite short and sometimes of different gauges and cars owned by one line were not permitted to operate on another, co-operatives owned by the railroads sprang up to conduct the interline transfer of goods. Except where different gauges were involved each rail-road member of a cooperative supplied freight cars to the cooperatives for interline hauls in proportion to its relative length of line or to its rela-tive volume of through traffic. Revenues were prorated on a formula that corresponded to patronage.

As the standard gauge came into general use the interline business was taken over increasingly by car-owning subsidiaries of certain railroads. Later the present system of interchange of cars among railroads evolved.[21]

In recent years there has been a surge of cooperatives in one type of freight forwarding, the assembling of small shipments into carload or truckload lots and the delivery of these shipments at the destination point.[22] The other and growing type of forwarding, the arranging for transshipment from one transport mode to another for long-distance hauls, such as between railroads and ocean steamers, seems not to have offered a comparable opportunity for cooperatives. In 1942 the rates of investor-owned freight forwarders were put under regulation by the In-terstate Commerce Commission, but those owned by "shipper associa-tions" were exempt.

A clarifying series of commission decisions dealing with the require-ments for exemption from regulation as a shipper association indicates that they are cooperatives as that term is used here, and they are so de-noted. Exempt shipper associations must handle only goods shipped (or received) by their members. Either by frequent adjustments of charges or by the end-of-the-year payments or assignments to capital to each of the member's account, the net charges equal operating costs.

The local freight-forwarding business has grown sharply in recent dec-ades as the railroads discouraged small shipments and even declined to receive them. Shippers in some small cities had no freight forwarder to turn to. But the more general situation was that forwarders could agree on rates charged small-lot shippers, subject to commission approval, a not very effective control. Generally forwarders charged common carrier (rail or truck) rates on small shipments, or somewhat less, and in turn paid car or truckload rates for the load they accumulated. Even with the ease of agreement and commission restriction on entry (except where deemed consistent with the public interest) freight forwarding has not been a very prosperous business. But the cooperatives, although exempt from regulation, could succeed only if their service and net rates (after patronage dividends) were better than those of the regulated investor-owned rivals. In a very real sense the cooperatives have been the means of actually "regulating" those formally regulated by the commission.

Long-Distance Van Lines

Today the predominant portion of long-distance moving of household goods is done by large vans operating over the highway network of the nation. While the householder who wishes to ship his goods to a distant point ordinarily deals with the local storage and moving company the latter functions only as agent of a nonlocal enterprise that carries on, or coordinates, van movements on a regional or nationwide basis. While most of these enterprises are investor-owned, two of them were cooperatives—owned (during the period of this study) by local moving and storage companies, and together accounting for 22 percent of the revenues from intercity transportation of household goods by common carrier van. The oldest of these enterprises, Allied Van Lines, Inc., was a cooperative until 1968,[23] and is the largest in the business, while the second cooperative, Atlas, ranks seventh.

Decades ago household goods moved long distances only by rail, but as the highway system developed and the size and quality of trucks improved this business was progressively won by the over-the-highway vans. Rail shipment involves picking up the goods at the home of the shipper, crating them and taking them to a railroad siding to be loaded in cars, then reversing the whole process at the destination point. The van provides home-to-home service without crating the goods.

A local moving and storage company that hauled its customer's goods to a distant city rarely obtained a return load. If a return load were possible, as it is for a large part of the railroad cars since they are adapted to hauling a variety of freight over a national network of rail transportation, the cost of shipping by van would have been reduced by nearly half.

An attempt to solve this problem was made in 1924 by a substantial number of local moving and storage firms who established the "Intercity Return Load Bureau." But close cooperation of members in providing return hauls did not follow. Allied Van Lines was formed in 1928 to provide a dispatching service. But business was still done in the name of the member firm originating the shipment, and each such firm had operating authority from the Interstate Commerce Commission for a restricted area only. For this and other reasons the composite of Allied Van Lines and of its members could not match the efficiency of the large investor-owned companies, each with a nationwide operating authority which used local moving and storage companies as agents.

Acting under the Motor Carrier Act of 1935 Allied Van Lines arranged to carry on long-distance hauling in its own name. Each member had to have at least one tractor and a van of minimum size marked as an Allied Van, with a driver, all available for dispatching wherever the Allied offices required. (In order to operate under Allied's master permit from the

Interstate Commerce Commission all of this equipment was technically leased to Allied, but all costs related thereto were borne by the members.) Allied itself did not own equipment or facilities other than four terminals located at strategic points for transferring small shipments from one van to another. All business of members that involved interstate shipments over 250 miles and some intrastate shipments had to be turned over to Allied in the sense that it was done in Allied's name and under its control. As of 1968 there were nearly 1200 members of Allied Vans scattered over the United States and in most free countries abroad. There is at least one member in every sizable city in the United States and abroad and several in each of the larger metropolitan areas. Ordinarily members are not located in close proximity but each is free to solicit business wherever it can be obtained.

Working from a central office in the Chicago area and from five regional offices Allied's role is to maximize the return-load use of members' vans, tractors, and drivers. Complete authority over the scheduling of shipments and routes is in the hands of the Allied dispatcher. A local member books the shipment but as an agent of Allied, whose published rates apply and also its terms of shipment and its insurance. Actually the rates are those agreed upon by the Household Goods Carriers Bureau, whose announced rates become effective thirty days after posting them unless disapproved by the Interstate Commerce Commission. Allied's operations will be described with reference to the years before 1968, when for reasons explained below Allied changed to an investor-owned company.

After deducting a percentage of the gross revenue to cover its costs, about 9 percent in the years before 1968, Allied divided the remainder among the members participating in a particular shipment according to specific rules. The agent who booked the order provided helpers for loading, and the shipment might occur in his van, hauled by his tractor, and driven by his employee. But it was also quite possible that the Allied dispatcher would order another member's van to pick up the load that was available for a return load to the general area of its owner. After deducting the cost of performing its own functions from the percentage of gross revenue it has retained Allied divided the remainder among members participating in proportion to the contribution made to the shipment.

While the revenues of all of the large long-distance operators grew sharply after 1950 Allied was the largest. Its share of revenue from intercity transport of household goods fell by over one-fifth between these years, but so did the composite share of the largest four. Among the rapidly growing haulers (although still relatively small) was the other cooperative, Atlas. Apparently the skill of the local agents rather than whether long-distance moving is warranted through a cooperative or through an investor-owned company has determined rates of growth.

Two aspects of Allied's organization may have tempered its growth. Years ago it had grown to have a member in almost every sizable local market, and hence it has not been easy to add more members. But that is not the only possible explanation of Allied's declining share of total volume. It is possible that with each member's primary interest being in the storage and local (and the potential up to 250 miles intercity) hauling household goods, booking long-haul shipments to be directed by Allied is not pursued aggressively, for the members own Allied, which can only use persuasion and member education. Doubtless the 1968 decision to change Allied to an investor-owned corporation reflected members' lack of support to the extent of investing more capital in the cooperative.

Railway Express Agency

Most people will be surprised to learn that the nationwide express business was conducted from 1929 until recently by a cooperative enterprise owned by the railroads. Until 1929 nearly all of the express was handled by the autonomous investor-owned American Railway Express Company. It paid the railroads for hauling express, for providing space in stations and terminals, and for services of some employees. There were, however, repeated difficulties about the basis for remunerating the railroads and other operating problems. After several years of study a plan of ownership, operation, and division of income was put into effect in 1929 that met the standard of a cooperative.[24] (American Express then used its capital to enter other activities.) Each large railroad company bought stock in what was later called the Railway Express Agency in proportion to its respective gross revenues from express business during the 1923-1926 period. In the "Standard Express Operations Agreement" the railroads contracted to supply railroad cars, transport personnel that attended express cars while in transit, provide space in railroad stations and terminals and in other ways facilitate the express operations. The agreement also stated that "it is the intent of this Agreement that the express company shall have no taxable income." To that end the Express Agency deducted from its gross revenues its operating and other expenses and distributed the remainder among the railroads by a formula that approximated shares of revenue arising on each railroad's lines.

Rates are publicly regulated, but the express company as the representative of the owning railroads was powerfully restrained by competition of parcel post, of private parcel-handling companies, and of common carrier truck lines.

The railroads were in a different situation. They had excess capacity in their basic facilities of track, yards, and buildings and perhaps in some types of equipment. Hauling express cars would add to their net income so long as the revenue exceeded the added costs attributable to express haulage.

If owned by the railroads there was no need to negotiate with an express company about, or have public commissions fix, the charges for hauling express cars. In the cooperative form all revenue of the express cooperative above its operating cost was paid to the railroads according to a patronage-type formula. Beginning in 1961 this agreement was modified and more recently REA Express, its current name, has become less and less of a cooperative, and by 1967 was an investor-owned company engaging also in nonexpress business. It and the Post Office parcel business then faced keen competition from the United Parcel Service.

In the early 1970s REA Express went into bankruptcy and ceased operations.

Conclusion

In only a few lines of activity have cooperatives owned by urban businesss obtained a dominant or even a substantial position in the operation into which the cooperative integration took place. It is not surprising that a cooperative had a monopoly of the express business; the nature of the service favors monopoly whether done by a cooperative or an investor-owned business. In both cases the charges to the public were regulated. Similarly the minimizing of duplication in news gathering and transmission calls for very few enterprises; and the success of AP points to the value of a cooperatively owned company that sets the standard for investor-owned rivals. This still held after the court order opened the door for local rivals of what had been largely a one-member-per-locality arrangement. In the Allied Vans case the cooperative solved a problem local, van and storage companies had before the large-scale development of investor-owned companies to provide long-distance van service. But as years passed it was checked by equally successful investor-owned enterprises and has converted to the investor-owned form. Cooperative service companies now supply many sizable local wholesale bakers with some equipment and with all but the large-volume materials used. In wholesaling groceries and to a lesser degree in hardware and department store lines vertical integration by retailers by forming buying organizations has become a significant influence on investor-owned companies over much of the country. Less successful have been the reserve supply companies in the building material field.

Where urban investor-owned firms have successfully integrated downstream cooperatively the activity entered usually was ripe for changes that would reduce members' buying prices. Often this involved introducing methods of operation that reduced costs significantly to the benefit of members in their primary activity. The latter were relatively small compared to chain retailers or large baking companies.

In a few cases the cooperative integration was in response to the inadequacy of a service, as in the early freight forwarding, or the recent disappearance of a service, such as less than carload freight handling by the railroads. Then accumulating small shipments into large lots enhanced the opportunity for cooperative freight forwarders because those investor-owned either did not enter small markets or operated on margins above the necessary costs even though they were regulated.

Urban enterprises have not entered capital intensive activities by cooperative vertical integration. Even major facilities used by the express services were provided by the railroads. This suggests that entry is not invited where members must make a substantial investment when the expected reward is only a slightly better price or service. Some cooperatives even have little or no money tied up in inventories, particularly the department store buying cooperatives and the cooperatives that buy materials used by small baking companies.

Next it should be observed that all of the cases studied except those in transportation represent downstream integration. The exception was service auxiliary to railroad operations.

In downstream integration to reduce buying prices, rivals in selling usually are not members of the same cooperative, or that fact is not easily apparent to the members' customers. The Associated Press is an exception and has prospered even when it was forced to admit to membership rivals of old members.

9

Consumer Cooperatives

In sharp contrast to experience in western Europe and the British Isles, consumer retail cooperatives have not made a noticeable dent in the American economy. As reported by the 1963 *Census of Business,* consumer cooperatives accounted for only one-quarter of one percent of all retail sales to consumers and less than four-tenths of one percent of total food store volume in that year. Census data for 1973 are not available at this writing, but an official of the Cooperative League does not expect that the cooperatives' share will have changed materially. These market shares are miniscule compared to the cooperatives' 11 percent of all retail sales and 18 percent of food volume in Great Britain and 17 percent of all retailing and 25 percent of food store sales in Sweden.[1] A variety of service cooperatives also exists, ranging from cooperative housing and medical plans to memorial societies, nursery schools, and recreational facilities, but each provides a very small percentage of what consumers use.[2]

In contrast, households have integrated into some other activities more successfully. These include the rural electrification and telephone cooperatives to be examined in this chapter. The next three chapters report on financial mutuals and cooperatives, which are characterized by widely differing degrees of initiation and control by members.

123

Consumer Retail Cooperatives

The literature on the American economy contains little economic analysis of the limited cooperative integration by consumers into retailing. Fortunately the history and current status of these cooperatives can be examined against the background of the conditions facilitating or inhibiting vertical integration by farmers and by relatively small urban enterprises as portrayed in the five preceding chapters. Also useful is the analysis of the revolution in commodity distribution examined in chapter 8. After brief consideration of the present status and history of retail cooperatives generally, those engaged in food will be studied more fully.

Consumer Cooperatives Today

Of all the retailing done by cooperatives, only the volume and market share of those through which consumers purchase are of interest here. Of total volume of retail cooperatives as reported in the *Census of Business 1963,* three-fourths consisted of farm supplies and equipment members acquired for use in production (see table 6.1). When the farm supply volume is subtracted, the residual amounts to only one-quarter of one percent of total retail volume of consumer goods. The only cooperatives with a significant market share were book stores, with about 9 percent. Cooperative food stores' volume in 1963 was only four-tenths of one percent of total food store sales.[3] Despite their small market share, the record of retail food cooperatives will be examined because their very small market share in an era of large chain stores and nonchain investor-owned supermarkets suggests that these rivals are very efficient and intensely competitive.

A high proportion of the consumer-owned food stores are located in three north central states, the San Francisco Bay area, and the East Coast from Washington, D.C., to Massachusetts. Fifty-four stores had an average volume of $2.0 million in 1964,[4] compared to an average volume of only $460,000 for all cooperative food stores as reported in the *Census* of 1963. Many of the metropolitan area stores were established after 1956.[5] By 1973-1974 the number of cooperative food stores of supermarket size had advanced to sixty-seven (owned by twenty-two cooperatives), a count which did not include thirteen nonreporting cooperatives.[6]

Consumer Cooperative Stores over a Century

No phase of cooperative enterprise has had a more ragged history in the United States than that of retail stores owned by consumers. The record, detailed elsewhere,[7] has been strewn with dashed hopes for the "cooperative way," and is only summarized here.

Occasional consumer cooperatives were formed in colonial days, but nearly all were short-lived. The most significant development occurred at about the time of the Rochdale movement in England, though independently of it. The New England Protective Association, founded in 1845, grew rapidly to a peak of some four hundred outlets. The movement faded quickly, partly because of internal dissension, aggravated by stronger price competition from rivals than most cooperatives could weather. Some survived for decades and a few to this date. When the Mormons migrated to Utah they formed the well-managed Zion Cooperative Mercantile Institution as a cooperative, but it was changed to the investor-owned form after the depression of 1893. Falling prices and a series of depressions after the Civil War encouraged farm and labor organizations to sponsor consumer cooperatives, but most were short-lived. Unlike the Knights of Labor, who experimented with various forms of worker uplift, including cooperative stores in union buildings, and the Sovereigns of Industry, for whom cooperatives were a key project, the American Federation of Labor, the first large permanent labor union, directed its efforts toward better wages and working conditions.

In the first decade after 1900 retail cooperatives were formed in scattered areas outside the South. The most important and lasting was among immigrant groups from north and central Europe, especially the Finns. Fearing exploitation by merchants of their own nationality and experiencing a language barrier in dealing with other merchants, but united within a nationality group and by experience with cooperatives in their home countries, these immigrants formed cooperatives, some of which survive. Societies formed by Finnish farmers, miners, and lumber workers of Maynard and Fitchburg, Massachusetts, and in parts of Minnesota and Wisconsin and in Waukegan, Illinois (closed in 1972), are among the oldest but not among the largest today.[8]

During and just after World War I sharply rising retail prices, coupled with lagging wage rates and farm incomes, stimulated the highest rate of consumer cooperative formation in the country's history. Some were sponsored by farm organizations, but more by locals of labor unions. One of the largest was an ill-fated plan of Illinois mine workers, but the Akron (Ohio) Cooperative survives. Altogether 2600 local societies were reported for 1920, 83 percent of them located in towns of less than 25,000 people,[9] where chain food or general merchandise stores had not yet been established. The National Cooperative Association, formed in Chicago in 1919, built a chain of outlets in large cities. Its demise was hastened by a sharp drop of prices in 1920 and 1921 and by doubts about its cooperative character. Thereafter retail cooperatives declined. The country was prosperous and chain stores were entering smaller cities, which also became accessible by automobile to consumers who previously had shopped in small towns.

As the depression deepened and lengthened after 1930, interest in cooperatives spread from organized labor to white collar workers and from immigrants to native Americans. Government agencies, educators, and church groups became actively interested. Much publicity attended the establishment of the cooperative Greenbelt Consumer Services in a public housing project for government employees near Washington, D.C. Farm supply cooperatives in the Great Plains added food lines. The EPIC (End Poverty in California) campaign stimulated the growth of cooperatives from four in 1934 to fifty-six in 1935, but by 1938 only a handful of small-volume associations remained.[10] As in the early twenties a number of spurious "cooperatives" dimmed the glamour of that word.[11]

Since World War I retail cooperatives' experience has been varied but not clearly upward. Prosperity of farmers lessened their interest in buying consumer goods from cooperatives which increasingly faced the competition of mass distributor outlets. Even cooperatives formed by immigrant groups had hard sledding, for the new generations of customers had few ties with the homeland. Cooperative stores in many cases failed to keep up with modern developments in merchandising. Nevertheless there was a flurry of union-backed cooperatives during the sharp rise of prices just after the war, some of which were merely temporary outlets for case-lot selling. A plan by the United Auto Workers' locals to operate small stores near auto plants failed. But the society organized by the United Rubber Workers in Akron has become substantial and now has several stores. During this period a number of cooperatives were sponsored by Edward Filene's Consumer Distribution Corporation in the three so-called "green towns" adminstered by the Farm Security Agency. Two of these were eventually outbid by investor-owned firms, but the older Greenbelt Cooperative opened stores in twelve other communities. Other cooperatives financed by the Filene fund, including two department stores, did not fare as well.

Some associations have been formed because of a shortage (such as of milk or coal) which proves to be temporary, or because of dissatisfaction with the commodity lines carried in local stores (such as the lack of high-quality meat or of used text books), or because of the monopoly position of a retailer in an apartment complex. A quite different basis is family preference for nonstandard foods rarely handled by chain stores, which accounts, in part at least, for the marked success of cooperatives appealing to government, academic, and other professional families in the San Francisco and Washington, D.C., areas. When the investor-owned enterprises filled the competitive gap, such as in a housing development, enthusiasm for the cooperative usually declined except where the organization developed a broader patronage basis and attained the efficiency to compete. Clearly some of supermarket type and scale are doing well.

Currently, and reminding one of earlier founding of cooperatives to alleviate hardship, there is much interest in establishing cooperative food stores in low-income neighborhoods because, allegedly, the "poor pay more." They do in the small shops that grant credit. But this claim has not been demonstrated when price comparisons between low- and high-income areas have been made by valid statistical sampling of prices in stores of similar size and which sell for only cash.[12] Comprehensive information about the number and record of cooperatives in low-income neighborhoods is not available, but most of what one reads indicates that few have done well for long.

Performance of Retail Food Cooperatives

The monetary advantage from cooperative patronage is measured by comparing rivals' prices with the cooperatives' initial charges to members less patronage dividends. The stated policy of most consumer cooperatives, as shown in a survey of 1955 operations, is to charge going prices of the locality, a practice that minimizes the possibility of a price war.[13] Net savings (if any) are then paid as patronage dividends or withheld to add to capital. While twenty of the twenty-eight associations claimed to have the lowest net price level in their communities, eight admitted that one or several rivals charged lower prices, an issue for which a comprehensive recent study provides a more definite answer.[14]

Net prices (after patronage dividends) paid by members of a large sample of cooperatives were compared with net prices (after value of trading stamps to customers) of investor-owned stores for a market basket of forty-three grocery items. Each cooperative store was "paired" with a "twin" investor-owned store in another very similar city that had no consumer cooperative. The variance of relative prices in the "paired" stores was quite wide; the cooperative's prices were several percent higher in some cases, equal in some, and several percent lower in others. On the average, net prices of the cooperative were neither lower nor higher. There is, however, an advantage to members of small-town cooperatives because of the availability of CO-OP brand goods of high quality, as is explained further below. Also the study showed quite clearly that prices in chain store outlets of a given company were lower in larger cities with a cooperative than in those without. In general I conclude that the advantage of cooperative membership is far from uniform among markets and is rarely large.

Frequently cooperative food stores have not been able to buy goods at delivered prices comparable to those paid by rivals. While there are five wholesale warehouses owned by the retail cooperatives, in many areas the cooperatives' volume will not support an efficient wholesale operation. One warehouse's volume was only $18 million in the late 1950s,[15] or less than half the size of the seven large retailer-owned warehouses studied whose operating expenses were similar to those of chain stores for performing similar functions (table 8.2). Now some warehouses owned by a number of urban-area cooperative supermarkets approach efficient size. But their member cooperatives buy varying percentages of their requirements from the retailer-owned cooperative warehouses studied in chapter 8.

The average gross margins and operating expenses of cooperative and of investor-owned supermarkets are quite similar. This is evident from the gross margin data in table 9.1. Investor-owned supermarkets' average operating expenses as percentages of sales (which I have seen but am not free to quote) were slightly lower than for the cooperative supermarkets in most years in the 1960s.[16] The average net operating margins before income tax were not greatly different in the two types of stores.

Table 9.1. Average Gross Margins of Consumer Cooperatives and of Investor-Owned Supermarkets, 1955, 1963, 1969, and 1974

	Percentage of sales			
	1955	1963	1969	1974
Consumer cooperatives	17.8%	19.0%	19.7%	19.4%
Investor-owned supermarkets	17.4	19.1	19.3	20.9

Source: Cooperatives stores' margins in 1955 from the survey by Raymond Nordstrand. Data for 1963, 1969, and 1974 supplied by Consumers' Cooperative Development Association, Berkeley, California. Investor-owned supermarket margins for 1955 and 1963 refer to single stores with less than $1.0 million sales and are reported in National Commission on Food Marketing, *Technical Study No. 7* (1966): 222. Percentages for 1969 and 1974 supplied by the Supermarket Institute, Chicago, Illinois.

Another useful comparison is between cooperative supermarkets and chain store companies. Chains with annual sales less than $20 million,[17] like cooperatives, do little purchasing directly from manufacturers. In 1967-1968 these chains' average expense rate was about two percentage points above the median for cooperative supermarkets. If the latter compete with chains with more than $100 million of sales, one should subtract these chains' expenses of warehousing and delivery, equal to about 3 percent of retail sales. The remainder, or the average gross margin for the more clearly retailing operations, is quite similar to that for cooperative supermarkets. Net savings rates differ widely among cooperative supermarkets, but the median rate of about 2 percent of sales (after the nominal income tax paid) was quite comparable in 1969 to that of the large chains. Altogether the data do not indicate a substantial monetary gain from cooperative membership and patronage except for the cooperative whose costs are well below average or whose competition permits a higher than average gross margin.

Consumer cooperatives succeed in selling goods under their own "private" brands at a substantial savings to members. Prices of manufacturers' highly advertised brands must cover the costs of advertising to gain brand preference and, in addition, usually result in profit rates above the competitive level. Consequently where retail cooperatives' members are convinced of the quality of CO-OP brand goods, the net price can be significantly lower than for manufacturers' well-known brands, as was shown for farm supply cooperatives (chapters 6 and 7). This possibility is particularly promising for proprietary and even for prescription drugs. Their prices when sold under their generic names are substantially lower than for the advertised brands of the same medicine.[18] Several cooperatives in urban areas operate pharmacies successfully.

The CO-OP brands have been pushed effectively by the larger cooperative supermarkets. The California Associated Cooperatives' group sells a quarter of their packaged goods under CO-OP labels, a higher percentage of distributor-brand goods than was reported for the retailer-owned warehouses in chapter 8. Also, the California group's turnover rate of articles carrying the CO-OP labels (as reported to the author) is twice that for manufacturers' brands, while generally the turnover rate is lower for retailer brands in food stores.[19] The smaller cooperatives have not developed CO-OP brand business as much. This was quite evident in the responses to the survey made in the 1950s, particularly for the stores not located near a warehouse owned by retail cooperatives. There is some evidence that the situation has changed, in part because of more member education and the limited offering of private-brand goods by rivals in small towns.[20]

The pervasive problems of single-outlet cooperatives, lack of capital, varying experience in purchasing advantageously, and inexperienced managements have been tackled by some successful single-store cooperatives that have established additional outlets. Sixteen supermarkets of this sort were opened between 1955 and 1970, each with annual sales volume above one million dollars. Five were started by the Greenbelt Consumer Services near Washington, D.C. (at least two of which suffered severe competition from new investor-owned competitors), which now has its own wholesale warehouse. Three were initiated by residents of large New York City cooperative apartment buildings. The Berkeley society established two new supermarkets and also bought a five-outlet chain and converted three into branches of the parent cooperative.[21] A branch of a successful cooperative has the advantages of capital and experienced management, two handicaps of a newly established society.

Reasons for Nominal Success of Consumer Cooperatives

The reasons for consumer cooperatives' nominal share of retail business in the United States, probably the lowest percentage in any industrial country, differ sharply between those applicable prior to about 1920 and those relevant to recent decades. Except as noted earlier with respect to the northern tier of states, before World War I conditions in the Midwest and the South were generally unfavorable to consumer cooperation and also to the effective unionization of other than the skilled crafts. This was an era of heavy immigration and of geographic movement within the country. Personal relations were usually short-lived, and interest in a particular locality was tentative. There was widespread expectation of doing better by moving geographically or occupationally, or even into the ownership class. Society was not structured into classes in which generations of a family retained the same status, a condition which stimulates a search for means to improve the welfare of one's class. With the country growing, increasing income seemed more promising than decreasing outgo, particularly if the latter required investment of a small sum and of the time to organize a cooperative in the uncertain hope of saving a few percent on the grocery bill.[22] In order to accomplish even that small gain, one must be prepared to pay cash.

The opportunities for savings were far greater before the revolution in distribution than since in the then more numerous quite isolated communities, each with one or at most a few retail outlets of a type. At the extreme were the company stores in mining and lumber towns whose margins usually were outrageous. No wonder there were repeated attempts of these labor groups to form cooperatives. The typical shopping center of farming communities was not much better. Not infrequently the local merchant was also the source of the farmer's credit for living and farm operating expenses. The very families that stood to benefit the most from a cooperative had neither the capital nor the experience to initiate it, nor the certainty of cash income to meet the cooperatives' necessary cash trading rule.

One might have thought that immigrant groups in New York City or in the steel towns of the Midwest would have had the cohesion that led to small-town cooperatives in the northern tier of states of that region. But they did not have enough common interest to form effective unions in most cases until almost a century later.

Some credit must be given also to antitrust and other legislation. Uncertain quality of goods at retail stores contributed to early interest in consumer cooperatives in Britain. The Pure Food and Drug Act was passed in the United States in 1906, and there had been strong interest in the subject earlier. The antitrust laws did not restrain local monopolies but did the regional or national ones. Sugar, petroleum, and meat monopolies were prosecuted, and those in flour, bread, and a number of other foods were investigated several times. Significantly the British cooperatives have had high market shares in making and retailing bread and tobacco,[23] which reflects the long-existing monopolizing in these industries. In 1960 the registrar of the British Restrictive Practice Court ordered the flour milling industry to prove its price agreement was in the public interest. Apparently the industry concluded that it could not supply such evidence for it promptly cancelled the arrangement. Put these facts together with the cooperative's substantial share of flour milling, and one can visualize a monopoly situation in Britain that consumer cooperatives got around. In the United States the flour milling industry is quite competitive, and the wholesale baking industry is held in restraint in the larger cities by the very successful bakery operations of the chain food stores.[24] But from what was seen in chapter 4 of the oligopolistic character of milk distribution in urban markets, there may be room for consumer cooperative action on a broader scope than merely retailing milk in cooperative food stores.[25] Few cooperative dairy stores have succeeded.

The United States rapidly urbanized after World War I, a condition favoring consumer cooperatives, but by then mass distributors had seized the lead in the revolution in distribution. Also they were engaged in a struggle among themselves for survival and growth. Everywhere (except for the segment of consumers willing to pay for more service) cost-cutting practices were forced. As was seen in table 9.1 and the attendant discussion, cooperatives do well to hold their own in this contest.[26] There has been little opportunity to show the fantastic saving rates of early farmer-owned petroleum, feed, and fertilizer cooperatives recounted in chapters 6 and 7.

Rural Electric and Telephone Cooperatives

Started in 1935 as a New Deal program to provide jobs and to bring electricity to the 89 percent of farms then without central station power, the rural electric cooperatives (usually called REAs) now supply electricity to slightly more than half of the 98 percent of farm homes electrified.[27]

In addition they serve a substantial percentage of rural nonfarm homes and commercial and industrial users. Partly in response to the REAs' success in demonstrating the rural demand for lower rates than had prevailed earlier, the investor-owned power companies have extended their lines from the 11 percent of the farms served in 1935 to supplying nearly half the farms now receiving central station power. In part the increased percentage of farms served by all electric power enterprises reflects the 50 percent decline in the number of farms. Numerous commercial and industrial establishments and persons employed in incorporated towns have moved to rural areas; the REAs and the investor-owned utilities have fought vigorously over who shall serve these customers.

Development of Rural Electrification and Telephone Cooperatives

The chief obstacle to earlier extension of central station power to rural users, particularly farmers, was the high cost of distribution of electricity to widely scattered customers. Costs of generation are a surprisingly small part of the cost of power delivered to small users. Because farm customers are sometimes less than one per mile, distribution costs are far higher than in cities. Power company executives were not (prior to World War II) optimistic about the latent demand for power in rural America. This may reflect the fact that the companies usually required that farmers, individually or along a road, pay as much as $2000 per mile to cover the cost of additional distribution lines, an unusual practice now. Prior to 1940 few farmers could make such outlays and also pay for wiring homes and for appliances. Only in recent years has much electric-powered equipment been used in farm operations.

The Rural Electrification Administration, established in 1935, was empowered to lend money to cooperatives or to investor-owned power companies to extend lines into rural areas. No requests came from the latter until recently. A 1936 amendment required that preference be given to cooperatives and "people's utility districts." The agency instituted a campaign to organize cooperatives, aided by its ability to lend up to 100 percent of the funds required to build distribution lines. Where power could not be purchased at satisfactory wholesale rates, loans to finance generating capacity were available and also for REA cooperatives to re-lend to users for wiring and purchase of electrical equipment. Later legislation gave the cooperative preference in purchasing power from federal generating plants.

The financial arrangement for the REAs augured well for their future. The Rural Electrification Administration was empowered to borrow from the Federal Treasury and to re-lend to REAs the amount of money Congress appropriated each year at the interest rate the government then paid on long-term bonds. Later the interest rate was set at 2 percent and remained low for decades. The cooperatives' net revenues and the patronage dividends received by members are exempt from federal income taxes.

Starting at a slow rate but mounting just before World War II restrictions on critical materials, a strong surge got underway in 1947. In the early 1950s about 20 percent of the REAs were operating at a loss, possibly because of the time required for members to electrify homes and farms. This situation passed quickly. By the end of fiscal 1974 REA had loans outstanding to nearly 1094 borrowing cooperatives plus a number of public utility districts and a few investor-owned companies. The REAs owned nearly 1.6 million miles of lines and served seven million users.

In recent years about 90 percent of the users have been in the farm and nonfarm residential categories, but they provided only 71 percent of the revenues. The remainder was from rural commercial and industrial users and nonfarm residences. Five out of six connections added in recent years have been to nonfarm customers. Much to the surprise of the investor-owned companies, whose special committee stated in 1935 that "additional rural consumers must largely be those who use electricity for household purposes," the electrification of farm operations has substantially increased the power consumption per farm. Between 1941 and 1969 the REA nonindustrial customers' use of power increased sevenfold.

After World War II Congress authorized the Rural Electrification Administration to assist in forming and financing rural telephone cooperatives. The plan is almost identical to that for the REAs with advances from the Treasury also at a low interest rate. By now there are 878 rural telephone cooperatives.

The REA Versus Investor-Owned Utility Controversy

Because the REAs took over distribution of power in sparsely populated rural areas, they were welcomed at first by many investor-owned power companies but are no longer. As per-farm use of power rose and as the REAs entered actively into supplying rural nonfarm users the investor-owned companies reacted vigorously. Under the 1936 law borrowers from REA, mostly cooperatives, may furnish "electrical energy to persons in rural areas who are not receiving central station service." Opposition from investor-owned power companies centers on invasion of what they consider to be their rural territories, facilitated by REA-subsidized capital and income tax exemption.

In addition much is made of the preferred position of REAs as purchasers of power from federal hydro-electric generating plants, particularly in the Rocky Mountain or Pacific states. Part of the objection is directed to the fact that often such electric plants do not pay their own way from power revenues. REA supporters assert that preferential access to federal power plants protects the cooperatives against refusal by investor-owned companies to sell to REAs at wholesale prices comparable to those charged other large-volume purchasers. As additional sites for hydro-electric power production have become fewer and with the high costs of steam generation in these western areas, the investor-owned companies hold that all buyers of federally generated power should be on the same basis.

A large plant is needed to supply not only its customers but also to send power up to several hundred miles to other cooperatives or to municipal district distributors. In the same areas investor-owned companies claim either to have excess capacity or, in spite of using more expensive capital and paying substantial income taxes, that they could afford to build very large and economical plants to supply this power.

The power companies allege that the REAs have often invaded the established utilities' "natural" territory. The REAs have not only aggressively pushed their lines into unoccupied or partially supplied rural areas but in some cases also have built lines parallel to those of their rivals. On occasion the cooperative borrowed at 2 percent from the Treasury and re-loaned the money to industrial users who located on their lines. Then the subsidy issue became very hot.

The fact that the REAs are exempt from state utility regulation irritates their rivals but not for easily identifiable and valid reasons. In contrast to their rivals' usual practice, the REAs charge the same rates to widely scattered and to more densely located users for whom distribution costs are lower. Except for some industrial users, the REAs base their rates on average cost per KWH, while their rivals' rates may be well above or below average cost according to the elasticity of demand of the class of customers. These facts minimize the competitive effects of unregulated REA rates.

The REA Subsidy Issue

Because of the unusual importance of the REA interest rate and income tax subsidy issues, they will be considered here rather than in chapter 13. Comparing revenue and the composite net income of the REAs with those of a private power company with the same assets is complicated.

In the first comparison, adjustment is made only for the difference between the rate the Treasury paid on its long-term bonds and the 2 percent charged REA borrowers for decades. Had the REAs as a group paid 5 percent, a typical Treasury rate on its long-term bonds, in 1969-1970 their interest cost would have been $289 million, not the $78 million actually paid.[27] The former sum would have exceeded the REAs composite net revenue of $223 million by $66 million. To have met the higher interest cost the REAs would have had to increase net revenues from sale of electricity by over 4 percent.

The next comparison is between a typical target return on capital which state commissions use in regulating rates of investor-owned utilities. Assuming a target 7 percent return on total capital, and for the moment disregarding the corporate income taxes paid by the utility companies, the REAs as a group would have had to earn $404 million to cover interest payments and provide net income that together would have been 7 percent of net assets. That $404 million is nearly twice the $223 million of interest actually paid plus the net revenue of the REAs. The "deficit" in return earned on capital would have equaled about 12 percent of 1969-1970 receipts from sale of power.

Finally, introduce the corporate income tax of about 50 percent of before-tax income, but after interest payments have been deducted as a cost. To earn a target return of 7 percent on total assets (or $5,770 million times .07, or $404 million), the following computations are made. Interest at the lower 6 percent rate on 40 percent of composite net assets capital of the REAs assumed to be borrowed equals $162 million. Deducting this part of the return on capital from the target total return on capital of $404 million leaves $242 million as the target return on capital stock *after* corporate tax. Multiplying this sum by two because of the approximately 50 percent corporate income tax would result in an after-interest, but before-tax, net income of $484 million. Adding this figure and the $162 million interest charge, it follows that $644 million is the before-interest and before-tax income that, after allowing for the corporate income tax, would equal 7 percent of assets. This is the sum to compare with the $78 million of interest actually paid plus the $145 million net revenues of the REA in 1970.

To have earned $644 million before interest of, say, $233 million, and also before the corporate income tax, the REAs' rates would have had to be increased by 27 percent on the average without any loss of volume! But that condition is impossible. One study indicates that the price elasticity of demand for electricity is unitary, or −1.0.[28] On that basis a 27 percent increase in rates, for example, would reduce electricity purchased also by 27 percent, and the target 7 percent return on capital, allowing for the tax, would not have been earned.

Clearly had 7 percent return on capital, either before or after adjustment for corporate income tax, been required years ago, the capacity added in recent years by the average REA would have been far less because its power rates would have been much higher.

The opposition to the REA interest rate subsidy has become so strong that funds appropriated by Congress from the Treasury in recent years have been so far below the amount requested by electricity and telephone cooperatives that new sources of capital are being developed. Initiated by the REAs and the REA officials, a National Rural Utilities Cooperative Finance Corporation has been formed with existing REAs as stockholders. The CFC, as it is called, can borrow on its own bonds in the securities market. By 1975 CFC borrowed $250 million in the investment market. As a counterpart of CFC, a Rural Telephone Bank has been established, but it borrows from the Federal Treasury and re-lends to rural telephone companies. The subsidization of both REA's and RTB's interest cost has declined sharply.

Conclusion

The times have favored the tremendous growth of both the electrification and telephone cooperatives, aided as they have been by the sizable interest rate subsidy. Initially all of the fixed and working capital needed was borrowed, though like other debts this obligation has been paid off in depreciated dollars. Both the higher absolute level of farm and nonfarm rural families' dollar incomes and the further development of the quality of electricity-using equipment helped. But there would not have been electrification of 98 percent of the farms by cooperative effort without subsidy or by investor-owned power companies unaffected by the cooperative threat. There is merit in the contention that the power companies have concentrated their rural line extension in areas of more dense population, a policy made necessary in some states by the rates they are allowed to charge rural customers by regulatory authorities or because farmers in sparsely populated areas would not pay distribution costs where one to several miles of line is required per customer. But this is history and does not provide an economic appraisal of the continuance of any REA or RTB interest rate subsidy.

10

Mutual Investing Institutions

Savers can invest directly in earnings assets such as bonds, mortgages, and corporate stocks or place their funds in a financial intermediary. The latter accumulates a pool of funds from many savers and invests in a large number of particular earning assets in order to obtain more nearly average experience with respect to income from and value of the investments. For a small saver to invest directly in earning assets requires not only that he devote time to investigating various investments but that he have the skill to choose wisely. In addition, he must assume the risk that a particular debtor can meet his obligation or that the value of a particular corporation's stock will not fall. Furthermore in the event the saver-investor needs cash he may find that a mortgage is not easily salable for the amount remaining due or that the value of a particular corporation's stock has declined. But most financial intermediaries have a sufficient inflow of cash from additional savings placed with them, from the sale or maturity of assets, and from earnings and repayments by borrowers to meet requests by other savers to withdraw funds. Placing savings in a financial intermediary is risk reducing and liquidity increasing.[1]

Financial intermediaries differ in one or both of two characteristics. A deposit-type intermediary contracts to repay the exact sum the saver places with it, and ordinarily will return the money upon demand. The rate of interest on the deposit is not usually contractual. Similar in type are the policy reserves of life insurance and individually held annuity policies against which the policy holder may borrow or obtain part or even all of the policy by cashing it in.[2] In contrast mutual funds in which savers buy stock are "variable value investing institutions," as will be shown below. The saver who buys a fund's stock usually can, upon demand, obtain his pro rata share of the current market value of the securities owned by the fund.

Second, while an investor-owned financial intermediary is a clear concept the meaning of mutual varies. It would appear to mean that the enterprise is owned and at least formally controlled by persons who place funds with it. Mutual also connotes that all of the income above operating costs of the enterprise not re-invested is shared by member-owners in proportion to funds placed with it. Full sharing would provide also that a withdrawing member would be paid his share of the mutual's assets, although this might not be done immediately if this would embarrass the enterprise. To varying degrees the financial intermediaries denoted mutuals are organized and practice in harmony with these criteria, but, as will be seen, no one of them does so fully.

Relative Volume of Various Financial Intermediaries

The amount and percentage of total withdrawable savings held in 1975 by each type of fixed-dollar contract financial institution is presented in table 10.1. Together mutuals had deposits of $374 billion in 1975, or about half of the $760 billion total of deposit institutions. Of the mutuals' total of $374 billion, savings and loan associations accounted for 60 percent, the mutual savings banks for 27 percent, and credit unions for about 9 percent. Not shown in table 10.1 are the assets of the mutual funds, which were about $48 billion at the end of 1970.[3]

Radical changes have occurred in recent decades in the relative importance of various savings and investment institutions, with certain mutual institutions coming to the fore in recent decades.[4] The share represented by time deposits in commercial banks, all investor-owned, fell by half from 1920 to 1950. This trend was reversed after the late 1950s when the banks' loans and the rate they paid on time deposits advanced sharply. Policy reserves of life insurance companies, with mutuals accounting for an almost constant share, represented a growing percentage of fixed-dollar contract savings until 1940, but a falling share since. The long decline of the mutual savings banks' share seems to have stopped. Over four decades prior to 1964 the share of savings and loan associations, most mutuals, tripled, but declined slightly in the last decade due to avid competition in rates paid on savings by various types of deposit institu-

Table 10.1. Savings placed in Fixed-Dollar Contract Institutions, 1975

Type of institution	Amount (billions of dollars)	Percentage of total
Time deposits in commercial banks	$386	47%
Deposits in savings and loan associations		
Mutual	231	28
Stock	55	7
Deposits in mutual savings banks	110	14
Shares and deposits in credit unions	33	4
	$815	100%

Source: *Savings and Loan Fact Book 1976* (Chicago: United States Savings and Loan League, 1976), p. 14.

tions. Two newcomers to the list, credit unions and mutual funds, attracted a growing share of savings until recently. As one would expect the market value of mutual funds' assets declines when stock prices fall and vice versa.

More important than short-term oscillations of relative shares are the longer-term roles of financial mutuals vis à vis various investor-owned financial institutions and the reasons therefor.

Mutual Savings and Loan Associations

The premier place mutual savings and loan associations now have among saver-owned deposit institutions (table 10.1) was not achieved until after World War II. They had grown during the twenties but fell back during the Great Depression. Their primary function of accumulating funds of small savers and lending them to homeowners on more liberal terms than did other institutions fitted the demand for such financing. Mutual associations' deposits grew nearly twenty times between 1945 and the 1960s, but in 1976 were still only 60 percent of banks' time deposits.[5]

Evolution of the Savings and Loan Association

The early "building societies," as they were called, were established to accumulate funds so that each member in turn could become a homeowner.[6] Workers attracted to factory areas during the Industrial Revolution of eighteenth-century England and later in the United States often lived in squalid rented quarters. Because they generally could not borrow to buy a home except on terms they were unable or unwilling to pay workers formed "building and loan" societies. Each prospective homeowner who joined agreed to make a small monthly payment into a fund. If some members withdrew by death or upon change of savings plan, new members were admitted upon payment of the sum they would have paid had they joined when the association was formed. When the fund grew large enough to pay for a house the members bid for the privilege of obtaining the loan. The successful bidder had to pay the premium he had bid plus interest on the money and was required to continue his monthly deposits. In succession each member could acquire a house. When all had done so the association was terminated.

After several decades an organization arrangement evolved whereby a society could live indefinitely. Some societies introduced the word "perpetual" into their title to emphasize the change. Under this plan shares were issued to old or to new members at any time as they placed funds with the association. Now each member has an individual account and is treated as a depositor who usually may withdraw his money without penalty.

Modern Savings and Loan Associations

Through this evolution the saver-borrower identity was ruptured, and now members join in either capacity and do not necessarily or even typically have a continuing interest in the association. When the saver no longer had to become a borrower an entirely new element of the population became interested. Savers can be in and out depositors according to relative interest rates or liquidity and safety of funds in the associations compared to alternatives. The typical borrower also seeks the best terms regardless of the type of lender.

While both savers and borrowers are members, mutuality operates only for the savers. Interest rates on borrowing members' mortgages are fixed at the competitive rate at the time the loans are made. All earnings on loans and other assets above operating expenses and an assignment to general reserves or surplus which serve as the association's equity capital are available for dividends on the saving members' deposits.

In line with the savers' predominant position, they formally control the association but usually are not de facto controllers. Each saver has multiple votes; in federally charted associations he has one vote for each $100 deposit (but no more than fifty votes), while each borrower as such has only one. The overwhelming portion of the members do not participate in the election of directors, and the management-director group becomes practically self-perpetuating. When members join they may without knowing it assign their voting proxies to the management or do so later for annual meetings. A study sponsored by the Federal Home Loan Bank Board concludes that mutual associations "provide their members with minimal information," which "reduces members' control of the association," and that "a large majority of the associations appear to be effectively controlled by one or two strategic individuals or closely knit family groups."[7]

Given these characteristics of the modern association one is not surprised that they are usually initiated by persons who expect an executive position in the enterprise or who are engaged in businesses related to housing. These ancillary activities include real estate developers and agents, construction contractors, insurance agents, and those engaged in the escrow business. These men often dominate the going association's board and obtain business in connection with the lending operations of the association. Profitable fire insurance business going to savings and loan directors' agencies has been documented.[8]

Lacking active control,[9] members' immediate protection must be provided by the public agencies that charter, inspect, and in various ways regulate what managements do with respect to the quality of loans and adequacy of reserves of associations. Each association is also restrained by the performance of rival savings deposit institutions.

Conditions Favoring Entry and Growth of Mutual Savings and Loan Associations

To succeed in establishing a savings and loan association three conditions must exist. There must be a sponsoring group; who they are apt to be and their motives have already been pointed out. Having raised the funds required for the initial reserve, later repaid to sponsors from the association's net income, a federal or state charter must be obtained. Approval depends on evidence of need for the association, given the available insitutions that pay interest on savings and lend on home mortgages in the locality. There may exist the few buyer (deposit institution) or the few seller (lending institution) situations found frequently in local markets explored in this volume. Third, success of a new association depends on its ability to attract member-depositors and borrowers by offering the combination of rates and other terms of deposit and lending that appear superior to those of established lending institutions.[10]

Savings and loan associations pioneered the amortized mortgage, which was part of a package of lending terms quite distinct from those of other institutional lenders prior to 1934. Amortizing the principal of a loan by periodic payments, in contrast to a lump sum payment at the expiration of the loan, reduces the risk that would otherwise be involved in lending a higher percentage of the value of property and for longer periods than other lenders' had practiced. In the 1920-1929 period, 95 percent of the savings associations' loans on homes called for partial or full amortization within the period of the loan, compared to less than 70 percent for commercial banks, most of whose loans called for only partial amortization within the contract period. (Mutual savings banks did not enter the home mortgage market aggressively until recent decades.) In the 1930-1939 period the savings associations on the average loaned 60 percent or more on noninsured or "conventional" mortgages compared to 50 percent for the commercial banks. In many ways the most striking figure was the twelve-year average length of savings and loan associations' outstanding conventional mortgages in the 1930s compared to five years for commercial mortgages for the banks. Possibly these more liberal lending terms of the savings association explain why in the two decades before World War II their interest rates on home mortgages were distinctly higher than those for rival institutions, particularly in the southern and western states.[11]

The early 1930s were difficult times for most types of financial institutions—about 1700 savings associations failed in that decade—and the recovery of mortgage lending was aided by three new federal agencies. The Federal Home Loan Bank System lends to member financial institutions on the security of home mortgages. The Federal Savings and Loan Insurance Corporation, which insures all federal and most state-chartered mutual associations, restored savers' confidence in the safety of deposits. The Federal Housing Administration provides insurance on home mortgages which require a very small downpayment relative to the size of the loan, which can be amortized over twenty and later thirty years. After World War II the Veterans' Administration was authorized to guarantee mortgage loans to veterans with even more liberal terms.

Because savings and loan associations are limited by law to investing funds primarily in home mortgages, developments affecting the housing market become part of the background. In the decades since 1945 the demand for housing, a large part of it purchased by individual families, has been unprecedented because of the urbanization of the economy and the upward trend of real incomes. Also urban residents have been willing to assume higher debts relative to incomes than formerly. Their ability to do so has been enhanced by the upward trend of family incomes and also by the generally rising price level, while mortgage payments remain at the dollar amount specified in the contract.

The postwar radical changes in the percentage of savings deposits held by various types of lending financial institutions reflect both legal provisions governing their use of funds and the investing policies of managements. For decades national banks, and generally state-chartered banks, were sharply limited by regulation to short-period mortgages and to lending low percentages of value of properties. In 1916 the loan period could be only one year. These restrictions were relaxed over several decades, and well before 1955 they could make uninsured loans up to 60 percent of the value of the property.[12]

The commercial banks preferred the more liberal length of loan and percentage of value of property allowed under the FHA and VA programs. Such loans accounted for over half of their home loans in 1944-1955.[13] The mutual savings banks had moved into lending on four family dwellings but in 1945 primarily held conventional loans. Ten years later they had shifted heavily to FHA and VA loans, but recently still had half of their loans in conventional mortgages.[14] Throughout, the savings and loan associations preferred conventional loans.

Particularly after 1960 avid competition for savings deposits developed both among financial institutions of a given type and between types, with the mutual savings bank (considered below) lagging somewhat.[15] The commercial banks, which had paid much lower rates on savings deposits than did savings and loan associations, pushed up their rates to attract funds. Withdrawals from savings and loan associations rose from 72 percent of deposits in 1960 to a peak of 92 percent in 1969. Concerned about current developments, in 1962 the Federal Reserve Board imposed a ceiling on the rate banks could pay on savings deposits.[16] In 1966 the Federal Housing Administration imposed a deposit rate ceiling on the savings and loan association subject to its regulation, only to adjust the ceiling the next year and again in 1970. Fortunately for the associations they could obtain short-period advances from Federal Home Loan Banks and did so in large volume in several years of the late 1960s. To counter the competition of the savings associations the banks issued certificates of deposit carrying 5 percent interest or more and due in a few years and which were not subject to the ceiling on deposit interest rates. The savings and loan associations were then allowed to do likewise in this bitter competition.[17] Much of this bouncing around of savings was a by-product of fixing, and the differential adjustment of maximum rates on deposits, a questionable long-run policy.[18]

Nor is it evident that the recent more liberal lending terms would be valid in the event of a major slowdown of home building or a wave of defaults on mortgages.[19] Clearly the earlier margin of advantage seized by the savings and loan associations has been narrowed by the legal and loan policy changes affecting their rivals.

A major explanation has been that neither the federal government nor most states have chartered stock associations. In 1970 the stock associations accounted for about a fifth of total savings and loan deposits (table 10.1), double their 1962 share. About 60 percent of their assets were in the California state-chartered associations. There is nothing in the character of the business that should handicap this form of ownership.

The evidence about the relative efficiency of stock and mutual associations is conflicting. The growth rate of a mutual is limited by the portion of its net income that competition for savings will permit it to retain as equity capital. In contrast the stock association can sell additional stock to investors and thereby maintain the necessary net worth to deposit ratio as deposits are attracted by higher interest rates. A statistical analysis by George J. Benston found no significant difference in efficiency of the two types of institutions as measured by the ratio of operating expenses to assets.[20] Alfred Nicols rejected this test of efficiency and selected as the relevant test the costs related to new business of the associations, that is, to loans made and new savings. These costs are clearly lower for the California stock associations than for associations in states other than California which are predominantly mutuals.[21] The average of assets per California stock association is 2.7 times the average for federally chartered mutuals and 5.5 times the average size of stock associations outside California. Benston had already shown that there are clear economies of scale in this business,[22] which may explain in part the lower costs Nicols found for the California stock associations.

The conversion of state-chartered but not federally insured mutuals to stock form have increased, particularly in California. This development raises issues with respect to the control of mutuals and their efficiency, as shown in operating expenses, their aggressiveness in finding lending opportunities, and in growth of net earnings, regards in which mutuals rank below stock associations.[23] These issues arise to varying degrees with respect to all mutual financial institutions, including credit unions, and also in some cases to commodity-handling cooperatives.

Recent developments have occurred both in the stock-mutual association rivalry and in the conversion of the associations to the stock type. This has been of particular significance in states that charter stock associations and also have experienced a strong surge of residential construction. Aside from relative operation efficiency, mutuals' growth is limited by the need—indeed the legal requirement—of all associations to maintain a minimum ratio of surplus and reserves to deposits. This equity capital can be increased only to the extent that the mutual earns net operating income after interest rates on deposits necessary to deter withdrawals, a relatively slow process.

Consequently when a rapid increase in the demand for mortgage credit occurs the mutuals are handicapped. Stock associations can sell additional stock to investors and thereby obtain the necessary equity capital to support expanding deposits and loans.

Recognizing these facts the Federal Home Bank Board took two steps in 1973 and 1974. It modified its ten-year moratorium on the conversion of federally chartered and state-insured associations to state-chartered stock form. Apparently the 1973 step is viewed as an incomplete change of policy for, in addition, the board has asked Congress for the power to issue federal charters to stock associations. Again the mutuals' handicap in building its equity capital is cited as the rationale.

Mutual Savings Banks

Starting earlier, and with a purpose quite different from that of early building societies, mutual savings banks developed over a century ago in response to conditions brought by industrialization.[24] Investor-owned banks were not interested in the accounts of such small savers as factory workers. Recognizing this, persons of wealth interested in working families' welfare sponsored and provided the original capital for mutual savings banks. By the time industrialization spread to the newer areas to the west and south adequate depositories were provided by savings and loan associations, savings departments of commercial banks, and the later but now abolished postal savings. A substantial number of stock savings banks were started in the Midwest—753 were reported for 1910—but most of them actually began as primarily commercial banks. The true savings banks are all mutuals, but only eighteen states authorize them. By 1976 these mutuals held about a third of savings deposits in mutual deposit-type institutions but only 16 percent of total savings deposits.

Depositors in a mutual savings bank are not member-owners, even formally. As the initial reserve fund supplied by the sponsors was retired out of the earnings of the banks it was replaced by further deductions from net income, a continuous process as deposits grew. Persons withdrawing from the intitial board were replaced by others selected by the board or by a community committee of nominators. By these arrangements the mutual savings banks could become perpetual. The failure rate among them has been very low.

Following standards set by state supervision and augmented by the objectives of the directors, savings bank funds were invested primarily in high grade bonds until recently and not in mortgages on residences.[25] All income above operating expenses and an assignment to the bank's reserves is paid to depositors in proportion to the funds they have placed in the banks.

The relative decline of mutual savings banks from double the deposits of savings and loan associations in the 1920s to equality in the mid-fifties and then down to about half in 1976 is explained only in part by legal and policy restrictions on their investments. Also most of these mutuals are located where housing construction grew relatively slowly after World War II. Nevertheless by 1955 savings and loan associations were doing well in all states in which there were also mutual savings banks, except in New York where the bulk of these banks' deposits are. After 1950 the savings banks became stronger competitors in lending on housing though more to finance apartment buildings than family homes.[26]

This record indicates that the purpose of the organization and of subsequent control of these banks contributed to less entrepreneurship than savings and loan associations exhibited. In contrast to the savings and loan associations, board members of the mutual savings banks are engaged in largely unrelated activities. Not being concerned primarily with the savings banks' affairs nor benefiting from its operations it is easy for them to set investment policy that assures foremost the safety of their depositors' principal. Belatedly those regulating the banks and those controlling them turned to investing in mortgages, which enabled them to earn higher rates of return than on bonds. Presumably the reason the banks have not faced the equity capital for growth problem that has been so acute for mutual savings and loan associations in some states is that most saving banks are not located in areas of very rapid growth of urban housing.

Mutual Funds

A mutual fund is an enterprise through which savers invest in what amounts to a pool of earning assets of types that, compared to mortgages, usually have less certain but, it is hoped, rising market values. Except in a few mutual funds nearly all of the investment is in common stocks. Some funds emphasize growth stocks, others a diversified list of stocks with some bonds, and so on. As more savers buy the fund's stock or those who already own stock in it add to their investment additional shares of the fund are issued, and the fund then purchases additional securities. A stockholder in the fund can ordinarily turn in his shares and be paid his pro rata share of the value of the fund's securities as of that date. Because of the variable market value of common stock the amount of money an owner puts in by buying the fund's stock, or can claim by turning in his shares, depends on the market value of the securities the fund holds at that time. For that reason the full title of a mutual fund would be "variable-dollar-value" fund.

Mutual funds are neither established by, nor usually controlled in fact, by their stockholders. Most funds are formed and managed by an investment advisory firm. Once established the fund does have its own board but the majority of the members usually are officers or directors of the advisory firm or are persons selected by it. For its services the advisory firm charges the fund a small percentage of the fund's assets per year.[27] Some funds reduce the percentage when the assets of the fund exceed a specified size. Generally the advisory firm's net income from that service increases with the size of the fund. In addition to the payment to the advisory firm the fund has day-to-day operating expenses.

A feature of most but not all mutual funds is a "front-load," or a percentage of the sum the saver-investor pays, which goes for start-up costs, chiefly commissions for the salesmen. The percentage has varied from 7 to 9 percent, a rate that, along with some other practices, has been strongly criticized and appears to have been revised somewhat under the threat of legislation and pressure from the Securities and Exchange Commission.[28] A few funds charge an "end-load" to an investor who turns in his shares in the fund. There are also "no-load" funds sold at asset value per share at the time the investor buys the fund's stock, an arrangement that facilitates additional investment by the saver.

Penetrating studies by academic economists and the Securities and Exchange Commission have led to a number of suggestions for improving the funds' operations to the advantage of the investors in them. Little of the recommended legislation affecting selling and operating funds has been passed by Congress.

Comparison of the performance of mutual fund portfolios during the decade of the 1960s with that of a random sample of New York Stock Exchange common stocks leads to the conclusion that "random portfolios of New York Stock Exchange stocks with equal investment in each stock performed on the average better over the period than did mutual funds in the same risk class. The differences were fairly substantial for the low- and median-risk portfolios (3.7 and 2.5 percent respectively per annum)."[29] It must be recognized, however, that small investors do not have enough money to invest in a random selection of stocks on the New York Stock Exchange. The lesser performance, as measured by the increase in the value of the funds' stock, is the cost to such investors for being able to place their money in a diversified portfolio rather than in one or two particular stocks.

Three points should be made in appraising the degree to which the mutual funds are in fact mutual. One is that the management fee is sufficiently large to encourage the sponsoring firm to carry out fund sponsorship and management compared to other uses of its resources. In other words managing the funds is profitable business. Second, the front-load is a substantial percentage of the money placed in a fund by a small investor, particularly if he were to liquidate his investment after one or even a few years. To the extent that no-load funds are available and the investor is alert he can place his money in them. One would expect the relative percentages of the total mutual fund assets held by no-load versus front-load funds to be affected by choices of alert investors. Third, the possibility of conflict of interest between the managing firm and a brokerage operation leads one to inquire as to whether the turnover of the securities in the funds has been higher than prudent management would practice. The rate of turnover of securities held by mutual funds tripled between 1960 and 1968, and not because shareholdings in mutual funds fluctuated. These were years of a very active stock market rise, which suggests that persons investing directly in common stocks were also actively buying and selling particular securities. Turnover rates of funds whose managers were affiliated with brokerage firms were high also, but these were small funds which had higher turnover rates whether affiliated or not.[30] This volatility may reflect the fact that several times in recent years owners of stock in mutual funds have become disenchanted and have redeemed more shares than they added to their holdings.

A final comment is directed to the lack of effective direct control by stockholders. Even if they have the right to vote for the fund's board the minimal exercise of that right is similar to that observed for savings and loan mutuals, large farm cooperatives, most mutual insurance companies, and most sizable investor-owned corporations.

11

Cooperative Borrowing Institutions

Compared to the prominent role of mutual investing enterprises, cooperative borrowing from savers is limited. There are numerous credit unions, but they provide only an eighth of the installment credit consumers obtain from financial institutions. Although members are savers and many are never borrowers the primary purpose of credit unions is to provide a friendly and less expensive source of credit. Much larger in the volume and in percentages of credit supplied are several types of agricultural credit institutions sponsored by the federal government that obtain funds from the capital markets to re-lend to farmers. As originally set up these institutions had many of the formal features of cooperatives but were subject to such meticulous government control that they did not warrant that label. Whether they now have cooperative status will be assessed later.

No other significant cooperative-like borrowing organizations exist despite the capital needs of small nonfarm businesses. This limited development of cooperative borrowing could reflect either efficient and competitive performance of markets for loans to small-scale borrowers or the unique difficulty of cooperative vertical entry into this activity by borrowers.

The Federally Sponsored Agricultural Credit Institutions

At various dates between 1916 and 1934 the federal government established several types of permanent agricultural credit institutions, all but one of which gradually became owned by farmer-borrowers. Because of

149

the limited supply of long-term mortgage money and concern about the lending terms, including the level and geographic differences of interest rates, the federal government established a land bank system in 1916. After World War I Congress was impressed by the apparent inability or unwillingness of commercial banks in farming areas to lend to farmers for periods of from six months to a few years for the purchase of livestock and machinery. To fill this gap government-owned intermediate credit banks were established in 1923 to make advances for the periods just mentioned to cooperatives, commercial banks, livestock loan companies, and newly authorized agricultural credit companies. Few of the latter were formed. Except for credit supplied to livestock loan companies, the intermediate credit banks' role was quite limited prior to 1934.

All of this was changed radically when the Great Depression brought a credit crisis in agriculture. To alleviate the farm mortgage situation, land bank commissioner loans using government money were made to farmers who could not meet land banks' or other lenders' credit standards.[1] In the meantime the land banks had suffered such large losses that the government re-subscribed to their capital. Thousands of rural commercial banks failed, and as a consequence operating loans were scarce even for farmers with good credit ratings. Both long-term and short-term credit for cooperatives was scarce. In order to meet these situations two additional and permanent agricultural credit institutions were established, a production credit system to provide short- and intermediate-term operating loans to farmers and regional banks to lend to cooperatives.

The Structure of the Federal Farm Credit Institutions

With the exception of the intermediate credit banks these farm credit institutions were set up initially as cooperatives in form but not in substance. The basic pattern established in 1916 for the land banks has been followed for the added financial institutions. In 1954 the intermediate credit banks also started on the borrower-owned path.

There are twelve district land banks whose capital was initially supplied interest-free by the Treasury. Farmers who wish to borrow on the security of mortgages on their property form a local farm loan association. Each borrower-member must purchase stock in the association equal to 5 percent of the loan for which he applies. He usually borrows that much more. When the mortgage is paid off the borrower may sell his stock to a new borrower-member. Since the local association has no funds to lend it endorses the loan applications and sends them to the district land bank for approval. The local association must buy stock in the bank equal to 5 percent of the loans approved by the bank.

Backed by the pool of the mortgages it holds the land bank obtains most of the funds it lends by selling its bonds in the investment market. To attract investors, interest on the bonds was exempted from federal and state income taxes, a provision later removed. Local associations' ownership of the land banks was almost complete by 1931 but was blocked by the financial crisis of the early 1930s. The government re-subscribed to the banks' capital, but with the improved state of agriculture all of government-owned stock was retired by 1947. The banks are now owned by the local associations.

A similar but not identical plan was followed for the other types of lending institutions. The Treasury provided interest-free the initial capital of the fairly numerous (446 in 1970) local production credit associations and of the district banks for cooperatives. (These cooperatives have been subject to the federal income tax since 1968.) Farmer-members of the local PCAs purchase stock equal to 5 percent of the sums borrowed. Part of the funds a PCA lends to members may come from its own resources. Usually the association endorses members' approved promissory notes and uses them as collateral for loans from the intermediate credit bank of the district. (The role played until 1956 by regional production credit corporations is ignored here.)

From the viewpoint of this study the important credit source for farmer cooperatives is the banks for cooperatives. There are twelve such banks in the corresponding number of districts plus the Central Bank for Cooperatives. District banks can lend to farmer cooperatives for operating capital, to carry inventories of commodities, or to acquire or build facilities. When a district bank has inadequate funds it can apply to the district intermediate credit bank or to the Central Bank for Cooperatives. The latter obtains most of its funds by selling bonds which have high credit ratings. This credit system has been very successful.

All of these federally sponsored credit institutions have retired the government investment in them. Even the intermediate credit banks had done so by 1969-1970, although they had not become cooperative-like until 1954. Repayment was aided by the fact that the government money had been supplied interest-free.

Initiation and Early Control of These Credit Institutions

A federal agency took the lead in establishing each type of credit institution. It chartered and organized the district corporations or banks. Starting the local land bank associations was left largely to local initiative, but not so the production credit associations. They were founded under emergency conditions that required quick development. Field personnel representing the Washington headquarters stirred farmers to initiate local associations that in a very short time blanketed most of the country. Advances to the PCAs by the district intermediate credit banks were quickly backed by the promissory notes of farmers scattered over a large region. Starting large operations quickly could not have been accomplished without the organizing activity of the federal agency and the Treasury-supplied equity capital.

Little borrower control of these institutions was provided initially. They operated under the close supervision of the Farm Credit Administration in Washington, D.C. In each district there was a separate bank or corporation for each type of lending operation with a board of its own. (These have recently been consolidated into a single board.) The majority of the members of each board and its chief officer were appointed by the FCA. Detailed guides for appraising borrowers' credit were spelled out by Washington, and until the 1950s the land bank appraisers were employees of the FCA. The district organizations were largely routine administrators of FCA policies. To varying degrees by dates and types of credit FCA approval of specific loans was required. The recent extensive decentralization will be evaluated below.

Government, not borrower, control was necessary in the early years of these institutions if funds were to be obtained on favorable terms by sale of the banks' bonds and debentures in the investment market. The pioneering character of these systems of farm credit, the newness of the organizations, and the inexperience of their staffs all argued for initial centralized control of lending.

Pooling of Assets on Which to Borrow

Each credit agency could offer to investors bonds backed by a regional or even a national pool of farmers' or cooperatives' mortgages or promissory notes. It is the land bank or intermediate credit bank (according to type of credit) of the district that puts its bonds or debentures on the market, not the local association. While each district bank for cooperatives may sell its securities in the investment market, the Central Bank for Cooperatives may participate in very large loans and lend directly to large interregional cooperatives.

Borrowing on large scale has advantages. It reduces the cost of locating lenders. Pools of farmers' or cooperatives' notes or mortgages of a major region where there are various types of agriculture reduce the risk that the debtors will not be able to pay because of a local crop failure or low prices for a particular farm product. The mortgage credit pool is even larger, for the bonds of each district land bank are a liability of all of the banks. It is not surprising that except in a period of severe agricultural depression the bonds and unsecured debentures of these agricultural credit banks have enjoyed high credit standing.

It is doubtful whether these credit institutions, particularly the land banks, could have been started as easily or fared as well without the implication of government financial aid beyond the original capital subscription. Each bank's capital (invested largely in government securities) represents a very small percentage of the face value of the bonds the banks sold to investors.

As to actual government aid one can pass over the fact that the Treasury bought a large part of the bank's bonds from 1917 to 1920 because the constitutionality of the land bank system was then in question. The real test came from 1929 to 1933 when the value of farm mortgages was so uncertain that the land banks could sell bonds at or near predepression interest rates only to the Treasury or the federal reserve banks. In fact the land banks' situation became so bad that the Treasury subscribed an additional 125 billion dollars to their capital, all repaid by 1947. Such problems have not been faced by the other types of institutions, in part because of shorter-term lending, but primarily because, since their founding, agriculture has been much more prosperous. To facilitate holding to high credit standards during the 1930s by the land banks, other institutions using government funds (but not described here) were established to rescue farmers in serious financial straits because of low farm prices or to provide credit more continuously to marginal farmers.

Performance of the Agricultural Credit Institutions

The land banks have contributed to quite uniform farm mortgage interest rates in various regions of the country. In 1915 rates in the western and southern states were from 1 to 2 percent (of principal) above the average 5.5 rate in the North Atlantic states.[2] Not surprisingly, for two decades or more the land banks supplied a higher percentage of the mortgage credit in the areas of higher rates. This is no longer true,[3] but not solely because of the land banks. The volume of savings has become larger in the newer sections of the country relative to demand for mortgage credit, and capital has become more mobile geographically.

Compared to other financial institutions the land banks have varying degrees of advantage that enable them to offer lower interest rates. Initially they had the direct subsidy of interest-free capital stock supplied by the government plus federal income tax exemption for their bonds.[4] During the depression and until 1944 the federal Treasury paid the difference between the banks' rates to borrowers and a much lower target percentage rate, such as 3.5 percent. Aside from such years, investors have been impressed by the giant pools of mortgages held by the land banks.

To this is added the implication of government rescue in the event of substantial default of farmer-debtors as happened in the 1930s. Individual commercial banks or even giant life insurance companies do not have such large and diversified farm mortgage portfolios.

Available data do not permit a precise comparison between interest rates charged by land bank associations (during periods when the interest rate was not subsidized) and by other lenders. Generally land bank rates have been below the average rate on all farm mortgages, but the latter include loans of widely differing quality. Often, for example, the seller of a farm will lend to the buyer a far larger share of the purchase price than would an insurance company or a land bank but at an interest rate well above the land bank rate. The consensus seems to be that for loans of equivalent quality rates charged by the land bank through the local associations are somewhat lower than those of other financial institutions. In addition in recent years the land banks have paid dividends on their stock owned by local associations. In turn most of the latter have paid dividends to members, particularly when average interest rates on members' mortgages exceeded the rate paid on land bank bonds.[5]

Except during the worst years of the depression the federal land banks have supplied a widely variable but not often the largest percentage of farm mortgage credit supplied by financial institutions. The percentage was only 6 in 1920 and 12 in 1930 but boomed to a peak of 50 in 1935 exclusive of the emergency land bank commissioner loans. After the war the land banks' share fell to about 21 percent in 1950. By 1970, when interest rates generally were high, the land banks' share jumped to 46 percent.[6] These banks served as a residual source of farm mortgage credit when other financial institutions preferred alternative uses of their funds. In contrast the proportion of farm mortgages held by individuals has varied from nearly half a decade ago down to a fourth at the end of the war, but it is now back to two-fifths. The land banks' holding of farm mortgages has been far above that of commercial banks consistently since 1930.[7]

These facts suggest that the combination of credit standards and procedures involved in obtaining loans offsets the land banks' lower interest rates. Except during periods of acute emergency in agriculture a large portion of farmer-borrowers of good credit standing have preferred to obtain mortgage funds from other financial institutions or from individuals.

While the production credit system was established to meet a crisis it has become a permanent supplement to the farmers' other sources of short- and intermediate-term credit. Local associations obtain funds from the district intermediate-credit bank. The farmer-borrowers' notes must be of the quality that enables the intermediate-credit bank to borrow in the investment market at the favorable interest rates they have enjoyed. Nevertheless the PCAs have been able to lend to some farmers denied credit by commercial banks and still not incur significant losses because reliance was placed on the farmer's ability to pay from farm operations primarily and not on the assets he could pledge.[8]

Following these practices the operating experience of the associations has generally been quite satisfactory. Their losses on loans have been comparable to those of country banks.[9] Of course they were established after farm product prices had hit the bottom in 1932-1933. Since then no large segment of agriculture has been in a critical economic position for long. As the PCAs gained experience their operating costs have dropped sharply. Until recently local associations charged members the maximum allowed margin of 3 percent interest above the rate associations paid the intermediate credit banks. Progressively part of that margin has become net income and, after building up their equity capital, most associations have paid dividends to borrower-members and thereby reduced the effective interest rate charged.

The PCAs have never supplied the bulk of farmers' operating credit. Even during the trying 1934-1940 period the PCAs advanced only about 10 percent of what farmers borrowed from them and the commercial banks together. Their percentage jumped to 25 in 1961 and was about a third in 1971. These recent higher percentages reflect the more attractive outlets for funds of commercial banks in recent years; reportedly many country banks were loaned up. The PCAs' percentage would be cut in half if advances to farmers by sellers of supplies and buyers of farm products were included.[10] If one were to add short-term loans by other federal agencies based on less rigorous loan standards (but excluding Commodity Credit Corporation loans for price-support purposes) the PCA percentage would still be lower.

Many farmers do not look upon the PCAs as the preferred source of short- and intermediate-term credit. There were only 446 associations plus some branch offices in 1970 but they were not as conveniently located for many farmers as are the thousands of small-town banks and branches of larger banks. PCA borrowing procedures are often more involved and the time required to consummate a loan longer than when borrowing from a bank. The latter is also a bank of deposit, which adds convenience. But the PCA is an alternative source of credit, a fact that influences the banks as lenders.

The banks for cooperatives developed slowly and have always had to meet sharp competition from commercial banks in lending to the more successful cooperatives. In 1936 only 35 percent of total credit obtained by cooperatives was advanced by the banks for cooperatives, but during tight credit situations in 1973-1974 cooperatives obtained half of their credit from the expandable funds of the banks for cooperatives.[11]

Are the Farm-Borrowing Institutions Now Cooperatives?

Beginning decades ago and expedited under legislation from 1953 to 1968 more and more discretion has been placed in the hands of the district banks and boards and, by them, in the local associations. All but one of the members of the district board that coordinates the activities of all four types of lending institutions are now elected by the banks for cooperatives, the land banks, and the production credit associations of the district. Each of these boards now nominates a candidate to represent its district on the Federal Farm Credit Board and so far the president has appointed these nominees. All land bank appraisers are now employees of the district bank, but their work is checked on a sample basis by an employee of the Farm Credit Administration. Final approval of all but very large and some other special mortgage loans is in the hands of the district banks, but they often delegate this power to local associations. Each production credit loan is subject to the check for quality by the district intermediate credit bank.

Despite these developments, the district banks and local associations do not yet have the degree of autonomy that one associates with full-fledged cooperatives. Compare their situation with the kind of supervision that the federal and state governments exercise over commercial banks and the other financial institutions considered in the preceding chapters. Government agencies do not have any before-the-fact authority over the granting of specific loans by these institutions. After-the-fact inspection of them is concerned with compliance with regulations and with practices that would inhibit prompt availability and safety of depositors' funds. In contrast the Farm Credit Administration may at its election exercise much more control over specific decisions. Add to this the apparent willingness of the federal government to succor these credit agencies in the event of serious financial difficulty. Putting such considerations together, these lending institutions are not under full-fledged member control.

There is an important interconnection between the cooperative farm credit institutions and the success of farm marketing and supply cooperatives. This is most evident with respect to the banks for cooperatives and the production credit cooperatives. The former lends funds to cooperatives to finance construction of facilities and to carry inventories. The production credit corporations' financing of farmers' operations enables their members to pay cash for farm supplies. In a sense the cooperative credit agencies are the capstones of federal institutions affecting farm operations and marketing and supply cooperatives.

The Credit Unions[12]

Defined as a financial enterprise jointly owned and operated by "sovereign economic units," or consumers, credit unions are an integral part of their members' respective total "business" operations. Actually two vertical integrative functions are performed by and on behalf of these consumer units; a credit union is most simply defined as a "cooperative association, chartered either by the state or by the federal government, for the purpose of *accumulating the savings of its members and of making loans to them* out of these funds for provident or productive purposes at reasonable rates."[13] In other words a credit union is both a depository of members' savings and a ready source of credit for them. The primary motive for establishing credit unions was the latter, but they have tended to favor the savers, as will be seen.

While they follow the one-member, one-vote policy, credit unions have three unique characteristics as cooperatives: (1) as a matter of law, membership in credit unions is restricted to persons having some common interest or bond, such as employees of a single company or as members of some type of association or of a community;[14] (2) typically a maximum legal rate of 6 percent is specified for dividends on credit union shares, that is, deposits, but dividends have rarely been that high; and (3) until recently very few but now many more credit unions pay interest refunds on borrower patronage.[15]

Consumers' Borrowing Problems and the
Development of Credit Unions

Credit unions developed to meet the consumer credit problems of persons with quite low incomes, particularly as industrialization augmented the economic insecurity of the growing percentage of families dependent on wage income. Emergency needs for credit faced such families from time to time. In later decades wider availability of durable consumer goods sharply increased the demand for installment credit. Meanwhile the usury laws of the various states, by imposing unprofitable interest-rate ceilings (typically 6 percent a year), had resulted in the virtual monopolization of consumer lending business by "loan sharks" charging exorbitant and illegal rates of interest. In this "governmentally protected" position, fortified by widespread consumer ignorance of borrowing costs, "the loan shark throve; for many were his dodges to avoid the law. And the cries of his victims were loud throughout the land."[16]

Credit unions, started in 1909 under Massachusetts law, were one of several approaches to the solution of the "loan shark" problem.[17] From time to time other types of institutions have undertaken to supply consumer credit at interest rates more nearly equal to necessary costs.[18] But the credit union not only provides members with low cost credit, it also encourages them to adopt thrifty habits and to use borrowed money more intelligently. All of this is achieved by member control over lending policy, which thereby influences the consumer finance industry.

Four development periods in credit union history can be distinguished: (1) the formative stage from 1909 to 1935, when expansion of state-chartered credit unions paralleled the growth of the other important, and to a considerable degree competitive, sources of consumer credit; (2) from 1935 to 1941 came rapid advances in the number of unions and their membership, stimulated largely by rising employment and the passage of the Federal Credit Union Act in 1934; (3) 1941–1945 saw the wartime decline because of the Federal Reserve Board's regulation of consumer credit and the enormous labor turnover with its attendant problems for the continuity of credit union organization, although the chief influence was lack of consumer durables to buy; and (4) during the following decades of consistently high levels of employment and income credit unions experienced their greatest expansion.

In 1970 there were nearly 24,000 credit unions, with total membership of nearly 23 million and assets of $18.6 billion. While credit unions accounted for only 4 percent of savings deposits, they supplied an eighth of installment credit advanced to consumers by financial institutions.[19]

Performance of Credit Unions

Why the credit unions have not gained a larger share of the consumer finance business is surprising in light of certain facts about their operations. Their typical one percent per month on the unpaid balance charge on members' borrowings, with lower rates on large loans, has been below the net charges of financial institutions that lend to families with modest to low incomes, particularly those that cannot meet the commercial banks' credit standards. Comprehensive data on actual charges by various lenders are not available, but informed persons consulted hold that legal maxima are a good guide to rates charged on small loans, particularly by personal loan companies. Two or 2.5 or even 3 percent per month were the maximum in some states, but 1 to 1.5 percent is becoming the more general rate charged by banks on small loans.

The credit unions' interest rates on loans are made possible in part by using free services. Most or all officers are unpaid and often are given time off from their regular work to carry on the credit union's business.

Occupational credit unions, the principal type among the federally chartered, are usually provided with rent-free office space and equipment by
the employer. Add to this the low cost of credit checks on fellow employees and the availability of (voluntary) wage deductions by the employer
as the method of collecting payments, and it is not surprising that the
percentage of income charged to expenses by credit unions is well below
that of personal finance companies.[20]

The conditions under which credit unions operate have enabled them
to pay higher rates on members' deposits than do other savings institutions. When the average savings and loan association rate on deposits
was moving slowly upward from 2.5 percent in 1950 to 4.1 in 1962 the
dividend rates of most credit unions had been between 4 and 5 percent as
early as 1951. In 1970 about three-fourths of the credit unions paid 5 percent or more, while 5 percent was the average rate paid by savings and
loan associations.[21]

Considering the long period during which dividend rates paid by credit
unions were distinctly above those of rival savings institutions, why have
not credit union deposits grown more rapidly? In part their growth is
limited by the fact that membership of each union is limited to an occupational or other group. No general appeal to savers can be made. Also
the members are not assured that they can withdraw savings as promptly
as from rival deposit institutions.

Not unimportant is the fact that, in contrast to most rival institutions,
members' shares even in federal credit unions were not insured prior to
1971. The Credit Union National Association had fought insurance arrangements even though 3344 federal credit unions, mostly small ones,
were liquidated from 1934 through 1960, but not because of insolvency
in most cases. In 724 cases members were paid less than 100 cents for
each dollar of their shares, and in the others they experienced delay in repayment. Nevertheless, as will be seen in a moment, savings in credit
unions tended for some time to outrun members' demand for loans at the
one percent per month rate.

The growth of credit unions has been checked also by the development
of a variety of sources of consumer loans, some of which offer lower
rates for persons of good credit standing than do credit unions. Investor-
owned installment finance companies have entered and expanded with
the increase of demand for this type of financing. The most significant
change in recent decades has been the aggressive entry of the commercial
banks into the small-loan field. By 1970 they held nearly half of the
outstanding consumer installment credit advanced by financial institutions. In rates and availability of loans the banks have become active
competitors of all lenders to consumers whose credit standing is high.

During much of the period since the war credit unions were more attractive as a place for savings than as a source of consumer loans. During the early 1950s members borrowed from credit unions only about 75 percent of what members deposited. Much of the remainder was put in interest-bearing deposits in other financial institutions or in government bonds. While prudence requires that not all deposits be loaned, 25 percent of deposits was not required to meet withdrawals; the percentage had dropped to about 8 by 1970 and the credit unions were not embarrassed thereby. In the 1960s rising interest rates paid on savings deposits by rival institutions slowed the growth of credit unions' funds, while these rivals' rates on consumer loans generally advanced. The credit unions' unchanged lending rate became more attractive to borrowers, and their loans rose to 92 percent of deposits.

Like all deposit institutions, credit unions operate between two markets which govern what they can do. They must compete for savings with other deposit institutions in order to obtain funds to carry out their primary objective of lending to members on favorable terms. At the same time the credit unions must compete with other lenders to consumers, now chiefly the commercial banks and installment credit offered by retailers. The rigidity of the credit unions' lending rate is open to question. Only to a limited but slowly increasing degree have they "muted" both ways by also paying variable interest dividends to borrowers.

Problems of Entry into Cooperative Borrowing

Establishing a cooperative borrowing enterprise is more difficult than forming a mutual investing institution. As was seen in the preceding chapter the sponsors of the latter provide the initial reserve, or equity capital, which is repaid out of net earnings of the mutual. Further assignments from net earnings provide additional reserves required for growth of the mutual. More important, the members of mutual savings and loan associations and of mutual savings banks deposit funds which the mutuals invest in a variety of earning assets. Similarly, credit unions had to become cooperative savings institutions before the same or other members could borrow. The cooperative investing aspect of credit unions is indicated further by their practice of paying patronage dividends to savers.[22] While member depositors can borrow from the credit union it is doubtful whether most members expect to be in debt continuously.[23]

Savers cannot be expected to lend to (deposit in) a borrowing cooperative at interest rates that permit re-lending at competitive rates unless the volume of its borrowing members' promissory notes and the diversification of their sources of income forecast stability of the cooperative's earning and loss rates. This seems not to have been a serious problem for credit unions despite a substantial number of failures. Expectation of becoming borrowers influences members to place savings in the cooperative, which enables it to make short-term loans to other members.

Because farm incomes in a locality may be affected sharply by crop failure or by the low price of a specific farm product the pool of farmer-members' promissory notes or mortgages held by a new cooperative bank must at once be quite large and diversified. Consequently the cooperative should not start small and in one locality; it must be quite large initially and have member-borrowers from over a large region or the whole nation.

The continuity of interest of members of a federal farm credit association differs by type of loan. Once a farmer has paid off his mortgage the local farm loan association is of little interest to him. He can sell his stock in the association or hold it and may receive some dividends. If he obtains operating funds from a production credit association he may use this source repetitively. Likewise farmer cooperatives may borrow repetitively from the regional banks for cooperatives. But the wide differences and oscillations from time to time in the shares of farmers' and cooperatives' total credit obtained from the federal agricultural agencies indicates the degree to which they are these borrowers' preferred sources of credit.

In the light of these considerations it is not surprising that borrowing cooperatives have not often been established without outside sponsorship and temporary financial aid and even subsidy. The numerous occupational credit unions have been encouraged and even aided by employers. The agricultural credit cooperatives are the most notable cases of government initiation, financial aid, and control of operations. In contrast to what was observed in chapter 10 with respect to sponsorship of savings and loan associations these borrowing cooperatives have not been formed by persons or enterprises which expected to gain substantially in their primary income-producing activities from lower cost of credit. Without government sponsorship and provision of initial capital it seems likely that the cooperative agricultural agencies would have developed very slowly, if at all.

Of particular significance for this study the banks for cooperatives have gone far to solve the capital supply problem of farmer cooperatives, as will be seen in chapter 13.

12

Mutual Fire and Casualty Insurance

Compared to patron-owned enterprises in most other fields of activity mutual insurance is big business. In 1971 the total premium receipts of all mutual fire and casualty insurance companies was about $31 billion,[1] exclusive of small companies such as local farm and town mutuals. This sum is nearly one-and-a-half times the $21 billion net annual addition to funds in deposit-type mutual savings and investment institutions and over twice the $15 billion net sales of farm marketing and supply cooperatives as reported in earlier chapters. Mutuals' share of major types of fire and casualty insurance ranges from a third of the workmen's compensation insurance (other than that carried by state agencies) and an equal share of automobile casualty insurance to one-fifth of major categories of fire insurance.[2]

In contrast to patron-owned enterprises in any other field, many insurance mutuals are giants. The net premiums earned by each of four mutual fire and casualty (mostly automobile) companies exceeded $300 million and for State Farm Mutual was $1.7 billion. The giant life insurance mutuals are even larger,[3] but they were established in that form or were converted to it a century or more ago for reasons that do not fit into the analysis here. None of those now giants was formed by persons whose primary interest was to acquire insurance at lower cost. Frequently organizers had limited capital but expected to receive substantial salaries plus a percentage of the enterprise's premium income over and above the commissions paid to salesmen.[4] While a significant portion of the premiums charged by these mutuals is usually returned to policyholders, this reflects chiefly and perhaps entirely that life insurance mutuals, unlike those in fire and casualty insurance, charge initial rates substantially above those for investor-owned companies' nonparticipating policies. But the mutuals pay substantial dividends. Formally policyholders in these mutuals are members but rarely know that fact or vote even by proxy.[5] These comments do not apply to the same degree to life insurance mutuals formed in the last few decades by farm organizations and other groups.[6] Neither these nor other life mutuals will be examined here.

Some but not all of the reasons for omitting life insurance from further consideration apply also to fire and casualty mutuals. Their members are rarely aware of the right to vote, except in small farm and town mutuals. In all of them formally and to a high degree in practice premium rates charged member policyholders, net after dividends, reflect the mutuals' underwriting cost experience,[7] the economically significant feature of patron ownership. But the way some mutuals now of substantial size got started, and even more their current practices compared to those of the investor-owned (hereafter denoted "stock" as in trade practice), insurance companies pose questions about the mutuals' cooperative character. For example most mutuals may, with the same impunity as a stock company, cancel or refuse to renew a member's policy. Members who withdraw by ceasing to pay premiums are not paid their shares of that part of the mutual's equity capital which their patronage had produced.

Conditions of Entry into Fire and Casualty Insurance

Entry into fire and casualty insurance is relatively easy in some situations, but survival is often more difficult. States require only modest initial capital, usually less than a million dollars.[8] A century or more ago the required sum was much smaller, and often much of it consisted of the promissory notes of the founders. But a small company cannot count on the average loss rate that insuring a large number of risks makes quite certain. It could be bankrupted if policyholders' losses were unexpectedly high in a given year. Nor can it safely insure a single risk that is large relative to its total premium income unless it re-insures such a risk in a company specializing in re-insurance.

Survival depends on relative efficiency, of which acquisition or underwriting costs and payments for losses are the large items. Whether and to what extent small companies' expenses measured necessarily as ratios to net premiums are higher is not entirely clear. Mutuals' level of rates is quite often if not generally lower; so are the rates of some stock companies which deviate from the standard rates filed by most large stock companies. Consequently lower-rate companies' expense ratios are inflated to a small degree. The only data by which to compare insurance costs of various companies are their costs as percentages of net premium income.

A recent econometric study shows that large fire and casualty insurance companies have lower costs in some parts of their operations but often higher in others.[9] Operating costs as distinct from costs for administering and paying loss claims are lower on the average for companies above $300 million net premiums. But loss expenses tend to increase beyond that size of company so that total costs do not fall. Total costs tend to be higher for distinctly smaller companies inversely to their size. Selling expenses are distinctly higher for companies of all sizes if they sell insurance by use of brokers rather than through their own agents or by mail solicitation, a point that is developed at length below.

Cost disadvantage may be offset by the fact that a new company does not enter the national market or initially engage in several lines of fire or casualty insurance. The new mutual may be formed because the cost of insuring a particular category of risk is substantially less than established companies' rates. The success of the new mutual then depends on how long the established companies hold their high-rate "umbrella" over the new rival and the speed with which it can grow to relatively efficient size. It also may use the less expensive method of selling through its own agents, which may be more effective.

Clearly entry and survival of quite small companies has not been prohibitively difficult. In 1960, excluding local farm and small town mutuals, there were over a thousand fire-liability companies, most of them far smaller than $300 or even $100 million of net premiums. In 1970 the largest ten had only 34 percent of the industry's total property and liability net premiums.[10] Nevertheless the number of fire and casualty companies reported in Best's annual summaries (which excludes very small companies such as farm and town mutuals) has been declining for nearly two decades. A large portion of the supposedly new companies are really subsidiaries of old ones established to deal with a particular situation.[11] Additional evidence on size requirements needed to enter will be found in the following more detailed account of fire and major types of casualty insurance.

Fire Insurance

Mutuals provide about a fifth of total insurance against losses by fire and other property damage for which extended coverage and similar types of insurance are provided. Mutuals insure a far larger share of farm buildings and contents and of some types of manufacturing and commercial buildings than of urban residences, facts to be considered more fully below.

Development of the Mutuals

While most early fire insurance companies were mutual in form, the stock companies soon had a lead in America. Experience with uninsured losses led to the formation of such local mutuals as the one Benjamin Franklin helped start, which is now quite large. Often called "contributionships" to indicate that they levied assessments on members to reimburse those suffering losses these mutuals insured dwellings only and surely would have failed in the event of a conflagration. Many stock companies were also established early in the nineteenth century to insure all types of structures. From this point on the account is a composite of the adequacy of the information base for quoting rates, of the effectiveness of competition among stock companies as related to the entry of mutuals, and of the impact of public regulation on the fire insurance industry.

Before the formation of rating bureaus to provide data on loss experience, mutuals providing fire insurance were formed by owners of business (including farm) buildings who expected to obtain substantially lower insurance rates. In the vanguard were the famed factory mutuals, first formed by New England cotton mill owners in the 1830s.[12] They found that premiums charged by stock companies, ranging from 2.5 to 4.5 percent of the value of the insured building and contents raised far more money than was required to pay losses, particularly of mills that were constructed of fire-resistant materials and design. Refused lower rates by stock companies a few enterprising mill owners formed a mutual which charged 75 percent (in the form of a deposit) of the rates of stock companies and still was able to pay substantial dividends. Other factory mutuals sprang up in New England and elsewhere even though the stock companies rates' fell somewhat, but in 1873 they were still more than three times what members of the factory mutuals paid net after dividends.[13]

In recent decades the factory mutuals, now combined into four groups, have developed a nationwide business and provide somewhat broader insurance coverage. They now insure some large chains' retail stores and insure members against property damage other than by fire.

Much of the success of these mutuals is traceable to the reduction of members' fire losses. From their early history they have rejected many applicants and ejected those who would not comply with designated fire-prevention practices in the construction of plants or in operations, as uncovered by frequent and rigorous inspection of the member's plants and fire-fighting equipment. Consequently, while members' insurance costs are lower, other costs are higher than of plants that cannot meet the factory mutuals standards.[14] Presumably members choose the mutual because the sum of these costs and the lower insurance rates are less than the stock companies' rates for insurance alone.

Because the factory mutuals do not charge rates as such but require members to make deposits in advance much above a year's premiums and on which the mutuals earn investment income, it is not possible to make a direct rate comparison with either stock companies or other mutuals. Using a market test the factory mutuals' volume of insurance coverage (not premiums received) more than doubled in the decade ending in 1969, while the stock companies' volume rose only 70 percent.

Not long after the founding of mutuals identified as "factory" other mutuals were formed by businesses whose inventories and often buildings were of highly inflammable materials. Groups of flour mills and grain elevators, millwork plants and lumber retailers, and hardware stores in a number of areas found fire losses to be a small fraction of the insurance premiums collected from them. As if taking a leaf from the New England factory mutuals' book, at various dates between 1870 and 1915 fire insurance mutuals identified by the name of the commodity produced or sold by members sprang up, particularly in the Midwest.[15]

In nearly every case the establishment of the mutual and early years of its operation were guided by a strong leader from the insured industry. An unusually effective entrepreneur was James S. Kemper. After a meteoric rise in an Ohio-based retailer-owned mutual he became owner-manager of a sales agency established in Chicago to recruit member-policyholders for a group of fire mutuals of the region. Later he helped form other mutuals, notably what is now the giant Lumbermen's Mutual Casualty Company, and for years was president of some of them. He, not the member-policyholders, provided the entrepreneurship.

Far smaller in scale were the farm fire mutuals started around 1875, which grew rapidly for reasons similar to those just sketched. Rates charged by stock companies were well above those farmers thought to be the necessary cost.[16] Often they were right, at least for the properties that the farm mutuals insured. Probably the stock companies misjudged the net effect of the absence (until recently) of fire-fighting equipment in rural areas and the minimal chance of conflagration. Most early farm mutuals were very small and assessed members when losses occurred instead of collecting premiums to cover losses in advance, and many that remained local still do. Particularly as long as they remained small and local their operating expenses were very low. Much free time was given by the officers of the association, or only nominal salaries were paid. In 1921 these mutuals provided two-fifths of the fire insurance bought by farmers, and the members saved about half of the stock company rates. Mutuals' share was about the same in the 1960s,[17] but those that write only fire insurance have been shrinking in volume and number while the larger ones have expanded into other types of property and casualty insurance.

Of all fire insurance premiums, excluding the volume of the very small companies such as farm and town mutuals that do not report to Best's, the mutuals have obtained a small but recently an increasing share. Until 1951 the only available data assigned the whole of each company's volume to its predominant type of insurance. Of companies engaged primarily in fire insurance, mutuals obtained a stable 11 percent from 1900 to 1920. By this measure there was a steady growth in the mutuals' share to 16 percent by 1950, but some of this reflected the more rapid extension of mutual, than of stock, fire companies into casualty insurance. Best's reports since 1950 separate the fire and related insurance volume and show the mutuals' share to have been 14 percent in 1951 and about 20 in 1970.[18]

The entry and growth record of the mutuals must stem from the failure of stock companies' rates to be adjusted to the level of necessary costs of insuring particular types of properties. This lack of effective competition requires an examination of the rate-setting process and the relation of government regulatory agencies thereto.

Rate Bureaus, Regulation, and the Opportunity for Mutuals

With varying degrees of success after 1840 stock companies pooled their information on fire losses through rate bureaus and, on the basis of these data, established uniform rates for various types of risks. Early agreements did not last long, but over several decades they became increasingly durable and came under the general attack on collusion and monopolies that swept the country in the years before World War I. Many states then forbade the joint setting of insurance rates.

The companies protested strongly on two grounds. They were correct in claiming that no company had sufficient experience to provide a statistical basis for rates except perhaps a few large-volume types of property. But their further assertion that "open competition in fire insurance" necessarily forced rates below the cost of operations and payment for losses is questionable. No one seems to have argued effectively that pooling information permits computation of average loss experience for particular types of property but that collusion on rates was not a necessary corollary.[19] Nevertheless most states ceased to attack rate agreements arrived at through rate bureaus.

Soon several states that together accounted for a large share of all fire insurance volume required that rates be approved by a state agency. The companies usually filed the rates worked out by a bureau and rates for each category of fire risk became uniform. Most state commissions winked at and some even required joint action by the companies in arriving at the rates filed. Until recently some states either refused to approve lower rates filed by particular companies or handicapped those desiring to deviate from the bureau rates. Apparently the state agencies did not bar companies from paying dividends to policyholders. Thereby the door was open to mutuals whenever their costs of providing insurance could be significantly below state-approved rates.

Insurance rates arrived at by agreement (formally or not) can be expected to reflect, with a lag, changes in the loss experience for a particular category of risk. Bureau staffs do continuously examine loss experience, such as those affected by developments in building materials and fire-prevention equipment. But once a set of rates for various risk categories or the procedure for appraising risks, such as large buildings, has been agreed upon, it is much easier to leave the situation undisturbed. While rate structures were by no means unchanging there is more than a hint that they were less adaptable to new conditions before the mutuals forged ahead, particularly in nonresidential fire insurance. Until recently the pressure for uniformity of rates was enormous, aided by provisions of some state laws, the reliance of commissions on rate bureaus' schedules, and the organized pressure of most stock companies.[20]

The author has observed that those working out private agreements tend to simplify the task by having as few categories of risks (or products) and the corresponding rates (or prices) as possible. Indeed, under the four years of price control during World War II, the Office of Price Administration sought to simplify its task by setting a uniform maximum price for an article even though various sellers' prices had differed. Correspondingly, in rate agreements the tendency appears to have been to place what were significantly different risks in a common category. Once an agreement was reached, revising categories and rates was made difficult by the differing loss experience of companies.

The regulatory agency could appraise the adequacy of revenue compared to costs of fire insurance as a whole but less so of the rate structure and needed changes therein. The agency would be subjected to more criticism if, more than occasionally, a few of the companies' premium receipts were less than selling and other operating expenses and payments for losses than if rates were higher than necessary by a few percentage points. The staffs of regulatory agencies were far too small and often lacked the technical competence to check the validity of risk categories and of the corresponding rates. Changes in risk categories or of rates for particular risks have to be defended in administrative hearings and even in the courts. Not surprisingly as recently as 1957-1960 less than two-tenths of one percent of the rates filed by rating bureaus with state agencies were disapproved.[21]

To the extent that at various periods rate competition has been absent the only means by which a company could affect its volume was by "nonprice" competition. That term covers liberality in settlement of claims for losses and allowing policies to be canceled for which the premium had not been paid even though insurance coverage had been provided for a period. One finds references to misclassifying of properties so as to charge the bureau rate for a lower risk than that properly applicable to the particular property. Also the attempt was made to get captive clients, for example, those that borrow money from a financial institution with whom an insurance agency is associated in some way.[22] All but the last of these practices add to the loss experience and hence to costs of each company and of bureau-rate companies generally.

These practices were stimulated where insurance policies were sold through what has been called the "American Agency System." The reference is to agents, usually brokers, who do not represent a single company and whose clientele, owners of property, rarely designate the company with which the insurance is to be placed. Consequently the broker is in a position to choose the company that offers the best treatment of those insured; in a sense he is the seller of the policy in the eyes of the insured and in turn the broker is the buyer in the view of the insurance company. Added to the nonprice competition costs is evidence that the brokers' percentage of premiums paid tended to exceed the necessary costs of selling.

Usually brokers received a quite uniform commission of 25 percent of the premium on each annual or other short-term renewal of the policy. Such uniformity of commissions could not emerge from effective competition. Agreement was influenced by brokers' conferences. The brokers' position was strengthened until recently by court decisions that the insured's relation was with the broker not the insurance company. This aided the brokers in holding a common front against any insurance company's attempt to reduce commissions.[23] Recent federal court decisions, however, have held to be collusive and illegal the devices used by groups of brokers to "hold the line" on the prerogatives they had enjoyed.[24]

The Mutuals' Spur Rate Competition

By 1940 the contrast was sharp between the stock and mutual companies' selling expenses, loss and claim expenses, and underwriting profits. On the average, stock companies then incurred agents' compensation expenses equal to 27 percent of net premiums written compared to 15 percent for the mutuals. Stock companies' loss and claim expenses were 43 percent of premiums earned compared to the mutuals' 36 percent.[25] In part the contrast reflects that the mutuals insured industrial and commercial buildings primarily where each policy was large. Most insurance on individual homes was and is provided by stock companies. Another cost contrast is the policyholders' losses by fire, 43 percent of premiums earned for the stock companies compared to 34 percent for mutuals. The mutuals must have been more careful in selecting properties to be insured and possibly were less liberal in settlements of losses.

Separate from underwriting profits are the companies' earnings on their investment portfolios built in part by stockholders' or members' initial investment but for successful insurers primarily by assignments from underwriting profits to reserves and surplus.

In 1944 the rather artificial rate structure nurtured by the stock companies and reinforced by state regulation took a serious blow. Insurance had long been exempt from the federal antitrust laws but in that year was declared to be "commerce" and subject to the Sherman Act.[26] Much alarmed, Congress passed Public Law 15, which in part exempted insurance from federal regulation provided state laws assured rate competition. By 1950 these laws had been amended, but their administration in many states continued to place handicaps on individual companies seeking to file rates that deviated from the standard or bureau rates.[27]

Nevertheless by 1970 much more adjustment had occurred. About one hundred stock companies were deviating from bureau rates or selling participating policies, but the net premiums earned on these policies amounted to only 10 percent of total stock companies' fire and similar insurance. Of particular interest is that average stock company commission and brokerage rates had declined during the preceding decade by two to four percentage points by type of coverage. These companies' underwriting profit rates were lower than in the 1949-1959 decade, and underwriting losses were frequent and substantial on the homeowners' multiple peril insurance. In the 1960-1969 decade the mutuals' average commission and brokerage and total underwriting expense rate were still three to ten percentage points below that of the stock companies except on homeowners' mutual peril policies. But mutuals also felt the competition; their underwriting profits were substantially reduced and losses incurred frequently on homeowners' multiple peril policies.[28] Further comments on these developments and the effect of the mutuals are postponed until casualty insurance has been examined.

Casualty Insurance

Since ancient times individuals and businesses have faced potential losses from shipwreck, robbery, malfeasance of employees, or damage inflicted on others. Early mutuals to provide insurance against such losses varied from the Schaghticoke Society for Apprehending Horse Thieves and Robbers to more prosaic mutual boiler and plate glass insurance. Of particular interest has been the growth in the last half century of employers' liability for job-related accidents and of losses related to the operation of motor vehicles. Mutual companies now provide about a third of the insurance against each of these types of losses.[29]

Employers' Liability Mutuals

Starting just before World War I a wave of state laws made more definite and enforceable employers' financial liability for accidents to their employees. Stock insurance companies were not enthusiastic about offering employer liability insurance, which led some states to set up this type of insurance. Where stock companies entered this business many groups of employers thought the rates were much higher than necessary. This stimulated the forming of such famed mutuals as the Employers Mutual Liability Insurance Company of Wausau, Wisconsin, and the Liberty Mutual of Boston. Together these two accounted for about half of this type of insurance provided by mutuals in 1970.[30] In industries of more than average risk of accident, special casualty companies arose, such as the Lumbermen's Mutual Casualty Company referred to earlier, which has diversified into many types of nonlife insurance. Typically these mutuals charge bureau rates and pay patronage dividends equal to savings, less assignments to build the mutuals' reserves.

By 1921 mutuals provided a fifth of this type of insurance, a third by 1936, and the same share in 1970.[31] For ten years ending with 1969 Best's reports their premiums earned exceeded their costs by nearly 12 percent, almost three times the underwriting profit rate of the stock companies.

Development of Mutual Automobile Insurance

Automobile insurance developed later but otherwise the account is similar to that of fire insurance with the exception that existing fire insurance rating bureaus could be imitated. Stock companies' methods of selling automobile insurance were analogous to those for fire insurance and so were the effects of arriving at and competing under uniform rates.

Establishing automobile insurance mutuals was particularly difficult because most automobiles are owned by householders and are used for pleasure. Compared to the large savings from mutual fire insurance on business and farm buildings an individual's potential gain from promoting an automobile casualty mutual appeared minute. Nevertheless several such mutuals were formed, some as offshoots from farm and other organizations or from fire mutuals already established.

Of all the mutuals the most dramatic story is that of the State Farm Mutual Automobile Insurance Company, established in 1922 by G. J. Mercherle, who had retired from farming at middle age.[32] Investigation proved to him that accidents involving farmers' automobiles were far less frequent and serious than for city dwellers' cars, but they were charged the same rates. Also the stock companies' methods of selling automobile insurance included the usual brokerage percentage. While small local automobile insurance mutuals already existed, sponsored by county farm bureaus, they were not large enough to obtain stable loss experience. Bankruptcy was frequent.

Mercherle developed a plan with several unique features compared to stock company policies: (1) semiannual premiums at half the annual rate; (2) a fifty-dollar deductible on each accident, thereby saving the cost of administering small claims; (3) using the state farm bureaus as state agents; and (4) selling memberships at a nominal fee which, together with a small sum per policy, financed both the selling of memberships and policies and the employee costs of settling claims.

Mercherle formed a management company that assumed the task of selling memberships and policies and adjusting losses. For this he received a membership fee and a small payment for each renewal of the policy and hired and remunerated the salesmen and the adjustors. This arrangement had been terminated by 1950 and so had the use of state farm bureaus as agents. There is no formal connection now between any of them and State Farm.

State Farm's major operating economy has been in underwriting (selling) expenses. In 1970 these expenses were 17 percent of premiums written for each type of automobile insurance compared to about 23 percent of all mutuals and about 28 percent of stock companies' typically higher premium rates.[33]

Not surprisingly, State Farm was a quick success. Quite soon it insured nonfarmers and by 1942 ranked first among automobile insurers, a position not lost to this date. In 1970 its share of all automobile insurance premiums earned was 13 percent.[34]

Some Rate and Cost Comparisons in Automobile Insurance

Rate comparisons can be accurate only when the various companies' policies have essentially the same provisions for the same type of risk. A more serious difficulty is that the structure of rates differs according to the geographic area in which the owners live, the age of the operators, the use made of the vehicle, whether for pleasure or for driving in connection with work or to work, and other bases of risk classification.

The real cost of insurance may differ, such as in liberality of settlements. This possibility is minimized by comparing the rates for automobile users' liability insurance, for an automobile owner presumably is not as concerned about the promptness and liberality with which his insurance company settles damage claims against him as he is for insurance coverage for his car and its occupants. Table 12.1 reports the percentage by which State Farm's rates for automobile liability insurance in a partic-

Table 12.1. Percentage by Which Automobile Liability Insurance Rates Charged by the Largest Mutual and the Largest Deviating Stock Company Were Below Stock Company Bureau Rates, 1936–1959 (Applicable to "Remainder of State [of Illinois] Territory")

Period	Approximate percentages by which rates of designated companies were below bureau rates	
	State Farm Mutual	Allstate Insurance
1936–1938	50%	30%
1939–1941	25	8
1946–1948	15	17
1949–1952	20	27
1953–1954	20	27
1955–1959	34	23

Source: The two companies provided the author with their own rates and also the rates nondeviating stock companies had filed with the state regulatory agency. "Remainder of Illinois Territory" refers to all of the state exclusive of sizable cities.

ular area were lower than the stock company bureau rates during the period when the mutual share was rising most rapidly. For the 1936-1938 period automobile owners in the designated area who carried liability insurance with State Farm Mutual saved about half of the bureau rates. This savings was cut in half during the next four years and after World War II declined to 15 percent. It rose again and remained on a plateau of about 20 percent from 1949 through 1954 and then shot up to about 34 percent for the next five years. A similar comparison for recent years is difficult because companies now identify several and frequently changing classes of drivers with different rates and classifications.

Once it became clear that deviating rates would be approved by state authorities certain stock companies challenged the mutuals. Following selling and administrative methods analogous to those of State Farm, Allstate Insurance Company (a subsidiary of Sears, Roebuck and Company) years ago filed rates that deviated sharply from bureau rates. The last column of table 12.1 shows that Allstate's rates (for particular policy and area) were further below stock company bureau rates from 1946 through 1954 than were rates of State Farm, but not in other subperiods from 1936 to 1959. Such changing relative rates must reflect either temporary differences in the respective company's loss experience or a lag in the adjustment of rates to that experience. Allstate has demonstrated over several decades that a stock company that follows low-cost acquisition and administrative methods can approximate the record of a very efficient mutual.

Further evidence of the effect on rates of cost-saving methods of selling insurance, of billing policyholders, and of settling claims appears in a fairly recent study of four very large companies. Significantly two are mutual and two are stock companies but each practices "direct writing," or selling through its own agents. For the 1953-1957 period the net cost of insurance to these four companies' policyholders was almost exactly 20 percent below that of companies selling at standard rates through brokers. The savings fell to 15 percent in premium rates from 1961 to 1965.[35] The author of these comparisons has informed me that the complexity of rate structures prohibits a similar comparison for the years after 1965. It is noteworthy that companies practicing direct writing sold 44 percent of all automobile insurance in 1969.[36]

Given the facts just cited one insurance executive wrote, "since price is, of necessity, based upon pure loss and expense of operations and such pure loss is not readily subject to any rigid control, we shall, if we are interested in being truly competitive, have to do something about the expense of our operation [apparently meaning acquisition costs primarily]. Such a need is evident regardless of price levels."[37]

Facing such competition stock companies were forced to make adjustments. From 1949 through 1958 data in Best's show that on the average mutuals' acquisition cost was about 8 percent of their lower net premiums below that of stock companies. Even at the stock companies' higher rates they had underwriting losses on two major types of automobile insurance, while the mutuals fared quite well. From 1960 through 1969 acquisition costs as a percentage of net premiums of both types of companies fell sharply, but more sharply for the stock companies. The latter incurred underwriting losses quite steadily during this decade except on the "comprehensive" policy. Reflecting this greater rate competition, the net underwriting margins of mutuals were forced several percentage points below the level of a decade earlier.

During this decade both mutual and stock companies' net margins oscillated as companies experimented with marking off new and changing categories of drivers and with adjusting of policy provisions and rates to loss experience. The operating results of the decade reflect the extreme competition to which most stock companies were forced by the mutuals. Belatedly, but not markedly, the stock companies carried out varying degrees of cost-saving selling practices which reduced their average brokerage percentage and the number of companies offering deviating (from bureau rates) or participating policies increased.

Comments on the Current Situation

The success of the mutuals in property and liability insurance has forced reductions of stock company rates relative to their costs. The mutuals in turn have experienced reduced underwriting profits and even losses in several years. This does not necessarily forecast financial difficulty. Both stock companies and mutuals have earnings on very large investment portfolios relative to their insurance liabilities. These portfolios were built up over decades largely by transfers from underwriting profits and serve as a general reserve against large underwriting losses.[38]

Nevertheless, much concern is expressed about this situation in the insurance journals. Continued underwriting losses forecast reduction of the investment portfolio and lesser capacity to enlarge the insurers' volume of insurance. These possibilities are potentially serious for the mutuals for they cannot acquire equity capital by sale of stock.[39]

At the same time a debate has occurred about whether earnings (and possibly realized capital gains) from investments should enter computations of the necessary levels of insurance rates. The weight of economists' analysis points to an affirmative answer.[40] By 1972 about half of the states required that investment income be considered in determining the level of rates that may be charged by property and liability insurance.[41]

There is little reason to view the stock company-mutual competition as undesirable or as a serious threat to the industry. Competition has forced some economy in acquisition costs of the typical stock company, and possibly also in the liberality of settlements of loss claims under policies that are sold through brokers that do not represent a particular company. At the same time the mutual cannot, other than temporarily, charge rates that result in underwriting losses and certainly not losses that eat into investment assets.

These are unique features of stock company-mutual competition, traceable in part at least to state regulation. But adjustments forced by the mutuals' competition have benefited buyers of insurance.

13

Financing Cooperatives and Mutuals

A common thread runs through the preceding chapters: at the time of their founding cooperatives have difficulty in obtaining member-supplied capital. This situation is inherent in the cooperative form of enterprise organization and goes far to explain the types of economic activity they enter. Subscriptions of owner-supplied capital are limited to what members are able and willing to invest. Exceptions occur where the federal government sponsors and supplies the original capital, which is later retired out of earnings.

The sponsors of a new mutual savings deposit institution subscribe only nominal amounts of capital. Less is known about insurance mutuals, but my impression is that sponsors of a new mutual provide very little capital.

The amount each member of a new cooperative or a sponsor of a mutual will subscribe can be expected to reflect one or more of three considerations. First is the member's degree of confidence that patronage of the cooperative or mutual will add to his income more than he could obtain from the best alternative investment of the money. Second, because the success of an enterprise to be owned by numerous patrons does not depend on the participation of any one of them potential members may adopt a "wait and see" stance. If the venture proves successful the hesitant potential members could then join, for nearly all cooperatives and all mutuals welcome additional members. Third, potential members—farmers, retailers, consumers—usually have limited capital in liquid form.

These considerations go far to explain the small initial scale and the low capital-output ratio of nearly all newly established cooperatives. The exceptions are few, and those are made possible by funds supplied by an outside source, usually public as in the cases of rural electrification cooperatives and the federally chartered agricultural credit institutions.

Newly formed mutuals do not need much capital. They can rent facilities. Sponsors subscribe to the operating expenses and start building its reserves pending the time when loans are made and interest income can be earned by a savings institution or policies sold by an insurance mutual.

Sources of Equity Capital

Several interrelated aspects of the formation and financing of cooperatives and mutuals in various types of economic activity are presented in summary form in table 13.1. Some entries in the table are qualified or expanded in the table's footnotes and also in later sections of this chapter.

A clear relationship is evident between those who sponsor cooperatives or mutuals in particular activities and the source of the enterprises' initial equity capital. Where potential patrons took the lead in forming the enterprise they usually supplied this capital. This relationship holds for the commodity-handling cooperatives regardless of who the patrons are. Trade associations, farm organizations, and labor unions have aided in organizing insurance mutuals. Rarely have these organizations provided operating capital as distinct from paying some organizing expenses. New members of rural electricity and telephone cooperatives subscribe only nominal amounts.

Persons interested primarily in higher income from investment of savings or lower costs for insurance have not often either organized or provided the intitial capital of mutuals. There are exceptions among the insurance mutuals, usually those that have remained small and were initiated by potential members or by organizations of which they were members. Typically insurance mutuals and nearly all savings and investing mutuals were neither founded nor initially financed by persons seeking added income directly as member-patrons. While potential members at times led in forming credit unions the role of employers and social organizations was often important, and for the agricultural credit institutions the federal government's leadership was dominant. Sponsorship of mutual savings institutions and some capital subscription was often provided by persons involved in construction or other activities related to home ownership.

The far more important source of equity capital of successful cooperatives and mutuals has been additions to that capital obtained by withholding and adding to capital part or even all of the net savings (table
13.1, column 2B). The extent and forms these funds take vary con-
siderably and are sketched briefly in the following sections.

Farmer Cooperatives

For all local and regional farmer cooperatives, except REAs, members'
equity was almost three-fifths of total assets in 1954 and 1962 but had
fallen to 47 percent by 1970.[1] While the way in which members acquired
their equity differed widely among farmer cooperatives, for local and regional cooperatives as a group "almost 71 percent of the total allocated
[source can be identified] equity capital reported by the 7,289 local and
regional cooperatives in 1970 was acquired by retention of patronage refunds for payment at some future date. Fifteen percent was patron contribution by per unit capital retains from sales proceeds, and the other 14
percent was purchased outright by members, non-member patrons and
occasionally others."[2]

Most farmer cooperatives pay these retained funds in cash to continuing
and withdrawing members at later dates under the "revolving plan."[3]
This decision is strongly influenced by the income tax status of retained
savings, as will be seen below.

Consumer Cooperatives

Information on the financing of consumer cooperatives is far from
complete. Precise data are available only for food stores in the supermarket category. Additional information has been gleaned from conversations and correspondence with persons close to the operations of the
smaller and generally older cooperatives.

Upon joining, members are required to make very small and equal
subscriptions to the cooperative's capital. Some members may be per-
suaded to invest more and may receive interest-bearing notes. If the cooperative is successful additional capital is obtained from net savings
that would otherwise be paid as cash refunds. Comprehensive data are
available only for consumer cooperative food stores of supermarket
scale. During the years 1971-1972 through 1973-1974 the net savings of
these cooperatives as a group range between 1.3 and 1.8 percent of sales.
Because of the high turnover of inventory the return on assets of the
various cooperatives ranged between 5.3 and 7.6 percent of total assets.
Out of these net savings the reporting cooperatives on the average paid
patronage refunds ranging from 1.2 to 1.7 percent of sales.[4]

Until recently the rural electrification and telephone cooperatives (here
classified as consumer cooperatives) obtained their initial capital, and

Table 13.1. The Initiation, Financing, and Related Rights of Members of Cooperatives and Mutuals

Type of activity	Initiated by	Sources of equity capital		Right to share of equity
		A Initially	B Subsequently	
Commodity handling				
Farm marketing	Members, some by farm organizations	Members[a]	Retained earnings	Repaid, possibly delayed
Farm supply	Members; farm organizations	Members[a]	Retained earnings	Repaid, possibly delayed
Nonfarm business	Members primarily	Members[b]	Retained earnings	Repaid, possibly delayed
Consumer buying of Commodities	Members, unions, etc.	Members[a]	Retained earnings	Repaid, possibly delayed
Rural power and telephone	Federal agency	Members[c]	Retained[c] earnings	Repaid, possibly delayed
Mutual investing institutions				
Savings and loan associations	Persons in related businesses	Sponsors[d]	Retained[e] earnings	None
Mutual savings banks	Community leaders or persons in related businesses	Sponsors[d]	Retained[e] earnings	None
Mutual funds	Investment	[f]	[f]	Fully[g]
Cooperative borrowing institutions				
Cooperative agricultural credit agencies	Federal agencies	Federal government initially, now new members[h]	Retained earnings	Stock of locals retired or can be sold[i]
Credit unions	Consumers, employers, etc.	Members[e]	Retained earnings plus new membership fees	None
Mutual insurance	Members, trade associations	Sponsors[d]	Retained earnings principally[j]	None

[a]Generally equal amounts per member, but in some cases (e.g., some grain marketing cooperatives) initial investment varies with predicted patronage.

[b]Some types of these cooperatives require uniform initial investment in voting stock by all members, but this is minor compared to the required investment in nonvoting stock or in advance deposits that vary with some measure of the respective member's use of the coop-

erative's services. This applies not only to cooperatives that do not stock an inventory (e.g., the Associated Press and Associated Merchandising Corporation, which require an annual deposit according to the size of member's business) but also to cooperative wholesale warehouses owned by investor-owned firms.

ᶜNominal, for most capital obtained by federal government loans until recently (see chapter 9).

ᵈI assume that sponsors do not supply equal amounts of initial capital.

ᵉEquity capital does not appear as capital or retained net savings in balance sheets but consists primarily of surplus and general reserves.

ᶠExcept for preliminary outlays by the sponsoring investment firm, costs of organizing and operating the fund are paid by members when buying into the fund (front loan) and/or in annual charges. Either way, the members pay in proportion to their investment in the fund.

ᵍThe capital is the market value of the securities the fund owns. Each withdrawing member is paid his share of the fund's assets, except for the now rare charge of an "end load."

ʰThe borrowing member, however, presumably borrows 105 percent of loan in order to "buy" stock equal to 5 percent of the money advanced to him.

ⁱArrangements for repayment of the initial investment by a member have changed over time and differ among the various types of federally sponsored agricultural lending institutions, but a withdrawing member's share of retained net savings is not paid to him.

ʲSome mutuals charge membership fees.

most of that for expansion, by borrowing from the federal government. By the end of 1971 over a hundred of the 1092 REAs had retired their indebtedness out of net savings, and almost one-third of the total REA borrowings had been repaid.⁵ With rapidly rising electricity consumption in rural areas most REAs have invested net savings and have even borrowed more funds to add to their distribution capacity, while some have built generating plants.

Cooperatives Owned by Urban Businesses

The financing of these cooperatives differs quite sharply between those whose chief function is to act as buying agents for members and those that also carry inventories. Typically the operating costs of the former are financed by yearly advance deposits by members roughly in proportion to their actual or potential volume of business through the cooperative. Examples include the Associated Press and cooperative buying agents for medium-sized baking companies or for department stores.

Wholesale cooperatives that maintain a stock of commodities require a nominal purchase of voting stock plus either a substantial deposit or purchase of added but nonvoting stock (or debentures) roughly in proportion to the various members' volume. These cooperatives are in the grocery, hardware, drug, and building materials fields.

In addition to these sources of equity capital part or even all of net savings are withheld. For income tax reasons members' shares of withheld net savings are often distributed in the form of interest-bearing five- or ten-year debentures but which amount to member-supplied capital. Withdrawing members' deposits are refunded, nonvoting stock retired, and debentures paid off when due.[6]

Nothing will be added here to what was reported in chapter 8 about the limited development of transportation cooperatives owned by nonfarm shippers. Some of these have changed in the past decade or so to investor-owned form, in part at least in order to obtain more capital than members would supply.

Cooperative Borrowing Institutions

Because the original financing and subsequent retirement of the federal government's equity in the federal farm credit agencies was an essential part of the report on them in chapter 11, nothing is added here. This leaves the credit unions for brief comment.

Members of credit unions pay very small membership fees that qualify them to be depositors and potential borrowers. As depositors they are creditors of the credit union and provide nearly all of the funds it lends. The credit union's equity capital, or net worth, is built almost entirely out of the net income not distributed to members as depositors or, occasionally, as borrowers.[7] In the event of liquidation the members at that time are entitled to shares of net assets equal to their percentages of the deposits.

Mutual Investing Institutions

Since the initial and the subsequent financing of these savings deposit and investing mutuals has been detailed in chapter 10 only two points are emphasized here. The initial equity capital is usually provided by persons engaged in related activities such as home construction or who are concerned about the lack of savings deposit institutions in the locality. In the mutual's early years the sponsors are repaid out of net income. The reserves are built up to offset losses on loans, and the surplus account can be used when the current interest paid on deposits temporarily exceeds the mutual's income above operating expenses.

For all savings and loan associations, including stock associations, their net worth was only 5.8 percent of total liabilities in 1976.[8] As a further bulwark in the event of heavy withdrawals of deposits associations that are members of the Federal Home Loan Bank System (80 percent of the associations) may borrow from it, as many did in the late 1960s. Mutual savings banks that are members of the FHLB may do likewise.

Mutual funds are a unique case.[9] Since a mutual fund's assets consist of the market value of the securities it owns, plus a small amount of cash, it does not have a separate balance sheet entry for reserves. The investment concern that sponsored and manages the mutual fund does have a net worth, but this is not a part of the fund's assets.

Mutual Fire and Casualty Insurance Companies

To a considerable degree the account for the insurance mutuals parallels that for those engaged in receiving and investing savings. Local mutuals, most of which remained small, often charged small membership fees and also were aided by free time of sponsors. The mutuals that became large got advances from persons who expected to gain as agents or from other relations to the mutual and usually were repaid out of subsequent earnings. Capital for growth came from assigning to surplus a portion of each year's underwriting profits and income from the stocks and bonds in which the accumulated surplus had been invested. These surpluses have become gigantic, particularly for the old and large mutuals. The way they were built, the current debate about their adequacy, and whether the current income and capital gains realized from securities should be considered income when determining whether insurance rates are adequate were considered in chapter 12.

Comparative Treatment of New, Continuing, and Retiring Members

Further insight into the financing of cooperatives and mutuals, and also into the extent to which they are fully sharing arrangements, is provided by a comparison of the treatment of new, continuing, and retiring members with respect to the equity capital attributable to them.

Note first how these problems are handled in the ordinary investor-owned corporation. The new stockholder of a going enterprise ordinarily buys outstanding stock in the market. He pays the market value of his pro rata share of the enterprise over and above its debts. This sum need not bear any close relationship to what the corporation's balance sheet shows as the book value per share of common stock, which is the sum of what the original purchasers paid into the corporation and the per share amount of accumulated undivided profits. When additional stock is sold the offering price reflects the management's estimate of the value the market will place on the stock. When a stockholder sells his shares the price depends on the value potential buyers place on it. By this means the stockholders can withdraw at will and obtain the market value of their respective pro rata shares of the corporation.

New members of cooperatives rarely make more than a nominal payment into the capital of the enterprise. A notable exception is the new members of cooperatives chiefly engaged in wholesaling and owned by nonfarm businesses. A new member's initial investment in these is related in amount of his expected volume and is substantial but may take the form in part of his promissory note. Also new members of local farm loan or production credit associations buy stock (equal to 5 percent of funds borrowed) but may do so by borrowing that much more. Otherwise new members either pay nothing or only nominal membership fees, as in consumer- and farmer-owned cooperatives and in small insurance companies. A nominal fee is charged new members of credit unions. Savings and investment mutuals and most insurance mutuals charge new members nothing.

Consequently, upon joining financial mutuals, credit unions, and farm and consumer cooperatives, and to a lesser degree retailer-owned wholesale cooperatives, the new member benefits immediately from the enterprise's use of past withheld net savings attributable to the patronage of the old members. In the financial mutuals and credit unions this capital includes not merely the withheld net savings attributable to the patronage of present members but also that of former members, often of decades previously. In contrast most commodity-handling cooperatives "rotate" withheld earnings, and present and former members benefit often tardily but roughly in proportion to patronage. To varying degrees the new member immediately gets the advantage of the accumulated investment made by old members. Do these practices result in subsidization of new members?

Answering that question depends in part on the extent to which a withdrawing member is paid the share of the cooperative's or mutual's net worth attributable to his patronage. Rarely if ever is the withdrawing member of a mutual or cooperative financial institution paid any of the net savings attributed to his patronage that had been withheld and added to the financial enterprise's reserves and surplus. Furthermore only in the cooperative farm credit agencies is the withdrawing member repaid or allowed to sell the membership fee or stock subscription made upon joining.

Commodity-handling cooperatives, possibly including the REAs, are quite different. Recently the REA administrator suggested that the by-laws of each REA provide for payment to the heirs the remaining equity of a deceased member and for transfer of a member's claim to the future "capital credits" to "successors in interest or in occupancy."[10] Except for the small initial membership fee, a withdrawing member of consumer-, farmer-, or retailer-owned wholesale cooperatives can obtain past net savings attributable to the member's patronage. This may not be paid immediately because of the state of the cooperatives' finances.

This review indicates the varying degrees to which new members of established cooperatives and mutuals are subsidized in nearly all types of patron-owned enterprises by the current members and in financial mutuals and credit unions also by former members. The current members may approve because new members' volume may affect the cooperative's costs per unit favorably and offset the volume lost as old members withdraw. But none of this rationalizes the permanent withholding of net savings of withdrawing members, the practice of financial mutuals (except mutual funds) and of credit unions.

Income Taxation and the Accumulation of Capital by Cooperatives

After decades of controversy about whether cooperatives' net savings traceable to members' patronage should be subject to the federal corporate income tax, Congress worked out a system that potentially eliminates this tax on cooperatives. Consumer cooperatives are liable only for tax on net income attributable to nonmember business. Farmer- and retailer-owned cooperatives are chartered by states as corporations, usually under a special state law.

In order to minimize or eliminate the corporate tax on these cooperatives two steps can be taken. The cooperative must pay out each year at least a fifth of its net income as patronage refund, which are then subject to the members' personal income tax. Second, the cooperative must notify its members of their pro rata shares in dollars of the remaining net savings. The members then add these sums to their current taxable incomes. The effect of this law on the cooperative's operating capital is obvious. It can utilize up to 80 percent of its current net savings to augment its member-supplied capital or to pay previously withheld net savings. These provisions apply to retailer-owned wholesale cooperatives as well as to farmer-owned.

It should be added that investor-owned corporations with ten or fewer stockholders can elect to be taxed as a partnership in which each partner pays only his personal income tax on his share of the partnerhip's net income. Such partnership may compete with cooperatives in local markets. Of course single proprietorships are not subject to the corporate income tax.

Market Opportunity as the Source of Equity Capital

From the preceding sections emerge fundamental conclusions with respect to the financing of patron-owned enterprises. Setting aside the cases of financing (or guaranteeing of bonds) by the federal government the handicap of the very small initial investment by members has often been overcome. The cooperatives and mutuals whose efficiency and the conditions in the market entered enable them to generate net income usually add part or all of that money to their equity capital. This occurs often even though the cooperative or mutual is short of efficient size and smaller than its rivals. But the latter have not responded promptly by added efficiency, better prices to patrons in deposit or lending terms, or types or rates for insurance to forestall well-managed patron-owned enterprises from obtaining and re-investing substantial savings. By this means the latter attained the scale needed for doing well even though rivals' terms to patrons improved.

There are two qualifications to this conclusion. There must have been an opportunity for entry; the notable case of its absence except in some localities and periods has been in food retailing. The other qualification is the ineptness of management, a characteristic of many newly established ventures generally, but possibly more prevalent among cooperatives than the record suggests among mutuals.

The investor-owned firms in the various economic activities studied here have complained about government preference in various ways, with positive aid to patron-owned enterprises included. This was considered in the chapters dealing with the REAs, the federal farm credit agencies, and the mutual savings and investing agencies with respect to mortgage lending terms. In each case the particular public policy should be weighed against the validity of traditional lending policies of commercial banks, the mixed work relief versus improvement of rural life subsidy aspect of the REAs initially, minor preferences given to farmer cooperatives on occasion by the administration of federal programs, and the relevance of those issues today.

There remain two knotty issues. One that has arisen repetitively is the treatment of cooperative and mutual corporations—most patron-owned enterprises take that legal form—under the federal tax laws. The second, applicable to financial mutuals including those engaged in insurance, to credit unions, and to some degree to the farm credit agencies, is the absence of the members' right upon withdrawal from membership to his "share" of the mutual's equity. A similar issue has to do with who gets that equity in the event of the sale or liquidation of the mutual.

Sources of Borrowed Capital

The funds used by established cooperatives and mutuals need not be limited to equity capital. They may borrow from commercial banks if their credit standing satisfies the lenders. Indeed banks are the only institutions available as a credit source to cooperatives other than those farmer-owned. These other cooperatives include consumer cooperatives and cooperatives owned by nonfarm businesses.

Special federal loan agencies are available for farmer cooperatives and mutual investing institutions. The twelve district banks for cooperatives are such a source of loan capital to farmer cooperatives (see chapter 11). These banks are to a considerable extent the capstone of public policy toward farmer cooperatives. Likewise there are twelve district federal home loan banks to which savings and loan associations and mutual savings banks that are members of the Federal Home Loan Bank System can turn for loans. These loan agencies obtain the bulk of their funds by selling their bonds in the capital markets where their bonds have high credit ratings.

14

Entrepreneurial and Organizational Problems

The primary issue to which this study has been addressed is the efficacy with which groups of sellers or buyers can vertically integrate into the type of business of which they have been patrons.[1] Success in such ventures requires accurate appraisal of the opportunity for cooperative vertical integration. That opportunity exists where the established investor-owned firms' prices differ from necessary costs sufficiently to provide to a cooperative's members a higher return on capital than they could obtain from the best alternative use of the funds. The opportunity might exist if the patron-owned enterprise were able to develop monopoly power as the buying or selling representative of its members. The latter position to a significant degree has been attained by some farm marketing cooperatives, as was noted in chapters 4 and 5.

Once established the cooperative ordinarily faces issues with respect to the scope of its activity and its operating policies. How large must be its initial size in order to succeed in the long run? Later it must often decide whether to integrate vertically beyond the level entered initially. Should it enlarge the geographic area served and, if so, should it do so with another plant or merge with a cooperative already in the locality? The former choice may involve competition between cooperatives, a topic on which cooperatives' managements disagree. Operating policy decisions include the desirable or feasible degree of member control and whether

188

net prices to members should differ with the size of transactions or with their respective annual volume of business with the cooperative. A quite new issue is whether in some circumstances members' operations should be coordinated formally with those of the cooperative. Each of these topics will be considered briefly after reflections on the process and difficulties of initiation of patron-owned enterprises.

Initiation of the Cooperative or Mutual

A large number of patron-owned enterprises have been organized by persons whose only pecuniary reward could be from patronage but also many have been promoted by outside persons or groups. Two critical conditions for initial success are whether the enterprise must have substantial size in order to enter efficiently and the related issue of the amount of capital needed.

Initial Size for Effective Entry

Except in a few circumstances the primary economic units—consumers, savers, farmers, and relatively small urban enterprises—that have successfully carried out cooperative vertical integration initially formed only local market enterprises. The size needed for maximum efficiency in most of these activities was quite small, but most cooperatives and mutuals were not even that large at first. Insufficient volume has ranked high among the reasons for failure of farmer and consumer cooperatives and for liquidation of credit unions.[2]

Where the disequilibrium between established investor-owned firms' prices and necessary costs was wide enough and lasted long enough small but well-managed patron-owned enterprises have entered and obtained substantial net savings. Investing part or all of these savings in the enterprises rather than distributing the money as dividends aided them in achieving the efficiency required for long-period success. This was reported repeatedly in chapters 4-11 and summarized in table 13.1.

In some types of operations cooperatives and mutuals must start on a substantial scale if they are to fulfill their purpose. Several cooperatives owned by urban business enterprises had this characteristic. Examples include the Railway Express Agency, the Pullman Company, Associated Press, and Allied Van Lines,[3] but not the retailer-owned cooperatives. Had the federally sponsored agricultural credit institutions started on their own they would not have been of sufficient size initially to offer to investors a diversified portfolio of farmers' evidences of indebtedness as security behind the bonds sold in the general investment market. This handicap was offset by federal government sponsorship which included supplying the initial capital and detailed direction. Added was implied or actual government guarantee of the bonds sold by these credit institutions. Mutual insurance companies started on very small scales. Many failed, but others survived because stock companies' rates exceeded costs, and the well-managed mutuals thrived. But hundreds of mutuals insuring low-risk property remain quite small. Savings and loan associations were very small initially, but the likelihood of failure was reduced by the authorizing agency's appraisal of the need for the new association.

Effective action by farmer cooperatives in some situations required that members' volume represent a high percentage of the output of the product in a producing area. Many bargaining cooperatives have been organized in markets of small geographic size, which facilitated signing up a large portion of the volume, a precondition to effective negotiation.

Some cooperatives aimed for a large share of the market initially. It was logical for a cooperative to engage in aggressive merchandising of its brand in order for its sales promotion to be efficient. In contrast the ill-fated marketing cooperatives that undertook to control the price of a farm product in the 1920-1940 period often did not sign up a sufficient share of output for even temporary success. They acted like monopolists when they could not thwart expansion of members' and nonmembers' output. With some notable exceptions, the initial but not always enduring success of some fruit cooperatives in California stemmed in part from the time required for the growers to expand capacity in response to prices the cooperative obtained. In several situations prices were held above the long-run equilibrium level and the expanded capacity then forced prices to, or below, production costs for most of the output. The overwhelming percentage of successful farm marketing and supply cooperatives started as very small enterprises.

Potential Members As Promoters

To a significant degree the doubt expressed earlier as to whether small economic units could initiate cooperative vertical integration has not been borne out. Most farmer-owned cooperatives, early building societies, and local mutual fire insurance mutuals were started by potential members, usually in a locality and on a small scale. They engaged in simple buying or selling, home financing, or insuring operations. Only in dairy products did a large number of cooperatives engage in manufacturing. For local cooperatives and mutuals the only information needed to judge prospects was the prices at the level at which the cooperative would buy or sell and its operating costs. Farmers could compare the published price of gasoline in Oklahoma, plus rail freight, with distributors' prices in the north central states. Anyone good at figures could work out the deposit and lending programs of the early self-liquidating, fully cooperative building societies. The rates that a local insurance mutual should charge required an estimate of the probability of farm building fire losses. On the other hand the failure rate among consumer cooperatives has been high except in a few localities.

Often they, and at times farmer cooperative ventures also, were started because of the decline of workers' incomes or of farm prices. But these adverse conditions did not necessarily indicate monopoly in handling a farm product or in local retailing. Consequently the cooperatives' failure rate was high. Some of the California fruit cooperatives tried to hold up prices when excess capacity developed; they had hard sledding for decades. Nearly all regional or national cooperatives designed to hold up prices when they had no effective control of supply failed in that objective. Add the prices of rivals aimed at destroying cooperatives (chiefly in decades past) and the not infrequent inept cooperative management, and it is not surprising that the failure rate among farmer cooperatives was high for decades,[4] although not clearly above that of small ventures generally.

Well-conceived cooperative and some mutual ventures that required larger scale initially and more capital per member were established by nonfarm investor-owned enterprises. Some of these were of substantial scale in their primary activity. Their managements were able and willing to devote time and money to promoting cooperative vertical integration. Usually only a relatively small number of members was needed to provide the initial volume for cooperatives such as the regional news-gathering cooperatives later combined to form the Associated Press, for retailer-owned cooperative wholesalers, and even for the factory mutual fire insurance companies. Each potential member had a substanial stake in the collective venture. Whether he participated or not would have affected significantly the chances that the cooperative or mutual would be organized. But forming the mutual insurance companies owned by small urban enterprises was usually aided by the leadership of well-rewarded agents or managers of a trade association.

Promotion by Outside Persons or Groups

As has just been suggested, more frequently for mutuals than for successful cooperatives whose potential members were small economic units, the leadership has been provided by persons or organizations not motivated by the prospect of gain as members. Individuals selling equipment or wishing to dispose of a plant that a cooperative would use, or who wanted a better job than they had, have on occasion "sold" potential members on asserted gains from a cooperative. Failure has been frequent in such cases. In recent decades savings and loan associations and to some degree mutual savings banks have been organized by persons who expected officer positions in the institution or who owned a type of business related to the associations' operations and expected added volume to be obtained in that activity. Most mutual funds have been formed by enterprises which expected to gain in their primary activity (such as investment advising). Some very successful mutual insurance companies have been founded by individuals who expected to gain by commissions for promoting membership and purchases of insurance policies. Established farmer cooperatives have sponsored insurance mutuals. Credit unions have been aided by their members' employers and by labor unions and other groups.

Organizations of farmers for political and social ends, labor unions, and trade associations of urban enterprises have sponsored cooperatives or mutuals.[5] In the nineteenth century farm and labor organizations sponsored cooperatives for reasons not infrequently based on the assumption of an inherent advantage in cooperatives. These experienced high failure rates. The record has been far better in recent decades, particularly in the sponsorship of farm supply cooperatives by statewide or larger farm associations. Trade associations have had a good record in sponsoring insurance mutuals.

Government agencies have helped form cooperatives through publicity work and by specific acts of sponsorship. Aid has varied from the county agricultural agent organizing a cooperative for shipping pooled cars of lambs, through almost "buying" the formation of cooperatives under the Farm Board program of the 1930s because of the extent to which aid was funneled through cooperatives, to providing milk market order prices as an alternative to dealer-cooperative bargaining in fluid milk markets. The federal government led in organizing rural electrical and telephone cooperatives and the now essentially cooperative agricultural credit institutions and provided initial financial aid in both cases.

Role of Strong Personalities

One cannot read of the early history of many cooperatives and of some mutuals that have become large without noting the influence of men of unusual leadership ability. Not infrequently an enthusiastic leader has stirred interest in organizing a cooperative or incited loyalty to one in being at a critical time. But this role has not been effective for long except where the market reached by cooperative vertical integration proved to be clearly better than the one in which the members would otherwise buy or sell individually. Unfortunately in the pre-1940 history of cooperatives a few persons who had these persuasive powers were charlatans and others had more capacity to make ringing appeals than to judge the potential pecuniary advantage to members.

Of more certain and lasting influence have been leaders who were highly competent as well as persuasive. One cannot think of the Sunkist Growers without recalling the names of Powell and more recently of Armstrong, or of Land O' Lakes without the long and effective leadership of Brandt, or of the Washington Farmers' Association without Manton and, for decades, Beernink. Similarly factory fire insurance mutuals owe much to Taylor, and the vast State Farm Mutual to the vision of Mecherle.

Organizational Structure and Policies

In summarizing these features of cooperatives and mutuals, the objective is to compare or contrast their structure and policies with the "Rochdale principles" on the one hand and with the investor-owned enterprises on the other. The topics range from terms of ownership and degree of member control through form and direction of growth and the means thereof.

Term of Membership

The terms of membership in large-membership cooperatives and mutuals vary somewhat but rarely are onerous. Relevance of the prospective member's primary activity is taken care of by his interest in membership. Not often is attention paid to how well the prospective member conducts his primary activity, but ability to pay cash if a buyer or to wait for payment if a seller is often a de facto condition for membership. Only in buying cooperatives owned by urban businesses is attention paid to whether a new member competes in his primary activity with old members. Only in some businessmen's cooperatives and in the farm loan cooperatives is more than a small and usually equal capital subscription required. Members of some cooperatives, but not of mutuals, may be required to contract to do business exclusively with the cooperative.

For the most part the democratic features of membership are followed at least formally in cooperatives but not in most mutuals. One member, one vote is the rule in consumer and in nearly all farmer- and retailer-owned wholesale cooperatives.[6] Except in insurance mutuals associated with farmer or professional organizations members do not vote. Even formally members of mutual savings banks have no vote. Through the device of having members of savings and loan associations assign a proxy whereby the management votes for members, the latter have no control except through their behavior as depositors.

Some cooperatives campaign to increase member participation in annual meetings. Examples include consumer cooperatives, credit unions, REAs, and the farm credit institutions. Farm cooperatives do likewise, but the percentage of members that actively participate in the affairs of the larger cooperatives is usually small, although generally higher than in voting in person in large investor-owned corporations. Members of cooperatives owned by such nonfarm firms as retail stores and the Associated Press participate more directly in the cooperative's affairs.

Mutuals generally welcome additional members, and so do cooperatives except in businessmen's cooperatives where the new member would compete with an old member in his primary activity. Except in the latter case new members usually are substantially subsidized in the sense that they benefit at once from the capital past and current members have supplied out of retained earnings.

Limits on Membership in Many Businessmen's Cooperatives

Cooperatives (but not mutuals) owned by nonfarm firms often select members but not to limit the size of the cooperative.[7] Logically an application for membership by a close competitor of one or more old members is ordinarily denied in a line of business where members' enterprises are identified to the public by some common designation, such as Certified Stores of Chicago. Otherwise, additional noncompetitive members are welcomed by businessmen's cooperatives. Typically each member subscribes to the cooperative's equity capital and may vote on the basis of some measure of potential or actual patronage.

Growth Through Centralized or Federated Organizations

Growth of a cooperative into another geographic market or vertically can be carried out by means of a "centralized" or of a "federated" form of organization.[8] In the former a successful cooperative enterprise builds or purchases additional establishments in other localities, usually to engage in the same kind of operation. Often it also owns and operates plants that carry out the further vertical integration. Some substantial farm marketing and supply cooperatives and recently a few consumer cooperatives have expanded this way. Most cooperatives owned by businessmen are of the centralized type. Savings and investing mutuals have established branches where permitted by regulatory authorities.

Quite different is the federated form in which a number of locals form a "super cooperative" owned by them and not directly by their members. The super cooperatives may then take the lead in establishing local cooperatives in other localities. Except in a few cases where the federated organization is not much more than a trade association its primary function is to carry out further vertical integration two steps or more removed from the members' primary interest. Most farm supply and some marketing cooperatives are of this federated sort. Quite different in purpose are the subsidiaries established by large mutual insurance companies to engage in different types of insurance than that of the parent enterprise.

Which form of growth has been used does not reflect a clearly identifiable principle, and often has emerged from the history of the particular cooperative. One finds both the centralized and federated forms in agricultural marketing and in the farm supply business. Some successful consumer cooperatives operate branch stores.

One aspect of operations does indicate the relative effectiveness of the two forms. The federated is adapted to situations where the members of the locals produce or buy a standardized large-volume product. Then the cooperative's task is merely to minimize the costs between the locals and the prices in a more nearly perfect vertically placed market, two or more transaction steps removed from the members of the locals. Wheat and cotton marketing cooperatives are examples of this sort.

In contrast, where the cooperatives' success depends on market development a centralized cooperative's authority to coordinate selling of all members' output or buying of goods tends to be more efficient. A federated cooperative could have trouble, as did the Challenge Cream and Butter Association of California and Idaho, when its promotion of its brand of butter and of evaporated milk was undermined on occasion when autonomous locals reduced their output of butter because other dairy products were more profitable.[9] The merchandising of California citrus fruit by the Sunkist Growers has worked well but perhaps because Sunkist has taken over some functions ordinarily performed by local units and has demonstrated to the members and managements of locals the reasons for doing so.

Competition between Cooperatives

No issue brings to the fore more incisively one's conception of the basic character of cooperatives and of their role in the market system than the question as to whether each of them engaged in a particular type of operation should have an exclusive territory. No overlapping territories are allowed among local or regional farm credit institutions. The members of a credit union are often employees of a particular plant or members of a social or religious organization. A mutual savings and loan or savings bank may be formed only when the regulatory authorities find that there is need for it in a locality. But once established they do not confine either their membership or their lending to an exclusive territory. Except where tied to another organization mutual insurance companies rarely limit their activity to a given area or to members of a given primary interest. Some commodity-handling or buying organizations owned by urban enterprises overlap territories, as do buying organizations owned cooperatively by bakers or by department stores. Retailer-owned grocery wholesalers' territories do not overlap very much. Active competition among farmer-owned cooperatives is not rare.

The benefit or loss from intercooperative competition turns on a central point. If patrons are induced to join and maintain active patronage of a cooperative when doing so is not of pecuniary advantage to them then competition among cooperatives has been held to be inconsistent with the "cooperative way." A long-time student of cooperatives seems to agree in this statement, noting the "spectacle of cooperatives tearing each other down—fighting for each other's business organization for farmers."[10] Surely there is no better path to the demise of a cooperative than to insulate it from fair competition, that is, rivals' prices that are not below their costs. If it cannot withstand the competition of another cooperative will it survive in competition with investor-owned enterprises?[11]

The market is the great proving ground. If an enterprise, cooperative or not, is too small or inefficiently managed, that fact can be judged best by comparison with the performance of rivals. In the short run if there are too many and too small enterprises, cooperative or not, they will be injured by rivalry with those larger or more efficient for other reasons. This testing eliminates the excess number, presumably the least efficient. The competition cooperatives face from investor-owned enterprises may not be enough, for the latter may be backward.

Mergers among Cooperatives

Competition among cooperatives, which usually arises because at least one of them has grown beyond its original geographic market, has often led to mergers. This does not explain the formation of the Associated Press, for consolidation of a number of individual city or regional news-gathering cooperatives provided better service. Most of the numerous mergers among farmer cooperatives during the last half-century were designed to reach a more efficient size when the local market area had been enlarged by the improvement of rural transportation. Initially farmer cooperatives attracted membership within the area that one establishment could serve patrons who traveled by horse and wagon. As roads improved and trucks became the transport means the area served grew and not infrequently led to geographic overlapping of memberships. Enlargement of the local cooperative by merger may be inhibited by attitudes and interests similar to those that have slowed down school and local government consolidations.

Yet the pressure for efficiency accounts for the bulk of the nearly 1000 mergers among farmer cooperatives recorded prior to 1956.[12] Much of it has been facilitated by improvements in rural transportation. More recently the annual issues of the Farmer Cooperative Service's *Statistics of Farmer Cooperatives* has attributed the declining number of farmer cooperatives primarily to mergers to achieve more efficient size. It is not surprising that mergers among local cooperatives manufacturing dairy products ranked first. Supply cooperatives, generally more recent in origin, accounted for the next largest number of mergers from 1940 to 1956. Nearly all the local cooperatives acquired were quite small. Usually both the acquired and the acquiring cooperatives were in the same line of business. Some mergers enhanced the cooperative's share of the usually enlarged geographic market. Recent large-scale mergers of supply cooperatives referred to in chapter 6 usually represented the joining of a less successful with an aggressive cooperative. The merging of market-wide milk bargaining cooperatives into multimarket associations and the purposes of this kind of action were dealt with in chapter 4.

Second-Step Cooperatives

After succeeding in the first step in vertical integration, that of the formation of a local cooperative, further vertical integration has proven to be of advantage in important commodity areas. Associated Press was formed for this purpose. But to provide a service, such as various aspects of transportation, cooperative vertical integration has not gone beyond the first step. Consumer cooperatives handling food have established a few wholesale warehouses. Building on well-established local operations farm marketing cooperatives have entered terminal marketing operations with considerable success. But most attempts, as in the 1920s, to establish numerous locals and a terminal market cooperative more or less simultaneously, sometimes with the added objective of influencing the product's price, were not successful. Most local farm supply cooperatives have joined federated cooperatives which purchase directly from manufacturers or to a lesser degree engage in manufacturing of large-volume supplies, such as petroleum products or fertilizer, used in farm production. In some markets large unitary cooperatives perform second-level functions for local branches.

Member and Management Roles

The establishment of the cooperative is only the beginning of problems of leadership and decision-making. Because conditions surrounding the cooperative do not stand still entrepreneurship is a continuing need. But in a large-membership cooperative, as the conditions that stimulated its formation become dim with the years, it is easy for each member to "let George do it." This is the result of the size of the cooperative and number of member-owners; the same owner attitudes hold in the typical investor-owned corporation with thousands of stockholders. An important point is the extent to which similarity of problems have led cooperatives and mutuals, as they have become older and larger and have faced new external conditions, to adopt de facto managerial procedures and policies analogous to those of investor-owned corporations.

Managerial Personnel and Their Rewards

The early history of cooperatives (excluding those owned by urban businesses and most mutuals) is replete with evidence of managerial incompetence. Among the reasons cited for farm marketing cooperative discontinuances during two-thirds of a century "difficulties in the field of management" ranked first.[13] Similar conclusions are stated in other studies and in the interpretive literature on cooperatives. Much of the difficulty has stemmed from lack of understanding by members and even by boards of directors of the managerial abilities needed in the activity into which they integrated cooperatively. Being inexperienced in that activity the members held the traditional view that "what happens in the dark" between them and the more distant market should not cost much nor require much managerial competence. To members of limited income the salaries paid by investor-owned enterprises seem unnecessarily large. Aside from these attitudes it was rarely possible decades ago to find managerial personnel who were both experienced and in sympathy with cooperative enterprises.

This situation has not proven to be permanent. An increasing number of men have had experience in going cooperatives. Enterprises lacking managerial talent can now recruit from among the younger men in the employ of successful cooperatives. Regionals have helped the locals select and train managers. Also as cooperatives have become less feared as reformist there has been less concern about hiring managers with an investor-owned enterprise background. The complaint of ineffective management of cooperatives is now much less frequent. I have been impressed by the high level of ability of officials, particularly of the regional cooperatives.

The worst of the early penny-pinching attitude toward managerial salaries has disappeared. This never was a problem in the large nonfarm mutual insurance companies. But cooperatives generally, even those owned by urban enterprises, do not now pay salaries for top managerial personnel comparable to their rivals. Salaries alone are the monetary reward in cooperatives, while top officers of investor-owned corporations often are given options to buy the company's stock at favorable prices and other arrangements that minimize the tax impact of larger payments. Insofar as monetary rewards select managerial personnel, cooperatives (but less so mutuals) are still at a disadvantage.[14]

Locus of Control and Leadership

The extent of members' direct control depends on the degree to which they can and do exercise their franchise. Only in mutual savings banks and at least in some mutual funds does membership not carry the voting right. While members of savings and loan associations have the right to vote, typically they assign that right to the management or do not know of or attend annual meetings. In some mutual insurance companies associated with cooperatives a member upon joining assigns his vote to the cooperative of which he is also a member. Typically members of other insurance mutuals would have to apply for a ballot; few do. In cooperatives or mutuals composed of few members, such as small local farmer cooperatives, fire insurance companies, or the typical cooperative owned by urban businessmen, each member's share of the total cooperative is enough to make him an active member and voter. Large commodity-handling cooperatives often attempt to minimize the individual members' feeling of infinitesimal influence by having members of a district of a centralized cooperative's operations elect a member of the cooperative's board. In federated cooperatives members vote in the local only. The board they select then votes for or elects representatives to vote for members of the board of the federated cooperative. Despite such arrangements and "get out the vote campaigns" most studies show that only a small percentage of members usually vote in the large membership cooperatives.[15] Rarely does the state law governing cooperatives permit the member to designate someone else to vote for him as his proxy.

While the management group of a cooperative or of a mutual formally includes the board of directors who can veto major decisions and replace salaried officers this does not mean that the board exercises leadership. Members that are not active officers may have only limited knowledge of the business. Board members re-elected for several terms do acquire some experience. Ordinarily the board disposes of what the active management proposes. Indeed were the board to concern itself about operations very closely, an essential degree of imagination and planning might be inhibited. Once the operation becomes too large or complicated to be under the eyes of its owners effectively initiative tends to come from the salaried management.

An interesting and unusual arrangement for centralizing authority and responsibility is provided by the "Kirkpatrick" cooperatives established and ultimately controlled by the Illinois Agricultural Association. The largest of these cooperatives was the Illinois Farm Supply Company,[16] which united in 1962 with the Iowa Farm Bureau Service to form FS Services, Inc. Most of the locals in Illinois have issued sufficient voting preferred stock to FS Services, Inc., for the latter to exercise control if it so desires. On occasion this "control" stock is voted to postpone consideration of, but very rarely to block, action that the statewide organization deems to be unwise. Most locals have a management contract with FS Services, Inc., which further integrates their operations with those of the regional wholesale which they own.

As cooperatives became larger and engaged in other than their initial simple operations de facto leadership and much decision-making by the managerial group was found to be advantageous. This is but a logical consequence where the individual member's percentage interest in the cooperative is tiny and parallels the nonvoting (except by proxies assigned to the management) by stockholders of large corporations.[17] But the management of the large cooperative is less insulated from member-owners, for the latter can record disapproval by ceasing patronage, except when bound by a contract. Otherwise members' effect on the management in all large-membership organizations is nominal, as is evident with respect to investor-owned corporations owned by thousands of stockholders. Compared to these corporations the position of the management in the large-membership cooperative or mutual may be less secure for it depends on members' patronage more than on their votes.

Some Operating Policy Issues

Several operating policy issues unique to cooperatives and mutuals stem from their purpose and organization. These include methods of maintaining or increasing volume, which may be done by enlarging the line of products or service, the bases for determining capital contributions, and net prices to members as affected by the composite of initial prices and patronage dividends. Quite different are the questions as to whether the cooperative should try to influence members' operations or itself attempt an innovative role. Distinct from innovation is the issue as to whether the cooperative should add to its line of products or services.

Maintaining or Increasing Member Patronage

Because the volume of cooperatives and mutuals depends basically on members' patronage these enterprises are concerned constantly about member loyalty. Only members are patrons of mutuals, but members do not necessarily do all of their savings or insurance business with a particular mutual. Also most cooperatives, even some owned by urban business firms, accept business from nonmembers. But this volume cannot be counted on and if membership and patronage are unattractive so is patronage by nonmembers. Cooperative enterprises attempt to retain member-patronage in one of two ways, in addition to pecuniary benefits.

One method, not as widely used now as formerly, is the patronage contract with a penalty for nondelivery. First used, it appears, by a grain cooperative in Iowa whose investor-owned rivals offered members unusually favorable prices, patronage contracts became quite widespread among farm marketing cooperatives at one time. The five-year contract used in the early history of the California Associated Raisin Growers was attacked by the federal government as monopolistic. It was replaced by a contract providing an annual period for withdrawal, as is provided by many marketing cooperatives that today use a "continuing contract." Patronage is optional for members of farm supply and consumer cooperatives and of mutual financial institutions. Nonpatronage may be the basis for dropping a member in some retailer-owned wholesale cooperatives.

The reduced use of patronage contracts and their complete absence in important areas reflects a long-term view that, while a dissatisfied member can be held as a patron by contract, he cannot be forced to renew the obligation. Long-term success would then have been sacrificed to short-term stability of volume.

Consequently most cooperatives and mutuals rely for member loyalty on the combination of financial benefits and member relations campaigns. The former comes to the fore when the governing body of the large-membership cooperative is deciding the percentage of net savings to pay as cash patronage dividends. The higher the dividends, presumably the more attractive is patronage. But if it stimulates much added volume more capacity will be needed. That calls for additional equity capital immediately or later to repay borrowed money which usually can come only from retained savings. In other situations added capital is required to improve efficiency so that the existing patronage can be held.

The alternative patronage-winning devices are quite similar to those investor-owned concerns use when wooing patrons. Included are the way employees deal with members in day-to-day business, the promptness of service, the handling of adjustments, and the variety of products or services handled. There is some advertising directed at members, particularly by large mutuals. More pointed are educational campaigns designed to acquaint members with the cooperative's affairs and with the advantage of cooperative membership. Regardless of technique cooperatives and mutuals are engaged in selling the advantages of membership and patronage.

Substantial expense to get volume is in conflict with the fact that often the opportunity for some cooperatives has stemmed from the high level of advertising, service, and credit outlays by investor-owned enterprises. Avoiding such expenses has been the key to the success of retailer-owned cooperative warehouses. In farm supplies, but much less so for consumer goods, persuading members to buy has cost much less per unit of transaction than rivals' cost of persuasion, particularly where members have accepted the cooperative's skill in buying. Some managements now assert that members' confidence enables them to add new products or services with minimal sales expense. Generally member relation expenses of cooperatives have increased in recent decades but not to the level of their rivals' advertising outlays.

Adding to the Line of Products or Services

Patronage often can be increased by adding to the line of products or services, but this is not necessarily wise, as has been learned. Some product-supplying cooperatives and some mutuals have expanded the number of commodities, services, or financial transactions in which they do business. Mutual insurance companies were started to provide one kind of insurance but most have added other kinds. Marketing cooperatives established to handle one commodity have added others and farm supplies. Nearly all cooperatives established for the latter business have enlarged their line but have not become general farm supply stores. Some went into foods—but most have dropped this line—and their postwar venture into household appliances can hardly be called successful. Consumer-owned retail stores started with dry groceries, and their survivors handle other food lines, but few offer clothing as do many consumer cooperatives abroad. Retailer-owned wholesale warehouses initially provided dry groceries only, but many now distribute frozen foods and even fresh produce and meats.

Generally the cooperatives and most mutuals studied here have been cautious about expanding the scope of their activities, giving extensive service, or advancing credit. Insurance mutuals often charge lower initial rates for larger policies or for longer-period fire insurance contracts. Some production credit associations now charge different interest rates according to the credit standing of the borrowers. Farm marketing cooperatives have pioneered in reflecting in payments to members the value in resale of various grades of a product. Expected differential gains on products have been minimized by selection of items to handle. Quantity discounts usually reflected in initial prices for large purchases have been introduced gingerly by supply cooperatives except where the discounts exist in their rivals' price structures. Where cooperatives pick up or deliver goods the charges often do not reflect the costs by length of haul. The only rationale for not doing so must be excess capacity in the cooperative establishment combined with rivals' prices that do not reflect differential transportation costs. An effective quantity discount device used by some retailer-owned grocery warehouses is the minimum weekly charge, which becomes less per unit as more and more is bought by the member. Some farm supply cooperatives supply building materials wholesale, and hardware cooperatives often pay different dividend rates on various categories of goods according to estimated net savings. By no means have all cooperatives succeeded in demonstrating to members the merits of equitable treatment as that is defined here.

What the above considerations show is that the opportunity for most commodity-handling cooperatives lies not in being like, but unlike, their rivals. That usually means handling fewer items, offering less service, and not advancing credit. Net prices to members reflecting these economies maximize the members' gain. The effect is that these cooperatives are in fact selective in membership but do not have a closed-door policy. Instead those that can gain most because investor-owned firms' price discriminate against them have been those who chose to walk into the cooperative's open door. Failure to reflect in net prices to them the net savings traceable to their patronage, possibly along with failure to reflect relative patronage in voting, could drive away cooperatives' most valuable members.[18]

Cooperatives' Influence on Members' Operations

Considering the gain from patronage motivation of cooperatives an interesting development is the extent to which these organizations undertake to influence the performance of their members. The purpose may be merely to enhance the efficiency of the member's operations so that his survival in his primary activity will be more certain. Such aid is provided chiefly by education and advice and is free to the member. Nearly all cooperatives owned by grocery retailers and by baking companies provide technical and merchandising aids to members. Farm supply cooperatives provide counsel on what feeds or fertilizers to buy and how to use them.

More drastic are the cases where the objective is to urge or even to require that the member hand over to the cooperative certain functions usually conducted by him or carrv on his primary activity in a way that coordinates with the functions of the cooperative. Factory fire insurance mutuals specify types of construction and fire prevention practices as terms of membership. A few cooperative grocery wholesalers take an active hand in members' operations so as to enable them to match chain store prices. Some regional farm supply cooperatives have a management contract with their locals, such as that used by FS Services, Inc.[19]

One authority argues that some agricultural marketing cooperatives should undertake to shape farmer-members' operations more drastically. He means much more than the Sunkist Growers' practice of deciding when a producer's fruit should be picked and having it done by its own crews in order to preserve product quality. Closer to what he proposes is the provision of the Western Farmers Association's marketing agreement with members, which sets forth the quality of eggs acceptable and the time and quantities of delivery. But this does not go as far as the prediction, based on the assertions that "much of the food-future is already here," for "the old separated or open markets in the food economy are gone," and that consequently "it may be necessary actually to restrict memberships to those farmers who understand the goal of this kind of operation" and who "agree prior to commencing production that they shall merchandise the products under the terms wanted by their customers."[20] This clearly overstates the situation for agricultural staples but may fit for the growing portion of output composed of the specialties.

Quite different in purpose is "contract farming," now widely practiced in poultry production and in some livestock feeding. Investor-owned processing or feed manufacturing companies finance the production of broilers and supply some part or even all of the feed, the facilities, and the chicks. The farmer operates on a margin and supplies labor and such other inputs as his sponsors do not and escapes much of the uncertainty of feed or broiler prices. Some see in this arrangement the transfer of the farmer from an enterpriser to a worker on commission.

Contract farming and its apparent efficiency poses a serious problem for cooperatives. If they were to develop similar relations with members, a move requiring substantial added capital, they would become more like a production cooperative with associated marketing. Possibly the needed funds could be gotten from the composite assets and credit of the members organized as a cooperative.

Interpretation and Summary

Cooperatives and mutuals initially have unique organizational-managerial features which tend to change with age and growth in size. In businessmen's cooperatives, but less so in mutual companies formed by them, member control remains direct and active. The same tends to hold for the local farmer or consumer cooperatives. In some cases when locals become members of a federated cooperative they become less autonomous de facto. In the large cooperatives and in mutuals generally leadership tended to pass into the hands of a managerial group. The same is true of large federated cooperatives.

The latter tendency has been strengthened where an opportunity for a positive posture exists. Expertness in development of programs, consistency of policies over an extended period, and coordination of operations at all levels in which the cooperative (central office and local units) operates are the new requirements. The adaptations made have been in response to size of the enterprise and the pressures of and opportunities in the market.

Cooperatives and mutuals that have gone through this process have evolved toward de facto centralized control and decision-making (in a management group) and often to the positive stance that characterizes large investor-owned corporations. This is not a criticism, for thereby cooperatives and mutuals show adaptability to internal and external developments without losing their hallmark, the distribution of gains on a patronage basis. The reduced member control of the larger cooperatives and the impossibility of its exercise in the large mutual insurance companies raises some issues, but these are no more fundamental for the cooperative or mutual than for the large investor-owned corporation. The fact that being a customer or supplier goes with membership in the former makes the individual member's approval or disapproval more effective than would be the exercise of his vote.

A more fundamental change in the member-cooperative relationship occurs where leadership by the cooperative affects the efficiency of the members' operations and the coordination of those operations with the functions of the cooperative. In these cases a new division of activity and leadership between the members in their primary activity and the cooperative may be in the making.

15
Effects of Entry
by Cooperative Vertical Integration

The preceding chapters have been studies in the vertical organization of markets. By that is meant the extent to which various steps in the production and distribution of goods are coordinated by common ownership of the operations at particular steps rather than by market transactions between autonomous sellers and buyers. The vertical integration represented by cooperatives and mutuals may be "downstream," as by a farm marketing cooperative, or "upstream," as by a consumer cooperative or retailer-owned wholesale cooperative. Not all of the activities examined in the preceding chapters, however, fit precisely into this characterization of cooperatives.

One is the bargaining cooperative. It is an alternative to actual engagement in the operation at the next vertical step, which may be to supply goods to be purchased or to market output. The bargaining is usually about terms of sale of the output of a group of farmers. The largest development of bargaining has been in markets for milk to be consumed in fluid form and in the sale of sugar beets and of some fruits and vegetables for processing. By presenting a united front sellers attempt to obtain a better price than the members individually could get from investor-owned enterprises.

The other category of enterprise studied that may appear not to fit into the cooperative vertical integration concept is the financial mutual. This issue does not arise with respect to the federally chartered agricultural credit institutions as they matured, for they and the credit unions are fully cooperative. Much the same can be said of many small insurance mutuals. The doubt arises most strongly with respect to the large fire and casualty insurance mutuals and less so for the mutual savings and investing institutions. They were quite like cooperatives in origin, but as they became older and larger, members ceased to be aware of their ownership. Generally they do not vote for the mutuals' officers. Yet these mutuals are in competition with their investor-owner counterparts, which are pressed to offer as good or better interest on deposits or insurance rates than do the mutuals.

When vertical integration is successful in enhancing the members' real incomes the economic effects take two forms. The direct consequence is the better transaction terms the cooperative or mutual provides for members than they could receive from investor-owned firms. A potentially larger economic influence occurs when the success of a patron-owned enterprise forces the cooperative's or mutual's rivals to offer better terms to their remaining patrons. Altogether, successful entry of cooperatives or of mutuals tends to discipline the markets entered.

The Process of Entry

In the industries studied in the preceding chapters the first step in successful cooperative vertical integration has been into the "vertically adjacent" activity of which the members would otherwise be suppliers or customers. This applies not only to commodity-handling cooperatives but also to mutual insurance or savings institutions. The bargaining cooperative is an alternative to a cooperative that would handle the commodity and is seen most clearly with respect to farmer cooperatives.

Except for bargaining cooperatives, successful entry by cooperatives and mutuals has usually been on a small scale. Attempts have been made to establish farmer commodity-handling cooperatives that would encompass a substantial portion of the regional or even of the national market. Such cooperatives rarely succeeded for long. Instead successful cooperative activity usually encompassed a locality and rarely required a large investment in plant and equipment. Except for plants to process milk and some fruits and vegetables into storable products, most successful cooperatives were established merely to handle goods that members had for sale or wished to purchase.

Over time the vertical integration has frequently not stopped with entering the virst vertically placed activity. Once the first-step vertical integration has been established further integration into a second step has become feasible in a number of cases. Examples include local cooperatives handling petroleum products which, when well founded, integrated into petroleum wholesale distribution and later into refining and crude oil production. Similarly the formation and operations of regional grain marketing cooperatives represented second-step operations. Groups of dairy product cooperatives have formed associations to represent them in consuming markets.

Comparison with Bain's Entry Analysis

Of the twenty industries studied by Joe S. Bain in his path-breaking investigation of the conditions of entry into manufacturing industries (*Barriers to New Competition* [1956]) four are processors of farm products and three are producers of equipment or of petroleum products used in farming. Of these industries, Bain ranked canning fruits and vegetables to be quite easy to enter and meat packing and bakery flour milling as very easy to enter. Three industries were ranked as very difficult to enter: cigarette manufacture and the production and sale of large and complex farm machinery and of tractors. These estimates have proved out. Difficult but less high entry barriers characterize petroleum refining, which farmer cooperatives have successfully entered.

Some of the preceding chapters relate to the industries just listed. Despite the low barriers to entry into meat packing or bakery flour milling cooperatives have attempted only a little of the former and that not successfully. In my judgment the explanation is that these industries are quite competitive and hence do not invite entry. Significantly the chain food stores have not entered by vertical integration into either of these industries. Bain estimates that entry into fruit and vegetable processing is less easy but not seriously so. Cooperatives do a significant percentage of this operation.

More difficult to impossible for farmer cooperatives to enter characterizes the remaining three industries, according to Bain. Consumer preference for established brands of cigarettes built by advertising poses an impossible barrier to a cooperative or to almost any entrant. To enter the large-scale and complex farm machinery industry would involve hundreds of millions of dollars to build efficient large plants and to gain farmers' confidence in the equipment produced. The same holds for modern tractors. Cooperatives have not entered any of these three industries.

According to Bain petroleum refining is moderately difficult to enter because of the cost of an efficient refinery and buyers' preference for established brands. But the cooperatives have entered and supply 35 percent of farmers' purchases of petroleum products, as was reported in chapter 7. The explanation of this entry is found in that chapter. It is a combination of the investor-owned firms holding a price umbrella high enough that cooperatives could buy from small refiners at prices below what the large refiners charged distributors and the cooperatives then reselling the petroleum at prices significantly below what large investor-owned refiners charged for their branded products. Later the cooperatives amassed enough net savings to enter refining and some crude production and to engage in low-cost water and pipeline transportation of crude oil and of refined products.

Concluding Comments

The successful entry of cooperatives or mutuals disciplines the markets in which they engage. Their entry means loss of volume by the established investor-owned firms. They may be forced to operate on lower margins to survive. To that extent successful entry by cooperatives or mutuals does not fully measure their economic impact.

With two exceptions the preceding chapters portray cooperatives and mutuals as a competitive influence on markets entered. One exception is the fluid milk markets, particularly where the cooperatives are able to bargain for prices above those set in federal market orders. The other exception is where the cooperatives handle the dominant portion of the market supplies, as for the six fruit and nut marketing cooperatives listed in table 5.2.

Mutual savings and investing institutions provide the means of investing members' money in mortgage loans. In both activities these mutuals are now active competitors of commercial banks and for mortgage loans of the life insurance companies.

Mutual fire, casualty, and cooperative insurance is an alternative to insurance bought from investor-owned firms.

In sum, cooperatives and mutuals typically contribute to competition in the markets entered with beneficial effects. The members are the primary beneficiaries of these enterprises' entry and growth. At the same time the remaining investor-owned firms in the markets entered are pressed to offer better terms to their remaining customers.

In Bain's entry analsyis, vertical integration by established firms is a barrier to the entry of a new enterprise. In order to compete a new firm might have to integrate into raw material production, for example, or undertake distribution of its products. This would require substantial additional capital above that needed to enter only one step in the production-distribution processes.

In the preceding chapters vertical integration is inherently the means whereby groups of suppliers or of customers enter the market in which they would otherwise sell or buy. This is the essence of the cooperative or of the mutual. They are group mechanisms whereby the suppliers or customers do business at one or more vertical steps removed from members' primary activity.

NOTES
INDEX

Notes

1: The Cooperative Form of Enterprise

1   Readers may be surprised at the pairing of cooperatives and mutuals. Neither term is used consistently, i.e., "cooperative" for a group involved in commodity handling or rendering services and "mutual" for a group in financial activities—as will be seen in chapters 10-12 inclusive.
2   This is not true of mutual savings banks (owned by no one, as is noted in chapter 10), and the ownership of large mutual insurance and mutual savings and loan associations is far from clear (see chapters 10 and 12). Only recently have members fully owned the federally sponsored agricultural credit banks (see chapter 11).
3   Net savings of the enterprise may be reflected in initial prices to members, in subsequent patronage dividends, or partially or fully in added equity capital of the enterprise to members.
4   Most commodity or service cooperatives permit, perhaps with a lag, withdrawing members to obtain their shares of the equity capital, but financial mutuals rarely follow this practice.
5   J. A. Schumpeter, "The Creative Response in Economic History," *Journal of Economic History* 7 (1947): 149-151.

2: The Cooperative in Economic Theory

1   Quite different conclusions about whether the open-end cooperative is a firm (in economists' usage of that term) are found in the literature. I. V. Emelianoff's *Economics of Cooperation* (privately printed, Washington, D.C., 1948) compares views of European and American writers and concludes that (implicitly) the open-end cooperative is not a firm as that term is used in economic theory, for the surplus above costs is "accounts payable to or receivable from the aggregate on their [patron-members'] current transactions" (p. 251). Stephen Enke's "Consumer Cooperatives and Economic Efficiency," *American Economic Review* 35 (1946): 148-155, recognizes that the cooperative's function is to maximize members' benefits but is not always clear as to whether it is the group's or the individual member's benefits. In *American Cooperation* (Washington, D.C.: American Institute of Cooperation, 1960) George Mehren argues that "the association, not the member, is the firm in making decisions . . ." (p. 16), but that is true only so long as the individual member gains as much or more from patronage. The

most rigorous statement, similar to the theory of the open-end cooperative presented here, is that of Richard Phillips in "Economic Nature of the Cooperative Association," *Journal of Farm Economics* 35 (1953): 74-78, which builds on Frank Robotka's "A Theory of Cooperation," *Journal of Farm Economics* 29 (1947): 94-114. An identical stand is taken in a recent statement by Franz C. Helm in the *Economics of Cooperative Enterprise* (London: University of London Press, 1968), pp. 3, 4.

Quite different is the position of Peter Helmberger and Sidney Hoos in "Cooperative Enterprise and Organization Theory," *Journal of Farm Economics* 44 (1962): 275-290. They contend that a cooperative is an organized enterprise and is a firm because in large part management controls it. It is a vertically integrated firm (members plus the cooperative) brought under a single managerial control. But that managerial control (of the cooperative, not of the members' activities out of which their patronage arises) does not change the fact that in an open-end cooperative the real test of control is patronage, and members are free to be patrons or not, as sponsors of consumer cooperatives have often learned.

The closed-membership cooperative is clearly a firm, as is shown on pages 13 and 20. Unfortunately much of the literature does not explicitly distinguish between open-end and closed-membership cooperatives, though implicitly the usual discussion fits the open-end type.

2 The cooperative is then an association of many such relatively small "firms" or maximizing units. A brief summary of the literature on whether the open-membership cooperative is a firm is presented ibid.

3 For a challenging exploration of the leadership problem in various types of organizations, see Mancur Olson, *The Logic of Collective Action* (Cambridge, Mass.: Harvard University Press, 1965).

4 See Helmberger and Hoos, "Cooperative Enterprise and Organization Theory, 26-27."

5 This theoretical analysis of farm marketing cooperatives' exercise of monopoly power follows Peter Helmberger, "Cooperatives as a Structural Dimension of Farm Markets," *Journal of Farm Economics* 41 (August 1964): 603-607, 610-611, from which figure 3 is adapted.

6 For further analyses of worker cooperatives in Communist countries see Benjamin Ward, "The Firm in Illyria: Market Syndicalism," *American Economic Review* 48 (September 1958): 566-589; and Evsey Domar, "The Soviet Collective Farm as a Producer Cooperative," *American Economic Review* 56, no. 4 (September 1966): 734-756.

3: Entry by Cooperatives or Mutuals

1 See Joe S. Bain's path-breaking study, *Barriers to New Competition* (Cambridge, Mass.: Harvard University Press, 1956), pp. 1-41.

2 The list of potential entry barriers spelled out here differs somewhat from Bain's list.

3   Some writers have misunderstood Bain's statement on this point for his definition applies no matter who the entrant is (see Bain, *Barriers to New Competition,* p. 2). But in his empirical work, particularly when estimating the height of the entry barriers and relating their height to the organization of the market, Bain does not consider whether these barriers in fact would seriously inhibit entry by *established* enterprises.

4   In an essay in *Monopolistic Competition Theory: Studies in Impact,* ed. Robert E. Kuenne (New York: Wiley, 1967), pp. 170-180, I have developed more fully the reasons why problems of selling are ordinarily more difficult than those of purchasing.

4: Cooperative Marketing of Farm Products

1   Operating margins of distributive trades are quite stable over time. See Harold Barger, *Distribution's Place in the American Economy Since 1869* Princeton, N.J.: Princeton University Press, 1955), p. 92.

2   The figures cited in this paragraph are from, or computed from, data in "Changes in Farm Production and Efficiency: A Summary Report," USDA, *Statistical Bulletin No. 233* (1971): 29; and the USDA *Agricultural Statistics* (1910): 415, 477, (1972): 562. This dramatic development is not attributable solely to on-the-farm efficiency. Actually the power of earlier years (horses fed farm-produced feed) and the fertilizer used (manure) are now produced almost entirely off the farm in the form of tractors, petroleum products, and commercial fertilizers.

3   R. H. Elsworth and Grace Wanstall, "Farmers' Marketing and Purchasing Cooperatives 1863-1939," Farm Credit Administration, *Miscellaneous Report 40* (1941). A later report by W. W. Cochane and R. H. Elsworth, "Farmers' Cooperatives Discontinuances, "Farm Credit Administration, *Miscellaneous Report 65* (1943), examined the life history of nearly 15,000 farmer cooperatives that disappeared prior to 1940.

4   I estimated the cooperatives' share of farm marketings in the years prior to 1950-1951 by using cash receipts from farm marketings as reported in USDA *Agricultural Statistics* (1952): 691-692, and cooperatives' volume as reported in Anne L. Gessner, "Statistics of Farmer Cooperatives," 1959-60, Farmer Cooperative Service, *General Report 103* (1962): table 9 and appendix table 7. Since reported cooperative volume for the years before 1950-1951 included marketing cooperatives' farm supply volume, I deducted the latter back through 1935-1936 by use of estimates in note 4 to appendix table 7 of the Gessner report. For earlier years I deducted a progressively lower percentage to remove farm supply business to 1925, when I assumed that volume was zero. Also, except for 1935-1936 for which an estimate can be made by use of the net volume prior to 1950-1951, I assumed a gradually falling percentage of intercooperative business to 1935-1936, data for which are supplied in table 48 of Farm Credit Administration, *Bulletin 26* (1938). For the years prior to 1935-1936 I assumed (arbitrarily) that the percentage fell slowly back to 1925 and then more rapidly to a 5 percent level in 1913.

5   This summary was written by staff members of the Federal Trade Commis-
    sion in their *Staff Report on Agricultural Cooperatives* (1975): 45, 46. I have
    relied on this source in reporting the essential features of most of the court
    decisions considered on the following pages.

6   George C. Tucker, "Need for Restructuring Dairy Cooperatives," Farmer
    Cooperative Service, *Service Report 125* (1972): 2-4.

7   As shown by the more rapid increase of population than of class 1 deliveries
    in federal milk marketing areas. See USDA *Agricultural Statistics* (1972):
    450.

8   Federal Trade Commission, "Cooperative Marketing," *Senate Document
    No. 95*, 70th Cong., 1st sess., 1928, pp. 9, 10.

9   Herman Steen, *Cooperative Marketing* (New York: Doubleday, 1923), pp.
    156, 157.

10 Dana Durand and Frank Robotka, "Cooperative Creameries and Cheese
    Factories in Minnesota, 1914," Minnesota Agricultural Experiment Station,
    Bulletin 166 (1917): 27; B. H. Hibbard and Asher Hobson, "Cooperation in
    Wisconsin," Wisconsin Agricultural Experiment Station, *Bulletin 282*
    (1917): 10.

11 W. W. Fetrow and R. H. Elsworth, "Agricultural Cooperation in the United
    States," Farm Credit Administration, *Bulletin 54* (1947): 53.

12 H. H. Bakken and M. A. Schaars, *The Economics of Cooperative Market-
    ing* (New York: McGraw-Hill, 1937), p. 52; and A. H. Benton, "Marketing
    Dairy Products," North Dakota Agricultural Experiment Station, *Bulletin
    182* (1924), pp. 11-15.

13 By 1914 an estimated 61 percent of the butter produced in Minnesota was
    made in cooperative plants (Durand and Robotka, "Cooperative Creameries
    and Cheese Factories in Minnesota," p. 11), and in the three-state area of
    Wisconsin, Minnesota, and Iowa percentage was 65 in 1925 (Theodore
    Macklin and Marvin A. Schaars, "Cooperative Butter Marketing in Wiscon-
    sin," Wisconsin Experiment Station, *Bulletin 401* [1928]: 8).

14 Estimated by dividing the net dollar sales of butter by cooperatives in 1936
    (Farm Credit Administration, *Bulletin 26*, p. 92) and then by the average
    price of 90-score butter in Chicago. This puts the cooperatives' physical vol-
    ume at 670 million pounds, which was 40 percent of national output.

15 Bakkan and Schaars, *Economics of Cooperative Marketing*, pp. 52, 63.

16 Paul E. Quintus, "Operating Methods of Challenge Cream and Butter Asso-
    ciation," Farm Credit Administration, *Circular C-119* (1940): 1-3; and
    William H. Nicholls, "Post-War Developments in the Marketing of Butter,"
    Iowa Agricultural Experiment Station, *Research Bulletin 250* (1939): 369.

17 National Commission on Food Marketing, *Technical Study No. 3* (1966):
    tables 17.24, 18.15, 19.33.

18 Frank Robotka and G. C. Laughlin, "Cooperative Organization of Iowa
    Farmers' Creameries," Farm Credit Administration, *Bulletin No. 14* (1937):
    13, 70, 71; and T. W. Manning, E. Fred Koller, and O. B. Jesness, "Minne-
    sota Dairy Cooperatives," Minnesota Agricultural Experiment Station,
    Bulletin 420 (1953): 4, 5.

19 William H. Nicholls, "Post-War Developments in the Marketing of Cheese," Iowa Agricultural Experiment Station, *Research Bulletin 261* (1939).

20 For an analysis of relative farm returns, see R. W. Manning, Ralph Fedberg, and R. C. Kristjanson, "Milk or Cream: Which is More Profitable for South Dakota Farmers and Creameries," South Dakota Agricultural Experiment Station, *Bulletin 460* (1957).

21 For an unusually informative analysis of what are often denoted "nonprice" influences of farmers' choice of buyers, see Robert L. Clodius, Darrell F. Fienup, and R. Larry Kristjanson, "Procurement Policies and Practices of a Selected Group of Dairy Processing Firms," Wisconsin Agricultural Experiment Station, *Research Bulletin 199* (1957): 22-49.

22 The Federal Trade Commission, "Cooperative Marketing," pp. 29-44, and H. E. Erdman, *The Marketing of Whole Milk* (New York: Macmillan, 1921), give the history of major milk marketing organizations.

23 J. M. Cassels, *A Study of Fluid Milk Prices* (Cambridge, Mass.: Harvard University Press, 1937), figs. 36-39; and Federal Trade Commission, "Cooperative Marketing," pp. 29-33.

24 Erdman, *Marketing of Whole Milk,* p. 156.

25 Cassels, *Study of Fluid Milk Prices,* p. 250; and L. F. Hermann and W. C. Welden, "Distribution of Milk by Farmers' Cooperative Association," Farm Credit Administration, *Circular C-124* (1941), fig. 4.

26 Herrmann and Weldon, "Distribution of Milk," pp. 5, 6.

27 Alden C. Manchester, "Nature of Competition in Fluid Milk Markets: Market Organization and Concentration," USDA *Agricultural Economics Report No. 67* (1965), fig. 5. Since 1962 the number of handlers per market has probably decreased.

28 See Cassels, *Study of Fluid Milk Prices,* pp. 41-48.

29 An early post-World War II study reports the costs of producing milk in the fall to be from 50 to 150 percent higher than in the spring (N. T. Pritchard, "Fall Premium Milk Pricing Plans," Farm Credit Administration, *Circular C-147* [1952], p. 2). A study of the high-cost Boston milkshed reports that a price differential of $1.00 (or about 4 cents a quart) would be required to persuade farmers to incur the costs of evening out fall and spring production (M. S. Parsons, G. E. Frick, W. E. Pullen, and William Bredo, "The Seasonal Adjustment of Milk Production in the Boston Milkshed" [U.S. Department of Agriculture mimeographed report, 1950], pp. 40-47).

30 Floyd A. Lasley, *Geographic Structure of Milk Prices, 1964-65,* Bulletin 258 (Washington, D.C.: Department of Agriculture, Economic Research Service, (1975), p. 4.

31 Sheldon W. Williams and David A. Vose, *Organization and Competition in the Midwest Dairy Industries* (Ames: Iowa State University Press, 1970), p. 57-91.

32 Ibid., p. 65.

33 George C. Tucker, "Need for Restructuring Dairy Cooperatives," Farmer Cooperative Service, *Service Report 125* (1972): 42.

34 Truman F. Graf, "Present and Future Views of Dairy Marketing," University of Wisconsin, *Agricultural Economics Staff Papers No. 88* (1975): p. 6.

In addition there are state retail and wholesale price orders in seventeen states.

35 As determined by the Crop Reporting Board of the Federal Statistical Reporting Service.

36 "Over-order-prices expanded from 4 percent of the markets in 1956 to 65 percent in 1970" (Tucker, "Need for Restructuring Dairy Cooperatives," p. 42).

37 Ibid., p. 16.

38 Truman F. Graf and Robert E. Jacobson, "Resolving Grade B Milk Conversion and Low Class 1 Utilization Pricing and Pooling Problems," University of Wisconsin College of Agriculture and Life Sciences, *Research Report R2503* (1973): 27. To readers who desire to analyze more fully the Grade A supply problem this reference is recommended.

39 R. W. Bartlett, "Federal Order Markets: To What Degree Have They Encouraged Milk Surpluses in Excess of Adequate Supply?" *Dairy Market Facts* (Urbana: Agricultural Extension Service, University of Illinois, 1964).

40 A. W. Gruebele, "Unnecessary Surpluses of Fluid Milk and Competition from Filled and Synthetic Milk," Department of Agricultural Economics, University of Illinois, *Agricultural Economic Bulletin 17* (1968).

41 Ray A. Goldberg, *Agribusiness Coordination* (Boston: Harvard Graduate School of Business, 1968), p. 116.

42 Computed from Farm Credit Administration, *Bulletin 26,* p. 115, and reported in Thomas E. Hall, Walter K. Davis, and Howard L. Hall, "New Local Elevators: Cost-Volume Relations in Hard Winter Wheat Belt," Farmer Cooperative Service, *Service Report 12* (1955): 17, or in S. U. Van Ausdale and D. L. Oldenstadt, "Costs and Efficiencies of Grain Elevators in the Pacific Northwest," Washington Agricultural Experiment Station, *Bulletin 713* (1969).

43 This account of the conditions giving rise to and the failures and successes of grain cooperatives has been gleaned from the following sources: O. N. Refsell, "The Farmers' Elevator Movement," *Journal of Political Economy* 22 (1914): 872-895, 969-991; E. G. Nourse, "Fifty Years of Farmers' Elevators in Iowa," Iowa State Agricultural Experiment Station, *Bulletin No. 211* (1923); Federal Trade Commission, *Report on the Grain Trade,* vol. 1 (1920); Fetrow and Elsworth, "Agricultural Cooperation in the United States," pp. 78-88; Lloyd Charles Wilson, "Kansas Cooperatives, Their Development and Present Position" (M.A. thesis, Kansas State College, 1942); L. M. Brown and Harold Hedges, "Farmers' Elevator Operations in South Dakota," South Dakota Agricultural Experiment Station, *Bulletin 351* (1941).

44 See, for example, the *Nineteenth Biennial Report* of the Kansas State Board of Agriculture (1913-1914): 156.

45 Federal Trade Commission, *Report on the Grain Trade,* 1: 91-92, and Federal Trade Commission, "Cooperative Marketing," pp. 61-64.

46 As the locals became well-established, the penalty clause ceased to be used (Federal Trade Commission, *Report on the Grain Trade,* 1: 266).

47 "Farmer Cooperatives in the Central States," Farmer Cooperative Service, *Bulletin 1* (revised, 1965): 159.
48 Farm Credit Administration, *Bulletin 26,* p. 46.
49 Such a transition was underway in the Pacific Northwest at this time, and one year, 1930, saw the establishment of over half of the total of ninety-eight grain cooperatives which were in existence by 1939. Harry E. Ratcliffe, "Cooperative Grain Marketing by Local Warehouses and Elevators in the Pacific Northwest," Farm Credit Administration, *Bulletin 40* (1940): 2.
50 The sources of data and methods of estimating the cooperatives' market shares are the same as those in note 4 above.
51 A pool may apply to broad or narrow definitions of the product and refer to transactions over a short or a longer period.
52 See Joseph G. Knapp, *The Hard Winter Wheat Pools* (Chicago: University of Chicago Press, 1933), and H. C. Filley, *Cooperation in Agriculture* (New York: Wiley, 1928), pp. 131-134.
53 Knapp, *Hard Winter Wheat Pools,* pp. 148-155.
54 Fetrow and Elsworth, "Agricultural Cooperation in the United States," p. 83.
55 L. F. Carey, "Operating Problems of Farmers' Elevators in Nebraska," Nebraska Agricultural Experiment Station, *Bulletin 314* (1938).
56 E. J. Bell, Jr., "Current Problems of Montana Farmers' Elevators," Montana Agricultural Experiment Station, *Bulletin No. 226* (1930): 11, 17.
57 Edward B. Ballow, "Margins and Costs in Cooperative Grain Marketing in Kansas," Farm Credit Administration, *Bulletin 66* (1951): 11, 17.
58 Stanley K. Thurston and R. J. Mutti, "Cost-Volume Relationships for New Country Elevators in the Corn Belt," Farmer Cooperative Service, *Service Report 32* (1957).
59 Adlowe L. Larson and Howard S. Whitney, "Relative Efficiencies of Single-Unit and Multiple-Unit Cooperative Elevator Organizations," Oklahoma Agricultural Experiment Station, *Bulletin No. B-426* (1954).
60 Goldberg, *Agribusiness Coordination,* pp. 233, 234. It is difficult to see why the farmer may not delegate this role to other handlers than cooperatives.
61 Thirteen of the regionals, however, own 381 country elevators which, in turn, buy from farmers (Farmer Cooperative Service, "35th Annual Report of the Regional Grain Cooperatives," *Service Report 144* [1975]).
62 For information about regional cooperatives' structure, facilities, and operations, see the report just cited.
63 Computed from Farm Credit Administration, *Bulletin 26,* pp. 69, 161.
64 Minnesota Agricultural Experiment Station, *Bulletin No. 412, pp. 48, 68; Washington Agricultural Experiment Station, Circular No. 237* (1953), as computed from data on pp. 12 and 17, and Milton L. Manuel and Richard L. Epard, "An Economic Analysis and Recommendations for Improving the Management of Kansas Grain Cooperatives," Kansas Agricultural Experiment Station, *Bulletin No. 497* (1970): 11, 12.

65 Manuel and Epard, "Economic Analysis and Recommendations for Improving the Management of Kansas Grain Corporatives," p. 4.
66 "The Annual Report of the Regional Grain Cooperatives," Farmer Cooperative Service, *Service Report 144* (1975): 9, 15, 16.

5: Cooperative Marketing of Other Farm Products

1   The available evidence is presented and appraised by Peter G. Helmberger and Sidney Hoos, *Cooperative Bargaining in Agriculture: Grower-Processor Markets for Fruits and Vegetables,* (Berkeley: University of California Press, 1965), pp. 116-129.
2   W. E. Folz and A. C. Manchester, "Chainstore Merchandising and Procurement Practices," USDA, *Marketing Research Report No. 417* (1960): 20-24. The National Commission on Food Marketing, "Organization and Competition in the Fruit and Vegetable Industry," *Technical Study No. 4* (1966): 104-112.
3   For a more extensive appraisal of the character of the processor buying markets, see Helmberger and Hoos, *Cooperative Bargaining in Agriculture,* pp. 116-129.
4   My direct observation.
5   For a comprehensive analysis of this cooperative see Irwin W. Rust and Kelsey B. Gardner, "Sunkist Growers, Inc.: A California Adventure in Agricultural Cooperation," Farmer Cooperative Service, *Circular 27* (1960).
6   The points made in this paragraph are summarized from J. H. Heckman and G. H. Goldsborough, "Cooperative Marketing of Apples in the United States," Farm Credit Administration, *Bulletin 55* (1948).
7   Erich Kraemer and H. E. Erdman, "The History of Cooperation in the Marketing of California Fresh Deciduous Fruits," California Agricultural Experiment Station, *Bulletin 557* (1933): 39.
8   Estimate of S. W. Shear, formerly of the University of California Agricultural Experiment Station.
9   An exception is vegetables for processing.
10 For an intensive analysis of the bargaining process, particularly as applied to fruits and vegetables, see Helmberger and Hoos, *Cooperative Bargaining in Agriculture,* pp. 48-76, 169-175.
11 National Commission on Food Marketing, *Technical Study No. 4,* pp. 273-284.
12 Nearly half of the canned fruits and vegetables are sold under buyers', i.e., usually chain stores', brands and a substantial portion under small canners' little-known brands (ibid., table 7-18).
13 For background information on this bargaining operation see Helmberger and Hoos, *Cooperative Bargaining in Agriculture,* pp. 39-48; and John A. Jamison, "Marketing Orders, Cartels, and Cling Peaches: A Long-Run View," Stanford University, *Food Research Institute Studies* 12, no. 7 (1966): 117-142.
14 See National Commission on Food Marketing, *Technical Study No. 4,* pp.

287-358, for a description of federal and state legislation under which marketing agreements and orders can be issued. Most of the federal orders in effect in 1966 only restricted shipments of certain qualities of a product, but doing so limits volume.

15   For a brief discussion of how marketing orders work under this act, see Sidney Hoos, "Economic Objectives and Operations of California Agricultural Marketing Orders," California Agricultural Experiment Station, *Mimeographed Report No. 196* (1957). For developments under this composite bargaining-prorate program, one of which is to stimulate production in the more efficient orchards primarily, see Jamison, "Marketing Orders," pp. 125-142.

16   National Commission on Food Marketing, *Technical Study No. 4,* pp. 287-299.

17   Marc Nerlove and Frederick V. Waugh, "Advertising Without Supply Control: Some Implications of a Study of the Advertising of Oranges," *Journal of Farm Economics* 43 (1961): 813-837.

18   For a portrayal of how these various steps succeeded for a time, then failed and were rescued by proration, see Roy J. Smith, "The Lemon Prorate in the Long Run," *Journal of Political Economy* 69: no. 6 (1961): 573-586.

19   This paragraph reports my own observation of the operations of the dried fruit cooperatives.

20   W. W. Fetrow and R. H. Elsworth, "Agricultural Cooperation in the United States," Farm Credit Administration, *Bulletin 54* (1947): 75-77.

21   These sentences summarize the argument of James G. Youde and Peter G. Helmberger, "Marketing Cooperatives in the U.S.: Membership Policies, Market Power, and Antitrust Policy," *Journal of Farm Economics* 48 (August 1966).

22   Cooperatives' volume by states reported by Bruce L. Swanson, "Statistics of Farmer Cooperatives, 1964-65," Farmer Cooperative Service, *Gerneral Report 143* (1967): 18-19; and farm output as reported in tables for specific commodities in USDA *Agricultural Statistics, 1966.*

23   As computed from Farm Credit Administration, *Bulletin 26* (1938): 69, 161.

24   These facts are reported in Wells A. Sherman, Fred Taylor, and C. J. Brand, "Studies of Primary Cotton Market Conditions in Oklahoma," USDA *Bulletin No. 36* (1913): 6, 7, 15, 20; and in Fred Taylor, "Relations between Primary Market Prices and Quality of Cotton," USDA *Bulletin No. 457* (1916): 6, 7, 12.

25   R. H. Montgomery, *The Cooperative Pattern in Cotton* (New York: Macmillan, 1929), pp. 6, 7.

26   Wilson Gee and Edward A. Terry, *The Cotton Cooperatives in the Southeast* (New York: Appleton, 1933), p. 156.

27   Federal Trade Commission, "Cooperative Marketing," *Senate Document No. 95,* 70th Cong., 1st sess., 1928, p. 182.

28   Computed from data in Farm Credit Administration, *Bulletin No. 26,* pp. 69, 161.

29   O. J. Weaver and W. W. Fetrow, "Costs and Margins of Cooperative

Gins," Farm Credit Administration, *Bulletin 67* (1951). Several more recent individual state studies provide similar evidence.

30 The preceding events are summarized in Federal Trade Commission, "Cooperative Marketing," pp. 189-190.

31 As was shown in the American Tobacco Company v. *United States* (1946) U.S. 782-815.

32 See Federal Trade Commission, "Cooperative Marketing," p. 203. The failure of the attempt at monopoly of supply of tobacco and other deficiencies in these cooperatives' undertakings are spelled out in J. J. Scanlan and J. M. Tinley, "Business Analysis of the Tobacco Growers' Cooperative Association," USDA *Circular No. 100* (1929).

33 I estimated for earlier years by use of the sources and methods applied to other crops. See note 4, chapter 4.

34 Studies on this subject are summarized by James Seagraves, "Capitalized Values of Tobacco Allotments and the Rate of Return to Allotment Owners," *American Journal of Agricultural Economics* 51 (May 1969): 320-333, to which he adds recent evidence.

35 For a careful analysis and appraisal of this testimony and the court decisions, see W. H. Nicholls, *Price Policies in the Cigarette Industry* (Nashville, Tenn.: Vanderbilt University Press, 1951), esp. pp. 257-334.

36 See, for example, E. G. Nourse and C. W. Hamman, "Cooperative Livestock Shipping in Iowa in 1920," Iowa Agricultural Experiment Station, *Bulletin No. 200* (1921): 421.

37 L. B. Mann, "Cooperative Marketing of Range Livestock," Farm Credit Administration, *Bulletin No. 7* (1936): 71, 77.

38 Facts in this paragraph reported in Federal Trade Commission, "Cooperative Marketing," pp. 126 ff., 593-598; and in Farmer Cooperative Service, *General Report 29* (1957): 2.

39 As computed by me for 1936 from data in Farm Credit Administration, *Bulletin No. 26,* p. 92; and tables in various issues of *Agricultural Statistics.*

40 Data in this paragraph from National Commission on Food Marketing, "Organization and Competition in the Livestock and Meat Industry," *Technical Study No. 1* (1966), table 1.1.

41 R. L. Fox, "Farmer Meat Packing Enterprises in the United States," Farmer Cooperative Service, *General Report No. 29* (1957), and "Recent Developments in Farmer Cooperative Meat Packing and Processing," Farmer Cooperative Service, *Information No. 18* (1961).

42 See Joe S. Bain, *Barriers to New Competition* (Cambridge, Mass.: Harvard University Press, 1956), pp. 180-238; and testimony or affidavits of officers of relatively small packing plants, summarized in "Affidavits of Swift Defendants in Opposition to Motion of the United States for Summary Judgment in the United States District Court for the Northern District of Illinois, Eastern Division," May 1958, vol. 1, pp. 76-81.

43 R. C. Bell and W. D. Buchanan, *Partners in Progress* (privately printed, circa 1957), p. 41.

44 Data from Bruce L. Swanson, Farmer Cooperative Service, *General Report No. 134* (1966): 9; and USDA *Agricultural Statistics 1966,* pp. 418, 424, 430.

45 For descriptions of these arrangements and the problems posed for coopera-
    tives, see "Contract Farming and Vertical Integration in Agriculture,"
    USDA, *Agricultural Information Bulletin No. 198* (1958): 5-7.
46 National Commission on Food Marketing, "Organization and Competition
    in the Poultry and Egg Industries," *Technical Study No. 2* (1966), tables 2.1,
    2.2.

6: Farm Supply Cooperatives

1   Excluded are commodities used in family living or sold to nonmembers. Ex-
    cluded also are the volume of rural electric power (see chapter 9) used in irri-
    gation and service (chiefly transportation) cooperatives.
2   Computed from data in USDA *Agricultural Statistics* (1952): 701; Federal
    Trade Commission, "Cooperative Marketing," *Senate Document No. 95,*
    70th Cong., 1st sess., 1928, p. 5; and Farm Credit Administration, *Bulletin
    No. 26* (1938): 42.
3   I estimate the percentages through 1945-1946 (except for 1936) by the use of
    data and methods similar (except that figures are for supplies bought not
    farmers' marketings) to those used by the Farmer Cooperative Service. The
    percentage for 1936 was estimated by using the sum of feed, seed, fertilizer,
    and "operation of motor vehicles used in production" reported for that year
    in USDA *Agricultural Statistics* (1967): 575; and cooperatives' sales of the
    same categories reported in Farm Credit Administration, *Bulletin No. 26,* p.
    94.
4   Computed from USDA *Agricultural Statistics* (1952): 70, (1970): 56.
5   Changes in volume of livestock and products and of use of commercial feeds
    computed from USDA *Agricultural Statistics* (1952): 72, 660, (1970): 56; and
    from USDA, "Changes in Farm Production and Efficiency," *Statistical
    Bulletin No. 233* (1970): 5.
6   Computed from USDA *Agricultural Statistics* (1952): 691, 701, (1970): 475,
    477.
7   See F. A. Harper, "Cooperative Purchasing and Marketing Organizations in
    New York State," Cornell Agricultural Experiment Station, *Bulletin 544*
    (1932): 52; and W. G. Wysor, *The History and Philosophy of Southern
    States Cooperative* (Richmond, Va., 1940), p. 14.
8   L. F. Rickey and M. A. Abrahamson, "Role of Cooperatives in Manufac-
    turing and Distributing of Feed" (undated mimeographed release of the
    Farm Credit Administration).
9   A finding of the Wicks Committee of the New York legislature in 1917,
    quoted in Joseph G. Knapp, *Seeds That Grew* (Hinsdale, N.Y.: Anderson
    House, 1960), p. 18.
10 Federal law and most states now require that some means of identifying con-
    tents of mixed feeds be available to buyers.
11 Wysor, p. 16; and I. Harvey Hull, *Built of Men: The Story of Indiana Coop-
    eratives* (New York: Harper, 1952), pp. 53-58.
12 Hull, *Built of Men,* pp. 31-34; and Knapp, *Seeds That Grew,* pp. 15-17, 23.

13   Computed from Farm Credit Administration, *Bulletin No. 26,* pp. 50, 94; and USDA *Agricultural Statistics* (1952): 701.

14   Facts cited here are provided by Anne L. Gessner, "Integrated Feed Operations Through Farmer Cooperatives, 1959," Farmer Cooperative Service, *General Report 100* (1962): 6, 7. This report is probably a better indication of cooperatives' feed manufacturing activity than is the *Census of Manufactures,* vol. 1, *Summary and Subject Statistics* (Washington, D.C.: The census, 1963), p. 306, which reports that only 12.5 percent of shipments of animal feeds came from cooperative plants. Because many of the latter both mix feeds and sell them directly to farmers, the census may classify them as retailers.

15   Farm Credit Administrations, *Bulletin No. 26,* pp. 161, 239.

16   Figures are for 1964 in order to use data from the *Census of Agriculture* (Washington, D.C.: The census, 1964), vol. 2, Chap. 7, table 7. Cooperative volume by regions is reported in Farmer Cooperative Service, *General Report 143* (1966): 22.

17   USDA *Agricultural Statistics* (1952): 72, (1970): 56.

18   Ibid. (1961), (1973): 46 (following pages report more on the changes in feeds and their use).

19   Federal Trade Commission, *Report on the Fertilizer Industry* (1916): 12.

20   Jesse W. Markham, *The Fertilizer Industry: Study of an Imperfect Market* (Nashville, Tenn.: Vanderbilt University Press, 1958), pp. 187-192. There followed exchanges in the *Journal of Political Economy,* February and December 1960 issues, between Markham and Zvi Griliches, to which Vernon W. Ruttan added important facts as to whether farmers were irrational buyers. What comes out is that the market performance somewhat improved over two decades, aided by education of members by cooperatives.

21   For an extensive account of government investigations and prosecutions, see Federal Trade Commission, *Report on the Fertilizer Industry* (1950): 27-53; and Markham, *Fertilizer Industry,* pp. 171-186.

22   Federal Trade Commission, *Report on the Fertilizer Industry* (1916): 237.

23   Computed from USDA *Agricultural Statistics* (1952): 701; and Farm Credit Administration, *Bulletin No. 26,* p. 24.

24   J. Warren Mather, "The Mississippi Federated Cooperatives' System," Farmer Cooperative Service, *Bulletin 2* (1954): 23-24.

25   Farm Credit Administration, "Miscellaneous Report 149" (1951): 31, 36, 37.

26   Markham, *Fertilizer Industry,* p. 199.

27   Statements based on data in USDA *Agricultural Statistics* (1969): 2; and Farmer Cooperative Service, *Research Report 11* (1970): 23.

28   For further analysis of the influence of the mass distributors, see R. B. Heflebower, "Mass Distribution: A Phase of Bilateral Oligopoly or of Competition?" *American Economics Review: Papers and Proceedings* 17 (May 1957): 274-283.

29   The initial margin of automobile dealers is usually 20 percent of suggested factory city retail price. Surveys by the Office of Price Administration for 1941 (when initial margins were 24 percent) showed that dealer's realized

margins (on new and used cars together) averaged (the mode) 15 percent of retail sales volume, but were slightly higher in small towns. For 1956 the realized margin averaged about the same (Jack A. Pontney, "An Economic Analysis of the Retail Automobile Market" [Ph.D. diss., Northwestern University, 1963], table 31).

30 Recently an arrangement has been worked out whereby the members' credit purchases can be financed by the district production credit corporation. See Francis M. Hyre, "The PCA Cooperative-Patron Credit Plan," Farmer Cooperative Service, *General Report No. 135* (1966).

31 Most of the data (except recent market share estimates) presented in this paragraph are taken from Gerald M. Francis, "Distribution of Machinery by Farmers' Cooperative Association," Farm Credit Administration, *Circular C-125* (1941).

32 Joe S. Bain, *Barriers to New Competition* (Cambridge, Mass.: Harvard University Press, 1956), p. 170, places the tractor industry in the "very high entry barriers" category and the large and complex farm machinery industry in the "substantial entry barriers" class.

7: Farmer-Owned Petroleum Cooperatives

1 J. Warren Mather and John M. Bailey, "Integrated Petroleum Operations of Farmer Cooperatives, 1969," Farmer Cooperative Service, *Research Report 21* (1971): table 9. The number of refineries owned had fallen from twenty in 1950 to eight by 1969, by which date total volume of crude refined oil in cooperatives' plants had increased by a third. The average size of refineries had increased sharply, but four plants were quite small.

2 Despite that high average some cooperatives own little crude production and rely on purchases from nonintegrated producers or from oil imports. Government allocations to crude-short refineries have been a factor at times.

3 Based on the Bureau of Mines estimates of gasoline consumption less refinery output in this area.

4 The "Group 3" price quotations reflect the fact that the Interstate Commerce Commission placed all the Oklahoma (and later Kansas) refineries in a group for which all refineries' freight rates to a specific northern destination were identical. Trade publications reported a range of prices, f.o.b. Group 3 refineries (for northern shipment).

5 M. W. W. Splawn, "Report on Pipe Lines," *House Report No. 2192,* 72nd Cong., 2d sess., 1933, pt. 1, pp. 488-490.

6 Federal Trade Commission, "Prices, Profits and Competition in the Petroleum Industry," *Senate Document No. 61,* 70th Cong., 1st sess., 1928.

7 Farm Credit Administration, *Bulletin No. 26* (1938): 1-161.

8 Ibid., p. 50.

9 John H. Lister, "Cooperative Purchasing Through the Illinois Farm Supply Company and Its Member Supply Company and Its Member County Companies," Farm Credit Administration, *Bulletin No. 27* (1938): 35-36; and Mather and Bailey, "Petroleum Operations of Farmer Cooperatives," p. 6.

10   Net savings for years before 1930 for a number of locals are cited by Rudolph
     K. Froker and H. Bruce Price, "Organization and Management Problems of
     Cooperative Oil Associations in Minnesota," U.S. Department of Agricul-
     ture, *Circular No. 80* (1929): 25, 26, 36. Also see table 7.3.
11   Mather and Bailey, "Petroleum Operations of Farmer Cooperatives," pp. 5, 6.
12   Shown in "Petroleum Rail Shippers' Association v. Alton and Southern
     Railroad et al," Interstate Commerce Commission *Reports* 243, no. 28106
     (1941): 617.
13   Demonstrated by use of "the low of the range" of prices plus rail rates com-
     pared to tank wagon prices in northern cities, as reported in the annual edi-
     tions of *Platt's Oil Price Handbook*.
14   Information on price and margin developments obtained by interview.
15   The figures in table 7.2 were not fully applicable to two subparts of the west
     central area where the groups of cooperatives studied here are located. Some
     are so close to small refineries that rail and later pipeline transportation were
     not used. Prices in Montana were not affected by pipelines from midconti-
     nent, but for decades prices there were on the Group 3 plus rail freight basis
     even though the northern Rocky Mountain states produced a surplus of
     crude oil.
16   Computed from data in Farm Credit Administration, *Bulletin No. 26,* pp.
     69, 94.
17   In Farm Credit Administration, *Circular C-139* (1951): 20, Mather reports
     1947 net savings from *retail* operations only (i.e., sales to farmers) of all
     petroleum cooperatives to have been from 2 to 5 percent of sales. In that year
     of early postwar shortage, cooperatives were having great difficulty in buy-
     ing advantageously. That fact, plus the omission of "other income" from
     Mather's data, must account for the difference between the savings he re-
     ports and those shown in table 7.5.
18   The point could very well be made that the predominant portion of the mem-
     bers' equity represented by withheld net savings is a "costless" asset of the
     members, for they would not have had that part of their equity in the local
     had they not been members and had not the cooperative obtained the net
     savings which it withheld.
19   See note 17.
20   A compilation from refining companies' reports in *Moody's Manual of In-
     vestment: Industrials* reports the financial position of corporations' (after-
     tax) earnings to have been less than 5.0 percent of net investment in
     1936-1940 and to have been about 12 percent in 1954-1957.
21   Most of the information about recent developments is reported in Farmer
     Cooperative Service, "How Cooperatives Help Farmers in Time of Short-
     age," *Information 99* (1975).

8: Cooperatives Owned by Urban Businesses

1   The percentages reported in this paragraph were computed by use of data in

the *Census of Business: Wholesale Trade, Subject Reports, Area Statistics,* Washington, D.C.: The census, 1967), table 11, pp. 7-126 to 7-131.

2   At least to the early 1950s. See Harold Barger, *Distribution's Place in the American Economy since 1869* (Princeton, N.J.: Princeton University Press, 1955), p. 92.

3   A dramatic account of lagging by the chain stores and then of rapidly adopting supermarket retailing units is found in M. A. Adelman, *A and P: A Study in Price-Cost Behavior and Public Policy* (Cambridge, Mass.: Harvard University Press, 1959), pp. 59-64.

4   See, for example, UG, *The United Grocers Story,* a pamphlet published by United Grocers, Ltd., a California cooperative.

5   Federal Trade Commission, "Chain Stores: Cooperative Grocery Chains," *Senate Document No. 12,* 72d Congress, 1st Session, 1932, pp. 38-46.

6   Wilford L. White, *Cooperative Retail Buying Associations* (New York: McGraw-Hill, 1930).

7   See *Supermarketing* (March 1970) for a brief history and description of operations of voluntaries.

8   The preceding percentages were computed from data in the *Census of Business,* "Special Report: Voluntary Groups and Cooperative Wholesalers" (Washington, D.C.: The census, 1935), p. 13; *Census of Business,* vol. 5, *Wholesale Trade: Area Statistics* (Washington, D.C.: The census, 1948), p. 0.10; and *Census of Business,* vol. 3, *Wholesale Trade: Summary Statistics* (Washington, D.C.: The census, 1958), p. 5.2; and for 1967 the volume cited in note 6 to table 8.1.

9   National Commission on Food Marketing, "Special Studies in Food Marketing," *Technical Study No. 10* (1966): 16, 17.

10 See annual surveys of gross margins of various types of wholesalers reported in *Progressive Grocer,* e.g., 50 (April 1971): 86, 87.

11 Chain store purchasing, warehouse, and delivery costs were computed as follows: for 1955 data from Wilber D. England, "Operating Results of Food Chains in 1956," Harvard Bureau of Business Research, *Bulletin No. 151* (1957): 21, were used. To the reported warehousing and transportation expense was added a prorata share of administrative and general expense. That sum was divided by the reciprocal of the overall gross expenses of the warehouse and retail functions of the chains. The last step is necessary because all expense rates of chains are reported as percentages of retail sales. For 1967-1968 the data are from Earl Brown and Robert Day, *Operating Results of Food Chains, 1970-71* (Ithaca, N.Y.: Cornell University Press, 1971), p. 65, with the then separate category of merchandising and buying added to warehouse costs. Data for middle-size chains were used because they do part of their buying from wholesalers. For 1970 the *Progressive Grocer* (April 1971): 86, 87, reported that supermarkets which owned warehouses had expenses of 3 percentage points of retail sales for "warehouse, delivery, and headquarters expense."

12 *U.S.* v. *Von's Grocery Co.,* 384 U.S. 299.

13 Federal Trade Commission, *Economic Report on the Structure and Compe-*

titive Behavior of Food Retailing (Washington, D.C.: The commission, 1966), p. 50.

14   As reported to me by a Topco official.

15   These percentages were computed from data in the *Census of Business,* vol. 1, *Retail Trade: Subject Reports* (Washington, D.C.: The census, 1967), p. 4.2. Again the *Census* may understate the volume.

16   *Eastern States Retail Lumber Dealers Association* v. *U.S.,* 234 U.S. 600, 1914.

17   Fifteen of dealer-owned companies returned filled-out questionnaires, but only ten respondents proved to be cooperatives by the standard used here.

18   The *Census of Business,* vol. 3, *Wholesale Trade,* table 2, reports eleven wholesale cooperatives in dry goods and apparel lines, ten in stationery and in books, and four in furniture and home furnishings (excluding electrical appliances) but does not give sales volume. Again the *Census* count is incomplete, possibly because cooperatives that act merely as buying agents were excluded.

19   This paragraph is based on Kent Cooper and the Associated Press, *An Autobiography* (New York: Random House, 1959), pp. 4-8.

20   These facts and the ruling cited are from the district court decision of 1944, 52 F. Supp., p. 362. This decision was affirmed by the Supreme Court in 1945, 326 U.S. 1.

21   This paragraph is summarized from George P. Taylor and Irene D. Neu, *The American Railroad Network, 1861-1890* (Cambridge, Mass: Harvard University Press, 1956), pp. 71-76.

22   The business of forwarding is described briefly by Harry M. Baker and Richard J. Riddick, "The Role of the Forwarder in Efficient Transportation," *Transportation and Tomorrow,* ed. Karl M. Ruppenthal and Henry A. McKinnell, Jr. (Stanford, Calif.: Graduate School of Business, Stanford University, 1966), pp. 120-130. The role of the shippers' associations is described by Caughey Culpepper, "Shipping Associations—Bonanza or Bogeyman?" ibid., pp. 113-119.

23   Information about the history and organization of Allied was provided by its management and applies to the years before 1968 when it reorganized into an investor-owned corporation in order to obtain more owner capital. Data below on market shares were computed from *Trinc's Bluebook of the Trucking Industry,* annual issues for 1954, 1956, 1961, and 1968.

24   This description of the organization of the cooperative, supplied by its officials in 1958, applied before the important reorganization and enlargement of the scope of operations in 1959 that became effective in 1963. The basis of dividing net revenue was revised in 1961. Still more recently the railroads have disposed of their interest, and by 1975 REA was out of business.

9: Consumer Cooperatives

1   The percentages for Great Britain are reported by L. L. Mather, *Consumer Cooperatives in the Grocery Retailing Industry* (Ann Arbor, Mich.: Univer-

sity Microfilms, 1968), p. 3. Data for Sweden supplied by officials of the Co-operative Federation of Sweden.

2 Estimates of the number and volume of these service cooperatives are reported in the annual statistical issues of the *Co-op Report* published by the Cooperative League of the USA, Washington, D.C.

3 The number of cooperative food stores reported by the 1967 *Census* seems too high. The *Co-op Report* 15 (September 1967) asserts that some stores owned by individual proprietors who are members of retailer-owned wholesale cooperatives were included. The *Co-op Report* 18 (September-October 1970) lists 305 "consumer goods centers," which includes some nonfood outlets but acknowledges omission of some small stores.

4 As reported in the "1965 Figure Exchange" released by the Consumers Cooperative Development Association, Berkeley, California.

5 *Co-op Report* 15: 5.

6 The "1973-74 Figure Exchange" released by the Consumers' Cooperative Development Association.

7 Florence E. Parker, *The First 125 Years: A History of Distributive and Service Cooperation in the United States, 1829-1954* (Superior, Wis.: The Cooperative League of the USA, 1956), contains the most detailed history. Other books covering specific aspects of cooperative history include Leonard C. Kercher, Van W. Kebker, and Wilfred C. Leland, Jr., *Consumers' Cooperatives in the North Central States* (Minneapolis: University of Minnesota Press, 1941); Colston E. Warne, *The Consumers' Co-operative Movement in Illinois* (Chicago: The University of Chicago Press, 1926); and Orin E. Burley, *The Consumers' Cooperative as a Distributive Agency* (New York: McGraw-Hill, 1939).

8 The location of these and of most other retail cooperatives in 1968 is reported by Mather, *Consumer Cooperatives in the Grocery Retailing Industry,* pp. 157, 164.

9 Parker, *The First 125 Years,* pp. 66, 67.

10 Burley, *The Consumers' Cooperative as a Distributive Agency,* pp. 242, 243.

11 Ibid., pp. 247, 261; and Warne, *The Consumers' Co-operative Movement in Illinois,* pp. 163-198.

12 For a careful appraisal of fifteen surveys by various groups, see Donald E. Sexton, Jr., "Comparing the Cost of Food to Blacks and Whites—A Survey," *Journal of Marketing* 35 (July 1971): 40-46. There is some evidence that the quality of meat and produce is lower in low-income area stores. Also, the poor often do not live near supermarkets and because of irregular income rely on merchant credit.

13 Survey of retail food cooperatives' operations in 1955 was conducted by Raymond Nordstrand.

14 Mather, *Consumer Cooperatives in the Grocery Retailing Industry,* pp. 131-134 and appendix tables.

15 From the *Annual Reports* and *Yearbooks* of the Midland Cooperator, Minneapolis, Minn.

16 Figures for cooperatives from annual reports of the Consumer Cooperative

Managers' Association, Richmond, California; the "1973-74 Figure Exchange." See note 4 for more recent title of this group.

17   The chain store data are from Earl Brown and Robert Day, *Operating Results of Food Chains, 1970-71* (Ithaca, N.Y.: Cornell University Press, 1971), tables 40, 41.

18   See the extensive and sometimes conflicting testimony in "Administered Prices," *Hearings* before the Subcommittee on Antitrust and Monopoly of the Senate Committee on the Juciciary, 86th Cong., 2d sess., 1960, pts. 14-23.

19   As reported in National Commission on Food Marketing, "Organization and Competition in Food Retailing," *Technical Study No. 7* (1966): 133. For a report on the trials and successes of the San Francisco Bay area consumer cooperatives, see Robert Neptune, *California's Uncommon Markets: The Study of Consumer Cooperatives 1935-41* (Richmond, Calif.: Associated Cooperatives, 1971).

20   See Mather, *Consumer Cooperatives in the Grocery Retailing Industry.*

21   Annual report of Associated Cooperatives of Berkeley, California, and the *Co-op Report* 16 (September 1968): 5. These stores have faced more rigorous price competition in the recent years as the leading chain dropped trading stamps and reduced its prices by the cost of those stamps.

22   The mobility of the population in these decades and the consequent producer-minded focus of households is emphasized by Jerry Voorhis in *American Cooperation* (New York: Harper & Row, 1961), p. 158.

23   *Cooperative Independent Commission Report* (Manchester, England: Cooperative Union, Ltd., 1958), pp. 5, 15.

24   Charles C. Slater, *Baking in America,* vol. 2, *Market Organization and Competition* (Evanston, Ill.: Northwestern University Press, 1956), pp. 121-125, 246, 286-288.

25   See chapter 4 with respect to monopoly influences on the price of milk.

26   I reached this conclusion about the limited opportunity for consumer cooperatives before the long-time director of the Cooperative League of the USA wrote: "it is hard to persuade consumers that at present they actually need more food stores or supermarkets: . . . The situation is not like most of the other fields where cooperatives have proved successful . . . . But foodstores! Surely this is no keenly felt need of American consumers. Around the turn of the third quarter of the twentieth century it may be" (Voorhis, *American Cooperation,* pp. 157-158). This date has come but the cooperative food stores are not booming.

27   The data about REA operations in this and following paragraphs are from the 1970 *Annual Statistical Report* of the Rural Electrification Administration and USDA *Agricultural Statistics* (1971): 531. Much of the historical information is from earlier publications of the agency.

28   Richard C. Albin, "Misallocation of Electric Power in the Pacific Northwest" (Ph.D. diss., University of Chicago, 1960), quoted by George S. Tolley in Commission on Money and Credit, *Federal Credit Agencies* (New York: Prentice-Hall, 1963), p. 416.

10: Mutual Investing Institutions

1   See also comments later in this chapter about the introduction and extent of deposit insurance available or required of these intermediaries.

2   A life insurance policy reserve is built up to cover the higher mortality rate of policyholders as they become older. In an annuity the purchaser makes payments to the insurance company which accumulate until he reaches the target retirement age or other specified date.

3   Data for mutual funds are from the *1975 Mutual Fund Fact Book* (New York: Investment Company Institute, 1976), p. 7, but exclude assets of nonmembers of the institute which, in an earlier year, were estimated to represent 7 percent of total mutual fund assets.

4   Statements in this paragraph are based on figures in the current or earlier issues of the sources cited for table 10.1. Credit unions will be considered as "cooperative borrowers," the topic of chapter 11.

5   Data from *Savings and Loan Fact Book 1976* (Chicago: United States Savings and Loan League, 1976), p. 14. All figures for savings and loan associations cited in the following pages are from this source or are computed from data in it. If the information cited is from earlier issues of the *Fact Book* this will be noted.

6   For a fuller exposition of the evolution of these institutions, see H. Morton Bodfish, *History of Building and Loan in the United States* (Chicago: United States Building and Loan League, 1931).

7   Edward H. Herman, "Conflicts of Interest in the Savings and Loan Industry," in *Study of the Savings and Loan Industry,* vol. 2 (Washington, D.C.: U.S. Government Printing Office, 1969), pp. 789, 790, 802 (prepared under the direction of Irwin Friend).

8   Ibid., pp. 808, 847 ff. For further development of this point, plus emphasis on the opportunity for management of the mutual to have an easy life and to divert business related to lending to enterprises associated (via board memberships) with the mutual, see Alfred Nicols, *Management and Control in the Mutual Savings and Loan Association* (Lexington, Mass.: D. C. Heath, 1972), pp. 22-35.

9   Points to be considered at more length in concluding chapters are the extent of mutuality of all types of mutual financial institutions and who does or should own the accumulated net reserves of a mutual in the event of its liquidation or sale.

10   Small associations typically have a distinct disadvantage in operating costs; costs continue to fall, but less rapidly, the larger the association (George J. Benston, "Cost of Operations and Economies of Scale in Savings and Loan Associations," in *Study of the Savings and Loan Industry,* 2: 705, 706).

11   R. J. Saulnier, Harold G. Halcrow, and Neil H. Jacoby, *Federal Lending and Loan Insurance* (Princeton, N.J.: Princeton University Press, 1958), pp. 358, 356, 354, 350, 352.

12   Willis R. Bryant, *Mortgage Lending: Fundamentals and Practices,* 2d ed. (New York: McGraw-Hill, 1962), p. 65.

13 Saulnier, Halcrow, and Jacoby, *Federal Lending and Loan Insurance*, p. 305.

14 *National Fact Book of Mutual Savings Banks, 1970* (New York: National Association of Mutual Savings Banks, 1970), table 70, p. 44.

15 The events summarized in this and the next few pages indicate weaknesses in the legislation governing financial institutions and the effects of the multiplicity of regulatory agencies and of the policies that have arisen, particularly since 1930. A President's Commission on Financial Structure and Regulation, appointed in early 1970, investigated not only the mutuals considered in this chapter but also commercial banks, life insurance companies, and credit unions. The gist of the recommendations is to allow "greater flexibility and operational freedom in the financial structure," and to that end "to remove unworkable regulatory restraints as well as to provide additional powers and flexibility to the various types of financial institutions" (The commission's *Report* [Washington, D.C.: U.S. Government Printing Office, 1971], p. 8).

16 *Federal Reserve Bulletin* 48 (February 1962): 148. The rate maximum was increased later but is no longer in force.

17 *Savings and Loan Fact Book 1970*, pp. 65, 66, 117-120, 64-67.

18 Paul Samuelson, "An Analytic Evaluation of Interest Rate Ceilings for Savings and Loan Associations and Competitive Institutions," in *Study of the Savings and Loan Industry*, 2: 1589.

19 Foreclosures on nonfarm real estate rose from 1960 to 1967, but did not become a wave and declined after 1968 (*Savings and Loan Fact Book 1971*, p. 50). The FHA insurance and VA guarantee for the more risky mortgages, plus the opportunity of savings associations to borrow from FHLB and other sources, would have blocked a major crisis.

20 Benston, "Cost of Operations and Economies of Scale," in *Study of the Savings and Loan Industry*, 2: 710-719.

21 Alfred Nicols, "Stock Versus Mutual Savings and Loan Associations: Some Evidence of Differences in Behavior," *American Economic Review: Papers and Proceedings* 57 (May 1967): 337-346.

22 See note 10, above.

23 For Nicols's econometric study of the efficiency of stock versus mutual associations, see his *Management and Control in the Mutual Savings and Loan Association*, pp. 259-277. Nicols relates the lower efficiency of the mutual to the limited competitive pressures on the managements of mutuals.

24 The historical part of this section draws on John W. Lintner, *Mutual Savings Bank and the Savings Mortgage Markets* (Boston: Graduate School of Business Administration, Harvard University, 1948); and Weldon Wefling, *Mutual Savings Banks; The Evolution of a Financial Intermediary* (Cleveland, Ohio: The Press of Case Western Reserve University, 1968).

25 Lintner, *Mutual Savings Banks*, p. 235.

26 As shown by their share of savings deposits and of residential mortgages held. The savings banks continued to hold a higher percentage of mortgages on large residential properties than on one-to-four-family residences (*Savings and Loan Fact Book 1976*, table 23).

27 Irwin Friend, Marshall Blume, and Jean Crockett, *Mutual Funds and Other Institutional Investors: A New Perspective* (New York: McGraw-Hill for the Twentieth Century Fund, 1970), p. 52.
28 Ibid., pp. 52, 102, 103.
29 Ibid., p. 56.
30 Ibid., pp. 15, 81.

11: Cooperative Borrowing Institutions

1 The federal government established a number of other agencies for such purposes, particularly in the 1930s, of which one is the Farmers Home Administration.
2 See unpublished data from the Department of Agriculture quoted by William G. Murray, *Agriculture Finance* (Ames: Iowa State College Press, 1947), p. 119.
3 As is shown by data in USDA *Agricultural Statistics* (1962): 590, (1975): 477.
4 As long as the federal government owned any stock in a land bank (or any of the other agricultural credit agencies considered below) it was exempt from the federal corporate income tax but was subject to a franchise tax of 25 percent of net income. After retirement of the government-owned stock the banks and local associations are subject to the same tax provisions as are other cooperatives.
5 U.S., Department of Agriculture, "Supplement," *Agricultural Finance Review* 31 (December 1970): 37.
6 Farm Credit Administration, *41st Annual Report* (1973-74): 58.
7 Ibid., p. 58.
8 Earl L. Butz, *The Production Credit System for Farmers* (Washington, D.C.: The Brookings Institution, 1944), p. 48.
9 For experience through 1950 see R. J. Saulnier, H. G. Halcrow and N. H. Jacoby, *Federal Lending and Loan Insurance* (Princeton, N.J.: Princeton University Press, 1958), table 38. For more recent information see the *Annual Reports* of the Farm Credit Administration.
10 USDA *Agricultural Statistics* (1957): 612, (1971): 512; *FCA 29th Annual Report,* (1961-62): 7, *36th Annual Report* (1968-69): 33.
11 H. H. Hulbert, Nelda Griffin, and K. B. Gardner, "Methods of Financing Farmer Cooperatives," Farmer Cooperative Service, *General Report* 32 (1957): 31, 32. For recent developments see Farm Credit Administration, *41st Annual Report* (1973-74: 39.
12 The initial draft of this section was written by Irving Brecher.
13 Joseph L. Snider, *Credit Unions in Massachusetts* (Cambridge, Mass.: Harvard University Press, 1939), p. 3 (italics mine).
14 Required at least of those formed under Section 9 of the Federal Credit Union Act as amended on May 123, 1952. The contention has been made that homogeneity of membership is practiced less now. But in 1969 over half of the credit unions were listed as "occupational," nearly a fifth as "associational" (church, union, etc.), and 15 percent as "government" in the

International Credit Union Yearbook 1970 (Madison, Wis.: Cuna International, 1970), p. 9.

15 Years ago some large credit unions did refund part of the interest paid on loans despite governmental disapproval at that time. Eli Shapiro, *Credit Union Development in Wisconsin* (New York: Columbia University Press, 1947), p. 86. In 1954 the Federal Credit Union Act was amended to authorize interest refunds to member-borrowers, but in recent years credit unions' interest refunds amounted to less than 10 percent of total dividends on deposits and .35 percent of loans outstanding at the end of the preceding year (*International Credit Union Yearbook 1968* [Madison, Wis.: Cuna International, 1968], pp. 27, 31, 35, and *International Credit Union Yearbook 1970,* p. 35).

16 "The Big Business of Small Loans," *10 Close-Ups of Consumer Credit* (reprinted by the Bureau of Federal Credit Unions, Washington, D.C., 1940), p. 22. For further insight into the historical setting in which credit unions (and other "corrective" consumer-lending institutions) began operation, see "Combating the Loan Shark," *Law and Contemporary Problems* 8, no. 1 (Winter 1941); and R. Y. Giles, *Credit for the Millions: The Story of Credit Unions* (New York: Harper & Row, 1951), chaps. 1, 3, 4.

17 The so-called "remedial loan societies," or limited-dividend, semiphilanthropic pawnshops operating on a private capital basis, were active during the 1890s and the early 1900s. For a variety of reasons including excess conservatism in lending policy they were eclipsed shortly thereafter by the new agencies (credit unions, personal finance companies, and industrial banking companies) then being established.

18 The studies made forty years ago comprise the fullest analysis of consumer lending by financial institutions other than credit unions: R. A. Young et al., *Personal Finance Companies and Their Credit Practices* (New York: National Bureau of Economic Research, 1940), W. C. Plummer and R. A. Young, *Sales Finance Companies and Their Credit Practices* (New York: National Bureau of Economic Research, 1940), and John M. Chapman et al., *Commercial Banks and Consumer Installment Credit* (New York: National Bureau of Economic Research, 1940).

19 Unless indicated otherwise, all of the factual material about credit unions is from the *International Credit Union Yearbook,* especially the 1970 edition.

20 Over a period of years the average federal credit unions' gross income per year is about 10 percent of the loans outstanding and their expenses are about 4 percent of loans, or over one-third of gross income. For purposes of comparison it should be noted that expenses of personal loan companies in three states studied varied from 60 to 66 percent of income in the 1950s, and these were percentages of higher interest charged to borrowers (Young et al., *Personal Finance Companies,* pp. 1858-1860).

21 In 1970 credit unions as a group earned 8.5 percent of total assets, of which 78 percent consisted of loans to members. About 37 percent of gross income was absorbed by operating expenses. About 17 percent was assigned to reserves and surplus, of which a minimum percentage is required by law. The remaining 46 percent of the gross income was paid as dividends to members,

almost exclusively as depositors (National Credit Union Administration, *Annual Report* [1970], p. 10).

22 See note 15 above.

23 But young families in the second quartile of wage and salary incomes attempt to build their stock of consumer durables, and a higher percentage of them are members of credit unions than are savers in other institutions (The University of Michigan Survey of Consumer Finances in 1970, summarized in the *International Credit Union Yearbook 1971*), pp. 22-27.

12: Mutual Fire and Casualty Insurance

1 Fire and casualty data from *Best's Aggregates and Averages: Property-Liability* (Morristown, N.J.: A. M. Best Co., 1971), p. 1, excludes "reciprocals" and "Lloyds" and small farm and town mutuals. Hereafter, except where noted otherwise, all data about fire and casualty insurance were obtained from *Best's* for 1971 or computed from data in it.

2 Ibid., pp. 200-205. Net premiums earned are premiums written adjusted for reinsurance assumed and reinsurance ceded to other companies, and for premiums received during the year to provide insurance coverage applicable to future years.

3 Prudential's assets exceed those of any manufacturing corporation (*Fortune* 71 [May 1971]: 172, 194).

4 R. Carlyle Buley, *The American Life Convention, 1905-1952: A Study and the History of Life Insurance,* vol. 1 (New York: Appleton-Century-Crofts, 1953), pp. 42-54.

5 J. A. C. Hetherington, "Fact Versus Fiction: Who Owns Mutual Insurance Companies?," *Wisconsin Law Review,* no. 4 (1969): 1079.

6 Jerry Voorhis, *Cooperatives U.S.A.* (Chicago: Cooperative League of the U.S.A., 1961), pp. 38-39, lists nine "cooperatively oriented mutual insurance companies that differ from other mutual firms in the degree of policyholder control." Using a somewhat different definition, the *Annual Statistical Issue of the Coop Report* (Chicago: Cooperative League of the U.S.A., 1969), p. 25, lists twenty-seven.

7 Cost experience means the sum of the mutual's payments to members that suffer losses, operating expenses including selling or "underwriting" costs, and all taxes paid except those on real estate and the federal corporate income tax.

8 Roy J. Hensley, *Competition, Regulation and the Public Interest in Non-Life Insurance* (Berkeley: University of California Press, 1962), p. 48 ff.

9 Summarized from J. D. Hammond, E. R. Melander, and N. Shelting, "Economics of Scale in the Property and Liability Insurance Industry," *Journal of Risk and Insurance* 38 (1971): 181-191.

10 Computed from data in *Best's*, 1971, pp. 1, 29, with premiums of reciprocals and Lloyds omitted.

11 *Best's Review: Property-Liability Edition* 69, no. 11 (1969): 10, 11.

12 The information about the factory mutuals was obtained from Manufac-

turers Mutual Fire Insurance Company, *The Factory Mutuals, 1835-1935* (Providence, R.I.: The company, 1935), esp. pp. 43-45, 145, 189, 200 ff.; Dane Yorke, *Able Men of Boston* (Boston: Manufacturers Mutual Fire Insurance Co., 1950) pp. 71-73, 74; and from letters and conversations with officials of these mutuals.

13   John Bainbridge, *Biography of An Idea* (New York: Doubleday, 1952), pp. 102, 115.

14   The current operating practices of these mutuals are detailed by J. Finley Lee, "The Competitive Role of the Associated Factory Mutuals," *Journal of Risk and Insurance* 36 (1969): 401-418.

15   The history of these mutuals is sketched in Bainbridge, *Biography of An Idea,* pp. 205-300.

16   The information about these mutuals through 1921 is drawn from V. N. Valgren, *Farmers' Mutual Fire Insurance Company in the United States* (Chicago: University of Chicago Press, 1942), esp. pp. 11, 31, 61-76, 99-103.

17   Estimated by ratio of farm and fire insurance mutuals $67 million losses in 1962 to the $175 million to total farm losses from fire as reported in USDA's *Agricultural Finance Review: Supplement* (June 1964): 49.

18   Percentages through 1950 are based on information in National Association of Mutual Insurance Companies, *Growth of Mutual Insurance Business, Past and Future* (Indianapolis: The association, n.d.), p. 3; and for more recent years were computed from data in *Best's Aggregates and Averages: Property-Liability,* 1956, pp. 131, 194, and 1971, pp. 139 and 208. The three categories of insurance included are fire, extended coverage, and allied fire lines.

19   Even a report of a Joint Committee of the New York Legislature (Albany, N.Y.: J. B. Lyon Company, 1911), pp. 40-43, concluded that identical rates, or rather absence of rate competition, was necessary.

20   For a summary and economic analysis of the developments sketched in this and the next two paragraphs, see Werner Sichel, "Fire Insurance: Imperfectly Regulated Collusion," *The Journal of Risk and Insurance* 33, no. 1 (March 1966): 95-114; and the Senate Subcommittee on Antitrust and Monopoly, *Hearings,* 86th Cong., 2d sess., August 1960, pp. 136-137, 140, 150. The subcommittee's findings may be found in "Insurance Rates: Rating Organization and Rate Regulation," ibid., 1961, pp. 3-18, 93-127.

21   Even after the fundamental (potential) change in the state laws under pressure of federal government actions, hearings on rate structures and levels indicate that this situation had not changed much by 1960. See Senate Subcommittee on Antitrust and Monopoly, *Hearings,* August 1960.

22   See chapter 10 for references to the tie-in between some types of mutual investing institutions and insurance agencies. Also some states permit state-chartered commercial banks to have insurance departments.

23   For a summary of these influences, see Hensley, *Competition, Regulation, and the Public Interest,* pp. 32-35, 184-186.

24   See decisions in *U.S. v. Insurance Board of Cleveland,* Civ. A., No. 28042, District Court of N.D. Ohio, E.D., August 14, 1956; and *U.S. v. New*

Orleans Insurance Exchange, Civ. A, No. 4292, E.D. New Orleans Division, February 5, 1957.

25 As reported in *Best's,* 1941, pp. 52, 53. Mutuals' (and deviating stock companies') expense ratios somewhat overstate their cost levels because these costs are expressed as percentages of their lower rates.

26 *U.S.* v. *South-Eastern Underwriters Association,* 322 U.S., 533 (1944).

27 For a summary of early experience under the revised state laws, see Joel B. Dirlam and Irwin M. Stelzer, "The Insurance Industry: A Case Study in the Workability of Regulated Competition," *University of Pennsylvania Law Review* 107, no. 2 (1958): 202-215.

28 Percentages computed from figures in *Best's,* 1971, pp. 139, 210.

29 Computed from data ibid., pp. 140, 210.

30 Ibid., pp. 197, 198.

31 Computed from ibid., 1940, pp. 129, 133, 1971, pp. 140, 209.

32 Much of the information about the early years of State Farm is from Karl Schriftgrosser, *The Farmer from Merna* (New York: Random House, 1955), pp. 86-81, 105, 111, 117. Additional information has been supplied by officers of the company.

33 Computed from *Best's,* 1970, pp. 140, 141, 202-205, 209, 210.

34 Of net premiums earned as reported ibid., 1971, pp. 129-134, 201-205.

35 S. Alexander Bell, "Direct Auto Underwriters," *Best's Insurance News: Fire and Casualty Edition* 59 (August 1958): 18, 38, 39; and John W. Popp, "Direct Writers' Experience," ibid., 67 (October 1967): 122, 123.

36 *Best's Review: Property-Liability Edition* 39 (July 1970): 15.

37 Eugene E. Gallagher, *The Eastern Underwriter* 59 (1958): 28.

38 Which were substantial in 1962-1967 when the property-liability insurers as a group experienced an underwriting loss of over a dollar on each $100 of premiums received (L. W. Niggeman, "Capital Capacity and the Insurance 'Crunch,' " *Journal of Insurance Information* [July-August 1969]: p. 9).

39 Mutuals can and do form stock companies whose earnings add to the parent's capital. Also they may issue "surplus debentures," but usually only interested policyholders purchase them. During 1955-1966 63 percent of the stock companies got funds from outside, that is, not from underwriting profits, while only 16 percent of the mutuals obtained outside funds (Stephen W. Forbes, "Growth Performance of Non-life Insurance Companies, 1955-1966," *Journal of Risk and Insurance* 37, no. 3 [November 1970]: 355).

40 See Arthur D. Little Report and critique of it in "The Insurance Industry," *Hearings* before the Senate Antitrust and Monopoly Subcommittee, vols. 14 and 17 91st Cong., 1st sess., July and November 1969.

41 George B. Flanigan, "Investment Income in Rate-Making and Managerial Investment Attitudes," *Journal of Risk and Insurance* 41, no. 2 (June 1974): 230.

13: Financing Cooperatives and Mutuals

1 Nelda Griffin, "A Financial Profile of Farmer Cooperatives in the United

States," Farmer Cooperative Service, *Research Report 23* (1972): fig. 2, p. 13.

2 Ibid., p. 23.

3 This plan "provides for retirement of an association's oldest outstanding membership capital from funds furnished to the cooperative or accumulated by the cooperative from member and (non-member) patrons of later years" (Helim H. Hulbert, Nelda Griffin, and Kelsey B. Gardner, "Revolving Fund Plan of Financing Farmer Cooperatives," Farmer Cooperatives Service, *General Report 41* [1948, reprinted in 1967]).

4 "Figure Exchange," Consumers' Cooperative Development Association, Berkeley, California.

5 *Annual Report of the Administrator of the Rural Electrification Administration* (Washington, D.C.: The administration, 1971), p. 36. See also chapter 9, with respect to recent developments in the financing of REAs.

6 Information for this subsection was obtained by interview with officers and members of these cooperatives.

7 See chapter 11, with particular reference to the practice of paying patronage dividends to members as savers (i.e., on deposits chiefly) rather than to members as borrowers.

8 *Savings and Loan Fact Book 1976* (Chicago: United States Savings and Loan League, 1976), p. 81.

9 The "front load" paid by buyers of stock in most mutual funds does not become capital of the fund but provides the sponsoring investment firm funds to cover salesmen's commissions, to meet expenses of setting up and operating the fund, and to pay profits.

10 For example, of the $125 billion increase from 1924 through 1958 in the total equity capital of all manufacturing industries (including an estimate for the noncorporate sector), almost half represented retained net income after taxes (George J. Stigler, *Capital and Rates of Return in Manufacturing Industries* [Princeton, N.J.: Princeton University Press for the National Bureau of Economic Research, 1963], p. 74).

14: Entrepreneurial and Organizational Problems

1 Over decades of observing cooperatives and during the research for and writing of this volume I have obtained much information not specifically cited in previous chapters. Neither the sources of that information nor of information from more general sources will be cited in this chapter.

2 W. W. Cochrane and R. W. Elsworth, "Farmers' Cooperative Discontinuances: 1875-1939," Cooperative Research and Service Division, Farm Credit Administration, *Miscellaneous Report No. 65* (1943): 24-27. For consumer cooperatives see references in note 9, chapter 9; for credit unions see chapter 11.

3 Of these only the Associated Press and a small company in long distance highway transport of household goods are still organized as cooperatives.

Allied Vans changed to an investor-owned form in order to obtain more capital than members would supply.

4 Of the 21,000 farmer cooperatives known to have been established sometime in the three-quarters of a century prior to 1939, over half were out of business by that date, but not all because of failure (W. W. Cochrane and R. H. Elsworth, "Agricultural Cooperation in the United States," Farm Credit Administration, *Bulletin No. 54* [1947], pp. 29-186). Not more than a handful of these early cooperatives exist today. In contrast the failure rate has been very low among the "Kirkpatric" type of cooperative organization initiated by the Illinois Agricultural Association and over which the association may exercise control at its discretion (Mancur Olsen, Jr., *The Logic of Collective Action* [Cambridge, Mass.: Harvard University Press, 1965], pp. 153-157).

5 The highlights of farm organization-sponsored cooperatives are presented by C. L. Scroggs, "Historical Highlights," in *Agricultural Cooperation: Selected Readings,* ed. M. A. Abrahamson and C. L. Scroggs (Minneapolis: University of Minnesota Press, 1957).

6 The special laws governing the legal structure of cooperatives in three-fourths of the states require the one member, one vote proviso (Cochrane and Elsworth, "Agricultural Cooperation in the United States," p. 11).

7 Restraints on granting membership in the Associated Press and in the building materials reserve supply companies were altered or dropped as the result of actual or expected antitrust action (see chapter 8).

8 There is an extensive literature on the relative merits of the two forms of organizing the large cooperative. See, for example, J. D. Black and H. B. Price, "Cooperative Central Marketing Organization," Minnesota Agricultural Experiment Station, *Bulletin 211* (1924).

9 See, for example, Kenneth D. Nadem, "Economic Analysis of the Organization and Operations of the Challenge Cream and Butter Association" (Ph.D. thesis, University of California, Berkeley, 1948), p. 223.

10 Joseph G. Knapp, "Competition between Cooperatives: Meeting the Problem," *American Cooperation* (Washington, D.C., 1949): 366.

11 For a critique of the exclusive territory policy of British Consumer Cooperatives, see Basil Yamey, "Co-operative Competition," *Modern Law Review* (London), 22, pt. 2 (November 1959): 662.

12 Much of the information in this and the preceding paragraph is from Willard F. Mueller, "The Role of Mergers in the Growth of Agricultural Cooperatives," University of California, Division of Agricultural Science, *Bulletin 777* (1961).

13 Cochrane and Elsworth, "Farmers' Cooperative Discontinuances," p. 29.

14 In relation to this whole subsection the following statement in the *British Co-Operative Independent Commission Report* (London, Eng.: The commission, 1900), p. 66, is noteworthy: "We have no hesitation in asserting that under conditions of full employment, and looking ahead to the next generation, the present level of Co-operative salaries will prove too low to attract

the desired calibre of managerial recruit. . . . Co-operative salaries in general are substantially lower than those paid by the Movement's main competitors."

15 Similarly, in the long-established British retail societies "it can be taken that 2 percent of the membership is a normal attendance at a general meeting" (A. M. Carr-Saunders, P. Sargent Florence, and R. Peers, *Consumers' Co-operation in Great Britain* [London: Allen and Unwin, 1938], p. 256).

16 For a full analysis of the Illinois Farm Supply company as it was organized before the Second World War, see J. H. Lister, "Cooperative Purchasing through the Illinois Farm Supply Company and Its Member County Companies," Farm Credit Administration, *Bulletin No. 27* (1938).

17 For an analysis of management leadership in well-established cooperatives, see Peter G. Helmberger and Sidney Hoos, "Cooperative Enterprise and Organization Theory," *Journal of Farm Economics* 44 (1962): 275-290.

18 Ray A. Goldberg, *Agribusiness Coordination,* Cambridge, Mass.: Division of Research, Harvard University, 1948), pp. 235, 236.

19 See also J. Warren Mather and Jane L. Scearce, "Handbook on Major Regional Farm Supply Cooperatives 1954 and 1955," Farmer Cooperative Service, *General Report 25* (1956), which reports that only one regional had a management contract with all of its locals in 1954. Four regionals had contracts with a small percentage of their locals, but eight had no such contracts.

20 George L. Mehren, "Agricultural Cooperatives—Foundation and Forecast," *American Cooperation* (1960): 19.

Index

Agricultural cooperatives. See Farm marketing cooperatives; Farm supply cooperatives; Farm credit institutions
Agriculture: effect of developments in, on cooperatives, 35–36
Allied Van Lines, 118–19
Antimonopoly legislation: Clayton Act, 37, 38; Capper Volstead Act, 37–40 *passim;* Sherman Act, 38, 39, 170; and Associated Press, 115–16; effect of, on consumer retail cooperatives, 131
Associated Merchandising Corporation, 111–12
Associated Press, the, 113, 115–16, 181
Automobile insurance mutuals. *See* Insurance mutuals, automobile

Bain, Joe S., 208–9, 215*n3*
Baking company cooperatives. *See* Buying cooperatives
Bargaining associations: as distinguished from true cooperatives, 10; farm marketing cooperatives as, 33–34; and the Capper Volstead Act, 39–40; in the fluid milk market, 45; in the fruits, vegetables, and nuts market, 59–62; as exceptions to vertical integration, 206
Borrowing cooperatives: market position of, 149; market entry problems of, 160–61; necessity of outside source of capital for, 161. *See also* Farm credit institutions; Credit unions
Building materials cooperatives. *See* Wholesale cooperatives
Buying cooperatives: department-store owned, 111–12; manufacturer-owned, 113–14; baking company operated, 114–15, 181; news-gathering, 115–16; source of capital for, 181

Capital, source of: for savings and loan

associations, 140–41, 142; for mutual savings banks, 145; for federal farm credit institutions, 149–53, *passim;* difficulty of finding, 177–78; patron-members as, 178, 183–85; additions withheld from net savings as, 179; for farmer cooperatives, 179; for consumer cooperatives, 179–81; for urban business cooperatives, 181–82; for credit unions, 182; for investment mutuals, 182–83; for insurance mutuals, 183; disproportionate contributions by continuing members as, 183–85; income tax savings as, 185; market opportunity as, 185–86; borrowing as, 186–87
Casualty insurance mutuals. *See* Insurance mutuals, casualty
Consumer cooperatives: market position of, 123–24; history of, 124–27; nominal success of, explained, 130–31; effect of antitrust laws on, 131; effect of Pure Food and Drug Act on, 131; source of capital for, 179–81
—food: performance of, 127–30; compared to investor-owned stores, 128–29; development of "private" brands by, 129
—utilities: market position of, 131–32, 133; history of, 131–33; and Rural Electrification Administration, 132–33, 179; opposition to, by investor-owned companies, 133–34; interest- and tax-rate subsidies for, 134–36; methods of finance for, 136
Cooperative Marketing Act, 40
Cooperatives: defined and described, ix, 3; function of, 3, 8, 9, 10, 11, 15, 31; market position of, 4, 6; history of, 5–6; effect of entry into market by, 10–11, 24; voluntary membership in, 14–15; limited membership of, 15, 22, 112, 194; open-ended, 15–16, 17, 18–23 *passim,* 24;

241

COMPOSED BY FOCUS/TYPOGRAPHERS, ST. LOUIS, MISSOURI
MANUFACTURED BY CUSHING MALLOY, INC., ANN ARBOR, MICHIGAN
TEXT AND DISPLAY LINES ARE SET IN TIMES ROMAN

Library of Congress Cataloging in Publication Data
Heflebower, Richard Brooks, 1903-
Cooperatives and mutuals in the market system.
Includes bibliographical references and index.
1. Cooperation—United States.   2.   Mutualism.
I. Title.
HD3444.H37   334 '.0973   79-5407
ISBN 0-299-07850-7